Strategy in Action

Strategy in Action

HOW SCHOOL SYSTEMS CAN SUPPORT
POWERFUL LEARNING AND TEACHING

RACHEL E. CURTIS

AND

ELIZABETH A. CITY

HARVARD EDUCATION PRESS

Second Printing 2010

Copyright © 2009 by the President and Fellows of Harvard College

Library of Congress Control Number 2009927815

Paperback ISBN 978-1-934742-30-3
Library Edition ISBN 978-1-934742-31-0

Published by Harvard Education Press,
an imprint of the Harvard Education Publishing Group

Harvard Education Press
8 Story Street
Cambridge, MA 02138

Cover Design: Perry Lubin

The typefaces used in this book are Adobe Minion Pro for text and Adobe Myriad Pro and ITC Fenice for display.

For Robert D. City, from whom Liz learned:
appreciate people, cherish the small things, and sometimes,
you have to tack to get where you want to go.

For Carolyn and Joseph Curtis, from whom Rachel learned
the beauty of curiosity, the power of reverence, and
the belief that education is the answer.

CONTENTS

Foreword   ix
by Beverly L. Hall

INTRODUCTION   Three Questions, Two Paradoxes, One Focus   1

CHAPTER 1   Strategy, Part 1: Making Sense of the Work Under Way   19

CHAPTER 2   Teams: Creating the Conditions for Success   37

INTERLUDE   Finding the Parts in the Whole   63

CHAPTER 3   Data: Identifying Problems and Opportunities   67

CHAPTER 4   Vision: Keeping the End in Mind   93

INTERLUDE   Embracing Reality and Moving Beyond It   109

CHAPTER 5   Strategy, Part 2: Pulling It All Together   113

CHAPTER 6   Execution: Putting Strategy into Action   143

INTERLUDE   Look, Leap, and Learn   179

CONCLUSION   Toward Realizing the Potential of Strategic Action   185

APPENDIX A   Summary of Protocols and Tools by Chapter   195

APPENDIX B   Selected Protocols with Tips on Implementation   197

APPENDIX C   Further Resources   205

Notes   211

Acknowledgments   215

About the Authors   217

Index   219

FOREWORD

Shortly after I began as superintendent of the Atlanta Public Schools (APS) in 1999, we surveyed kindergarten teachers—some of the most optimistic people on Earth. Their students, only five years old, are eager to learn and full of promise. And yet, nine out of ten of our kindergarten teachers admitted they did not believe their students would complete high school. They based their opinions on the school district's 2000 performance data, which showed that more than half of Atlanta's students, in every grade and subject, were not meeting basic education standards.

Like many urban school systems, a majority of Atlanta's students come from challenging home environments and live close to or below the poverty line. Against this background of low expectations and poor achievement, our challenge was to transform our schools and break long-entrenched links between race, poverty, and educational outcomes.

In the years since this initial transformation, the Atlanta schools have made significant progress through comprehensive and multi-layered reforms. As a result, by state and national standards, very few districts in the United States can match the rate of student progress in Atlanta. We began this remarkable turnaround by asking: How does a school system bring about positive change? How do we ensure that the change is systematic and sustainable? How do we move a larger number of students to competency and proficiency across all subjects and grade levels?

This book answers those questions and rightly links the two essential elements—strategy and action—of all transformational change. While strategies for change abound, it is the process of aligning and linking them to effective actions that makes the difference. It is simply not enough to have strategies in place; we must be able to consistently execute them.

Transformational change *is* possible, but only when all forces—from those kindergarten teachers to board members—come together and commit to making the education of children the *number one priority*. Number one above power struggles, political whims, or practitioner and parental excuses.

In Atlanta, our journey to becoming a high-performing urban school district is driven by four key strategic elements: an unrelenting focus on quality instruction; robust community support; dedication to operational excellence; and strong leadership. All four elements are clearly defined and communicated, and are aligned to the strategic vision of the district.

QUALITY INSTRUCTION

Early on, to underscore that our core mission is teaching and learning excellence, we put research-based comprehensive reform models in every school, based on that school's profile. We also rolled-out nationally proven reform models, such as Project GRAD (Graduation Really Achieves Dreams), the K–12 International Baccalaureate Program, CORE Knowledge and others, complete with intensive professional development across the district. And before No Child Left Behind, we set accountability targets. We began offering financial incentives for every member of the staff in the schools that met 70 percent or more of their targets. From the cafeteria worker to senior staff—including the superintendent—we believed that every school employee has to own his or her unique role in student success.

Because research tells us that if a child has a quality teacher for three years, that child's performance can increase dramatically, we've also invested heavily in teachers and principals. We utilize Teach for America, The New Teacher Project focusing on mid-career changers, and the Visiting International Faculty as sources for new teachers. More than six hundred Teach for America teachers have served Atlanta Public Schools since 2000. But beyond hiring, the majority of our workforce is comprised of veteran teachers. To help support them, we've communicated clear performance expectations, designed meaningful evaluations, and invested in job-embedded professional development.

Our level of support is two-tiered: we have highly effective School Reform Teams, each operating under the direction of executive directors who employ a team of subject-specific model teacher leaders to target professional development for teachers within their geographic area. In addition, we invest in school-based instructional experts—mentors, instructional coaches, and facilitators. The job of our instructional teams is clear: to build teachers' knowledge and skills, especially in using data to develop their lesson plans and implementing best teaching practices in their classrooms. As a result of our investments, if you walk into any public school in Atlanta, teachers and principals know the data, they use benchmark tests and other formative assessments to identify the strengths and weaknesses of every child, and they use the information to guide instruction.

In mathematics and science, more than two thousand of our K–12 teachers have received intensive training since 2007 on how to retool the way they deliver math and science instruction beyond old-fashioned lectures and whole-group teaching. They are learning how to use our twenty-six best teaching practices, which are also linked to their evaluations.

Again, our focus as a school district begins and ends with instruction, and we can't ever, ever forget that.

COMMUNITY SUPPORT

One of the cornerstones of our transformation strategy has been the presence of an involved and strong community of business, civic leaders and parents. In the 1990s, a powerful coalition of community leaders said enough is enough. Atlanta—the city that had won the 1996 Olympics bid—was home to a school system that was stagnant and a burden on the wave of economic development envisioned for the area. Led by the Metro Atlanta Chamber of Commerce, the coalition vigorously recruited quality school board candidates—and threw support behind the board, superintendent, and schools. Metro Atlanta is privileged to rank in the nation's top-five areas with the largest concentration of *Fortune* 500 companies, and the city has a host of civic-minded small business owners. We were able to tap into that resource infrastructure in many ways.

One of the most vivid examples of the business community's role in our schools is Project GRAD. Through the GRAD reform model, we've infused our lowest performing schools with intensive teacher resources and social support services for students and their families. It's quite expensive, however, and we needed a tremendous amount of financial help to launch the program. After sharing program data—including the research-based approaches to teaching math and reading that were yielding excellent results in other cities such as Houston and Newark—with leaders of the corporate and philanthropic community, we raised $20 million in only three years.

Today, Project GRAD provides ongoing, sustained professional development in the teaching of literacy, math, and classroom discipline to teachers, and offers high school students the opportunity to attend summer institutes on local college campuses and earn scholarships. Another program strong point is the placement of social workers in schools to link families to outside services.

From medical care and emergency rental assistance to tickets for entertainment events, our partners step in to support and encourage students in ways the school system could never do alone.

GRAD is now in a third of our schools, and the outcomes are impressive – rising attendance and test scores, and much higher graduation rates and college enrollment. Remember, GRAD operates in what once were our lowest performing K–12 schools. If we could transform those schools, as we have, then we could make believers out of non-believers. And success is attractive.

We were able to build on those early results from Project GRAD to secure the expertise and financial resources of other businesses and foundations, such as the Bill and Melinda Gates Foundation, to help us transform our high schools into smaller, more personalized learning environments; and the GE Foundation to fund our Math and Science Initiative. In another show of support, a broad-based coalition of Atlanta leaders established the Atlanta Education Fund in 2007 as a way to unify and target community support for key APS reform strategies.

No matter what our role is as educators, we cannot go at it alone. We must involve the business, civic, parental and broader community in our strategic efforts.

OPERATIONAL EXCELLENCE

In our effort to become a high-performing organization, we've also implemented processes that are commonplace for the private sector, but are seldom employed in urban public school environments.

One of the best examples of this is our use of the Balanced Scorecard (BSC) as the foundation of our strategic management system. It gives us the ability to measure how each functional unit contributes to the district's overall goals, shows cause-and-effect relationships at all levels, and helps us bridge the divide between where the district is now, and our vision for children and their learning. The BSC strategic planning management system uses action plans to bring objectives to life by specifying the initiatives needed for the district to accomplish its goals. It also helps us translate our mission and vision into concrete measures, and then prioritize and allocate resources.

Reporting is a key part of the BSC, and we use data to inform strategy development, analyze progress, and make decisions for continuous improvement. Each functional unit establishes its own BSC to reflect its alignment and contribution to the district's high-level objectives. Employees at every level are able to demonstrate how their specific accomplishments help the district achieve its strategic objectives.

The BSC also enables us to more effectively communicate our strategic goals and performance to all stakeholders. Internally, it helps to mobilize employees to accomplish our shared vision. Externally, it helps to communicate the district's vision and progress, and promotes a forward-looking, results-oriented organization with accountability for results.

Another important element in our transformation strategy is our emphasis on obtaining efficiencies within business operations. We know that strategies must be partnered with effective execution, and so we established a Strategy and Development Office to drive system-wide implementations. We also evaluate all budget recommendations based on three criteria: their direct impact on student achievement, risk to the district if not implemented, and alignment with the district's strategic objectives.

STRONG LEADERSHIP

It takes strong principals and central office leaders to model, support, guide, and sustain the work. At every opportunity I get, one of the first questions I ask principals is: "How much time do you spend on instruction?" Again, the research is clear: if principals don't provide the instructional leadership, the school won't perform. Today's principal cannot get caught up in the minutia of building operations and logistics. To that end, we are piloting a school business manager position in our larger high schools and large middle and elementary schools. In addition, the School Reform Team serves as a one-stop shop for operational support to principals and their teachers so that, again, they can focus on instruction.

And as in the case of strong teacher supports, we invest heavily in professional leadership development, creating our own programs, such as the Aspiring Leaders Program (ALP) which partners with Georgia State University to provide an alternate route to leadership certification, and the Superintendent's Academy for Building Leaders in Education (SABLE), which provides two years of intensive leadership training for staff who already have their leadership certificate.

Strong, dedicated, and effective leaders—up and down the system—are the drivers of transitional change. One of the most important lessons we've learned on our way to becoming a high-performing district is that we need to make sure—regardless of the challenges—that we have the right people in the right seats on the bus.

Strategy in Action makes a valuable contribution to our understanding of what it takes to transform our schools and support more effective learning and teaching. It puts the focus squarely where it belongs—using systematic and strategically driven approaches to allocate resources, goods, and services based on placing the needs of children and schools first. It emphasizes focusing these resources on a few things that have the greatest potential to improve student learning, which, when done in concert, can leverage systemic improvement. The trajectory of our journey to reach these goals has proven simpler in theory than in practice and execution.

As educators, we have a great deal of hard work ahead. The path is clear, the time is now, and the future of our students lies in the balance.

Dr. Beverly L. Hall
Superintendent
Atlanta Public Schools
July 2009

Three Questions,
Two Paradoxes,
One Focus

> To the extent that it is possible . . . you must live in the world today
> as you wish everyone to live in the world to come. That can be your
> contribution. Otherwise, the world you want will never be formed.
> Why? Because you are waiting for others to do what you are not
> doing; and they are waiting for you, and so on.
>
> —*Alice Walker*

This book is aimed at helping educators address a problem we have encountered frequently since we first met nearly eight years ago.

At the time, Rachel was the director of school development for the Boston Public Schools (BPS) and had been part of "the System" for six years, playing an integral role in designing the system's strategy. Liz, fresh off an experience of starting a charter public school in Durham, North Carolina, as a teacher and later a principal, was a coach, still adjusting to being in a large district where "the System" was its own peculiar organism—one that people described with various degrees of reverence or irreverence.

We were at a citywide meeting of coaches to talk about the new, improved whole-school improvement plans, WSIPs in BPS-speak. Rachel noticed that Liz asked thoughtful questions. Liz noticed that Rachel was more focused on the purpose of the WSIP than on the due date and compliant completion of boxes on the plan template. We didn't cross paths again for many months. In the meantime, Rachel worked with the system's senior leadership team and district departments to launch the district's fledgling coaching strategy. Liz worked with teachers and principals at three schools to implement the new instructional model of writing workshop and to design their improvement plans.

The biggest adjustment for Liz in her new role, aside from the ever-present System beast, was the profound absence of the word *why*. Teachers wanted to know what they were supposed to do and how they were supposed to do it, not *why* they were supposed to do it, what it was intended to accomplish, and how it fit into their overcrowded schedules. Schools saw the system's revision of the WSIP process as "they can't make up their mind what they want us to do—just tell us, and we'll do it"—not as evidence of the system's learning. For us, the questions were inseparable. If you didn't understand the *why*, how could you make it work well in your own school and classroom? Rachel pushed with coaches and central office staff while Liz pushed with teachers: We're not doing this because "the System" says so, but because it's going to help children learn.

Our paths continued to cross, next in BPS's within-district principal development program (which Rachel founded and directed and in which Liz taught) and later, after Rachel left the BPS, in a Harvard leadership program for senior district- and state-level educators (in which Rachel coached a district and Liz taught and served on the management team). We also pursued separate paths, working with districts and leaders across the country. Even as we worked with districts in particular areas—Rachel in strategy and the development of leadership at all levels and Liz in data, resources, and instructional rounds networks (a collaborative practice of classroom observation akin to medical rounds)[1]—we noticed that most districts struggled to pull the various pieces of their work together. They faced enormous pressures to improve student achievement, but too often, they lacked a clear sense of what was the most important work to do on behalf of children. The districts tended, therefore, to apply a series of Band-Aids without examining the underlying illnesses. The result was too little progress for students.

THREE QUESTIONS

Systems that are making substantial progress for children have broken out of reactive, Band-Aid mode and are clear about their answers to three questions: *what, why,* and *how? What* are we doing? *Why* are we doing it? *How* are we doing it?[2] The simplicity of the questions belies the complexity involved in answering them. We have written this book to help school systems as they try to answer these questions.

What?

Most school systems we know have many answers to the question *What are we doing?* Therein lies the problem. Initiatives are taken on without a clear sense of how they relate to one another, and cumulatively they add up to a whole that is less than the sum of its parts. At the same time, school systems often underestimate or feel ill prepared for the organizational changes these initiatives demand and the implications of them for how the adults in the system function. As a result, the work of school systems is often fragmented, not well aligned, and limited in its effectiveness.

In short, most school systems lack a robust strategy. The word *strategy* is most commonly heard in school systems in the context of strategic planning, an exercise of setting direction and prioritizing work that districts go through every three to five years or with the arrival of each new superintendent. The sheer number of goals, strategies, and initiatives proposed in most strategic planning exercises makes it hard to focus, and the distance between many of them and the work in classrooms makes it unclear how implementation will lead to improved outcomes for students. These cumbersome plans often sit on a shelf and do little to focus the district's work on improving instruction and student learning. The result, paradoxically, is a strategic plan without a strategy. District staff work hard rather than smart, exhausting themselves with pockets of success and lots of wasted effort. Ultimately, students suffer.

What is a strategy? Strategy scholar and teacher Stacey Childress describes it this way: "The set of actions an organization chooses to pursue in order to achieve its objectives. These deliberate actions are puzzle pieces that fit together to create a clear picture of how the people, activities, and resources of an organization can work effectively to accomplish a collective purpose."[3] Developing strategy requires systems to identify a few high-leverage ways to improve instruction and student learning. These few carefully chosen things are well aligned, coherent, and mutually reinforcing and add up to a whole that is greater than the sum of its individual parts. This book is about how to develop and implement a strategy that drives the work of the system to improve teaching and learning.

Why?

Designing and implementing a strategy is hard work, countercultural, and difficult to do amid pressures to improve now. Why bother? Because it's the only way to help *all* children learn.

If we care about all children, then we need to care about systems, and we need to care about strategy. We cannot expect to improve schools, particularly schools in our large urban districts, without deliberate and concerted effort. This means bringing an end to the "Let a thousand flowers bloom," approach where teachers and schools find their way (or not) in isolation. True, most school systems could benefit from innovative ideas that bubble up from schools and teachers. But some flowers will bloom, and many will wither. This is not an indictment of individual schools, be they independent, charter, or within school systems—Liz has helped start more than one of those, and both of us have seen how powerful individual schools and teachers can be for students. But not all of our students have access to those schools and those teachers, and the magnitude and urgency of the opportunity before us to educate all children requires a systemic response.

That response has to include a strategy, or it will be more of the same old fragmented, Band-Aid approach. We have before us a great challenge and a great opportunity: to educate *all* of our children to succeed in a rapidly changing world we can scarcely imagine. There are numerous examples of teachers and schools successfully rising to this opportunity, supporting learning for all or nearly all of their students. There are far fewer examples of school systems doing the same. In an era when isolated examples of excellence are not good enough, when we want and expect *all* of our children to succeed, we need classrooms, schools, and systems that support improvement and excellence for *all*. We do not know how to do that work well, at scale, for all children. This book describes that complex, challenging, and crucial work and shows how systems can effectively engage in it.

How?

Over and over in our work, we see educators who despair when they hear of new initiatives or directives from the system's leaders. "How can we possibly do that, on top of the four thousand other things we are already doing?" they ask. In systems that are improving results for students, everyone works hard, but more importantly, everyone works *smart*. The educators have a strategy, but perhaps even more important, they are *strategic* in how they approach their work. Leaders in these systems are intentional in word, thought, and action. They weigh trade-offs, consider evidence, keep goals in mind. They check assumptions and consider the interrelationship of things. They have an idea of how an action might lead to a particular result, and they adjust their idea and action according to new information. They focus on what's most important amid the constant cacophony of options demanding their attention. Strategy is not just a thing you do; it's a way of being.

This book defines what strategy is, why it is important to school systems and student achievement, and how it can be designed and used to guide how systems function. This is the book that we wish we had in 2001, when we first met at the coaches' meeting. We have integrated what we have learned since then, from both inside and outside the education sector, and organized it in a way that can guide leaders toward systemic improvement.

Several assumptions underpin this book:

- School systems exist to support learning for all students. Both parts of this sentence are crucial: First, the purpose of school systems is student learning. Period. Everything they do should contribute to that goal, or it should not be done. Second, when we say "all," we mean each and every child in the United States. All.
- Teaching matters most. Of the things over which school systems have substantial influence, teaching has the strongest effect on student learning. Thus, the heart of the work of school systems is around the *instructional core*—the interactions of teachers, students, and content.[4] Activities at the periphery of that core should continue only if they affect the core.
- Being strategic, coherent, and well aligned is everyone's business. Senior leaders in the system make it their own work and help others to make it theirs.

TWO PARADOXES

Two central paradoxes make the work of school system leaders all the more challenging. The first paradox is about *diving in and stepping back*. This means committing to the work and making it personal while still recognizing that it is not about us, but about children. The importance of this paradox is most evident in systems that are experiencing persistent failure. To make progress, leaders must help people take ownership of their work and believe that what they do matters. Yet if people really embraced this in failing systems, it would be hard to come to work every day. They would interpret everything as signs of their own failure. To address this paradox, a leader helps people dive in, bring themselves entirely to the work, and believe in their own efficacy, while also helping them step back and get some distance on the work. Holding this paradox means helping people develop a professional practice in which they can separate themselves from their practice, yet acknowledge the role of emotion and identity in practicing with purpose.

Second, leaders must *recognize the complexity of the work and simplify it at the same time.* One superintendent we know described the need to "simplify, simplify, focus, focus."[5] This advice is something that successful school systems certainly do. But leaders also have to recognize complexity and help others recognize it. This means not oversimplifying—not turning definitions of learning and teaching into rigid checklists, not assuming that one intervention will transform teaching practice. Living in this paradox means simplifying while not ignoring complexity, focusing on what is most essential, clearing a path through the clutter, understanding that one person's clutter is another person's treasure, embracing ambiguity, and understanding the core work of learning as a dynamic and multifaceted endeavor.

This book describes why these paradoxes are so important in a system's strategic improvement efforts, as well as the large and small things leaders can do to help themselves and others hold these paradoxes and act within them.

ONE FOCUS

What is the purpose of our daily work? When answering this question, businesses ask themselves, "Are we making clothing or cars, bicycles or doughnuts?" What they make or do determines many things about how the organization functions. Their systems, processes, people, and daily routines are directed quite deliberately toward their product. In schools, we're in the business of learning. Sometimes we may act as if we're in another line of work (employment, enforcing regulations, administering tests, child care), but fundamentally, our business, our "product," is learning.

One of the most striking features of school systems where student achievement results consistently improve is a focus on learning and teaching that pervades all levels of all departments. No matter how stormy the seas get—budget cuts, reform fads, a thousand other distracting siren songs—these school systems resist being blown off course. Their focus on learning is their true north, guiding the system with constant reinforcement from senior leadership about what matters most. Meetings are about learning and teaching, not compliance and paperwork. Conversations include data and evidence of learning, not just anecdotes and opinions. Learning and teaching are everyone's responsibility, including those charged with balancing

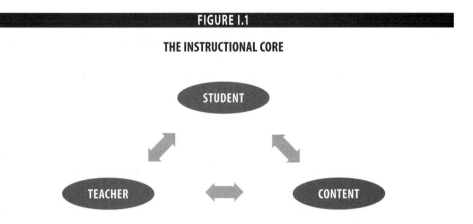

FIGURE I.1

THE INSTRUCTIONAL CORE

budgets and arranging bus routes. Individuals understand how their role connects to learning and teaching, and their responsibilities within that role are clear.

The Instructional Core

Because teaching and learning are at the heart of the enterprise, many education scholars and practitioners refer to these activities as *the instructional core.* Indeed, the very word *core* is rooted in the concept of "heart" (think Latin *cord, cor, cardi;* French *le coeur;* Spanish *el corazon*). What is the instructional core? It is what happens in classrooms every day. It represents the interaction of teachers (instructional practices) and students in the presence of content (curriculum).[6] This is often graphically represented in the form of a triangle (figure I.1). Each point of the triangle is critical.

Teaching Quality

When observing classrooms, people tend to focus on just one point of the triangle—the teacher. This is not surprising. In most American classrooms, the teacher does most of the talking, so our eyes and ears are naturally drawn to what she is doing and saying. What the teacher does truly matters. This is precisely why most of us became teachers; we wanted to affect children's lives in a positive way.

It's not just that teachers matter generally; it's that it matters quite specifically which teacher a child has. A host of research increasingly confirms this connection, which parents and students have long known. One district examined these data as part of a day-long leadership retreat at the beginning of the school year. Projected on the screen was a single slide with a pie chart displaying variability in student achievement gains (the favorite way of measuring "learning" in the United States these days). The data on the chart suggested that it matters a lot more which classroom students are in than which school they are in. There is much more variation *within* schools than *between* schools, and it is common to find an effective teacher in a classroom next door to a mediocre teacher.[7] The room, filled with about a hundred leaders, from across the system, including operations and finance personnel, principals, teacher leaders, board members, community partners, and parents, was abuzz after seeing the data. During the break, a parent said in private conversation, "I could have told you that. I've had two children go through this system. I offered to tell the people at my table which teachers are helping kids learn and which aren't, but they didn't want to hear the names."

While this issue can be interpreted as one of teacher quality (a popular policy topic these days), what is more relevant is the notion of teach*ing* quality—what teachers do rather than who they are. It is the *practice* that is highly variable across classrooms. And this variability is a product (and a failure) of our systems, which are not clear about expectations for teaching and/or have not created a coherent, aligned system of supports, incentives, and accountability to embody those expectations. While this describes the current reality in most American schools, it is not a foregone conclusion. Many other countries do not have nearly as much variability across classrooms as the United States does, and some schools within the United States do not reflect such troubling variability.

Rigorous Content

The *content* point of the triangle currently captures less attention in education discourse. The standards movement of the early 1990s introduced the then-radical notion that there might be some content that all students should be responsible for mastering (and, to a lesser extent, that educators should be responsible for helping students master). In other words, *what* do we want students to know and be able to do? While most of us have come around to the notion that standards are part of how we ensure equity and quality for all students, there remain several wildernesses where we are collectively reluctant to tread. First, all states have standards, but the standards vary a great deal. What it means to be proficient in Arkansas (where Liz went to high school) is quite different from, and reflects a less rigorous standard than, what is considered proficiency in Massachusetts (where Rachel went to high school).[8] Second, our American propensity to favor breadth over depth means that American fifth-graders are taught twice as many math concepts as their Japanese counterparts. No wonder Americans don't learn them as deeply. As U.S. children stagger under the weight of their textbooks, teachers stagger under the weight of covering the material.

Yet even if the standards—the intended curriculum—fall short of what students need to learn in order to succeed in the twenty-first century, the sad and little-known reality is that what students are asked to do in classrooms—the "enacted" curriculum—is often even less demanding. Put bluntly, too many students are not being taught what the standards' crafters would expect.

Research from the Education Trust confirms our own observations of classrooms: The higher the grade level, the bigger the gap between what students are supposed to be doing and what they're actually asked to do (figure I.2).[9]

When we see these task data, it should not surprise us that teachers say ninth-graders are unprepared for high school work; we've only asked the students to do sixth-grade work! Nor should we wonder why ninth-graders drop out when they are abruptly faced with a sharp increase in rigor and expectations from eighth to ninth grade or that colleges and businesses are often appalled at recent graduates' level of knowledge and skill; we were only asking high schoolers to do ninth-grade work in twelfth grade!

To be sure, these trends are not universal; Liz has often winced when looking at fourth-grade writing assignments that matched or surpassed the rigor of assignments she gave her seventh-grade students in years past. Yet again and again, when we are in classrooms, we are astonished at how little is asked of students, how greatly their capabilities are underestimated, and how willingly students by and large tolerate adults' limited imaginations.

Students As Learners

As teachers and school systems feel the pressure of increased scrutiny on their instruction and content, they understandably redirect some of that scrutiny toward the third point in the instructional core triangle, students. Though in some cases this is clearly a "not my problem" reflex, it is valid to point out that students play a role in the dynamic relationship of learning and teaching. As with teachers, what students bring to school— their knowledge, skills, beliefs, talents, interests, cultures, and dispositions—does affect the classroom. Many educators in the United

FIGURE I.2

THE ASSIGNMENT-LEVEL/GRADE-LEVEL GAP

As grade level increases, the assignments given to students fall further and further behind grade-level standards.

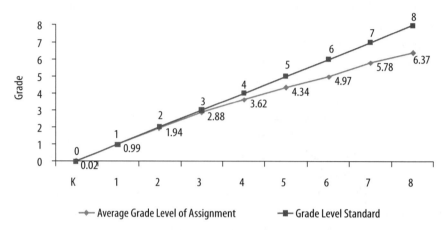

Source: Education Trust; John Holton, South Carolina Department of Education, analysis of assignments from 362 elementary and middle schools in South Carolina. Reprinted with the permission of the Education Trust.

And this pattern continues in high school.

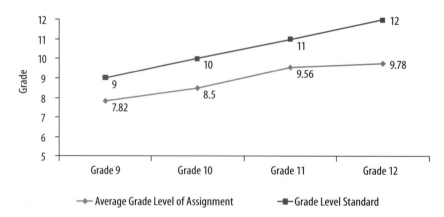

Source: Education Trust; John Holton, South Carolina Department of Education, analysis of English language arts assignments in fourteen high schools in South Carolina. Reprinted with the permission of the Education Trust.

States tend to either attribute excessive agency to students (students are who they are; we can't do much about it) or discount student agency altogether (to affect students, we should focus exclusively on influencing the adults and content). These are oversimplified assumptions, both of which sell students short and underutilize a powerful resource for learning—the students themselves. Involving students as active agents in their own learning and directly addressing the student point of the triangle acknowledges the important and complex role that students play in their own learning.

Why Focus on the Core?

Thus far, we have discussed the points of the triangle—teachers, content, and students—separately. The power of the core, however, is realized in the interactions between the three; the lines that link the points, enclosing the triangle and creating a core. The core is precisely that interaction. Without interactions, there is no learning. We have been in many classrooms where the focus is on interactions between two of the three elements: The teacher is teaching content, not students (a condition that plagues many high school classrooms); or the teacher is teaching students, not content (a condition we most recently observed in a small high school focused on relationships, where the teachers and students were all engaged in dialogue and reflection, with very little content present). The simplicity of the instructional core triangle belies the complexity of the interactions that produce learning. The more time we spend in classrooms, the more reverence we have for that complexity.

If you're not paying attention to the instructional core, you have little chance of improving it. In fact, if you haven't organized every part of the system to relentlessly focus on and support the core, the best you're going to realize is some learning for some students, and it will often be in spite of the system, not because of it. Some learning for some students—and we are not the first to say this—is not good enough.

Our schools and what we do in them can make children smarter. Alas, the converse is also true: We can also make children less smart. Consider an oft-cited study by William Sanders and June Rivers, who followed children who scored average on a standardized test. After three years, some of the children scored fifty percentile points higher than other students, an incredible difference for students starting at the same score just three years before. The difference? Teaching.[10] What students do matters; what families do matters; what society does matters. But what we do when children are in school matters most for what they will know and be able to do as adults—a simultaneously inspiring and terrifying thought.

Some people would argue that the proper combination of incentives and accountability, whether within or outside a system, would ensure high-quality learning for all children. This theory works best if you ascribe to the assertion that the adults know exactly what to do to improve student learning, but they're just not doing it.

Others might argue that school boards and teachers unions and piles of regulations and the media culture are what stand between us and high-quality learning for all children. Let the professionals be professionals and do their jobs. This theory works best if you ascribe to the notion that the adults know what to do to improve student learning, but conditions keep them from doing it.

No doubt, we educators can and should be considerably more sophisticated, purposeful, and effective with our incentive and accountability systems. No doubt, conditions sometimes hinder educators' ability to focus purposefully on the instructional core. However, another theory speaks more to what is (and is not) happening in the core: The adults don't exactly know what to do to improve learning for all students and therefore aren't doing it.

In some cases, adults may know *some* of what to do, but that skill and knowledge isn't systemic. Telling people they need to improve may motivate them to learn, but it won't motivate them to do what they don't know how to do. All the accountability systems in the world and the most supportive conditions won't work if the adults don't know what to do and if there is not some way to support them in learning to do it. If we're serious about all children, then we have to be serious about focusing school systems on the core. Systems, not just individuals, must steward the core.

How Do School Systems Focus on the Core?

School systems focus on the core by paying attention to what is happening in classrooms every day and making classroom practice *everyone's* work. The systems use incentives and accountability to reinforce the priority on the core, and they direct system resources (especially people and time) toward improving the quality of instruction, curriculum, and student learning. School systems that focus on the core with a coherent strategy, executed and refined over time, are making progress in fulfilling their vision of supporting all children to learn at high levels, to contribute to their communities, and to be ready for career and college. To be sure, this is harder than it sounds; school systems face numerous competing demands. But it is the only path toward improvement.

The paradoxes of complexity versus simplicity, and diving in versus stepping back, play out constantly vis-à-vis the core. Often, systems try to duck the complexity of the instructional core by improving only one element of it. But as Richard Elmore and colleagues point out, if you improve one area of the core, you have to improve the others, or you won't get the hoped-for learning.[11] When investing in a high-level math curriculum (i.e., *content*), the system must also address the other two elements of the core. It must invest in the *teachers*, increasing their math knowledge and math-teaching skills, which need to differ from how teachers learned math and currently know how to teach it. Moreover, the system must invest in *students*, helping them learn how to seek understanding rather than only a "right" answer and how to persist in the midst of uncertainty and complexity. Similarly, school systems that are improving the instructional core learn how to help everyone in the system (and those who support the system) own and work on their part of the system without being overwhelmed into paralysis. This means that responsibility is not a hot potato passed from person to person in the system and then to someone outside the system (e.g., from high school to middle school to elementary school to parents, or between central office departments such as learning and teaching, to special education, to English language learners, to human resources). Without pointing fingers, improving school systems look at evidence of what is happening in the core and figure out what they can do next to improve it. To use Rick DuFour's metaphor, they hold up mirrors rather than looking out windows.[12] They ask, "What's the next level of work here, and how can I improve my practice to support it?" In school systems that are improving and succeeding in helping children learn, people embrace the notion that what they do matters, focus on improving what they can control rather than excusing results on the basis of what they can't control, and look at student learning data and other evidence of their practice as information, not as a commentary on their personal value.

The good news is that making organizations effective is not rocket science—and in many ways is less challenging than helping a room full of eighth-graders learn. Effective organizations are clear about their purpose, understand their core business, have a picture of what it looks like when done well, have ideas about how to meet their goals, and continuously learn. This is not so very different from effective teaching practice: clear objectives, focus on student learning with a picture of what successful learning will look like, instructional strategies for helping students succeed, and a continuous process of assessment, reflection, and improvement. Unfortunately, most school systems are currently unable to do what our best teachers (and principals and other leaders) do as a matter of regular practice. The good news is that systems can learn and that many examples of school systems that are improving can show the way.

OVERVIEW OF THE BOOK

This book describes how a school system can develop its skills in the areas outlined above and work strategically to help all children learn. The book is for school systems, traditional and charter, as well as the partners (educational, philanthropic, community, and policy) that work with them to bring school improvement to scale. Systems are, of course, collections of individuals who gather together for a purpose. This book is for the people who are our school systems, for educational leaders and those who support them. This group includes superintendents, central office staff, principals, school boards, and external partners working with schools and systems to facilitate improvement. Most educators we know appreciate an understanding of theory and research and want guidance on how to *do* the work in a way that will work in their own setting, preferably now. In this book, we have tried to provide a mix of information, ideas, and tools, drawing from our experience in multiple roles inside and outside various schools systems as well from the literature on effective organizations—educational and otherwise. Our goal is to help readers think strategically, ask the right questions, and act in ways that build their system's capacity to support the learning of children and adults.

Each school system operates in its own unique context, yet school systems in very different contexts share common tasks and challenges in supporting the learning of children and adults. In this book, we focus on the common tasks and challenges and provide frameworks, questions, and tools to help you apply your learning to your own context. We weave the story of one school system, which we call Moorwood, throughout the book to illustrate what it looks like when a district engages in strategic work. Moorwood is a composite of many school systems, and we hope you see your own system in that story. We also share examples from other systems and offer more general ways of thinking about the issues. We provide tools and protocols to help you assess, organize, and focus your work, and to generate fruitful dialogue in short periods of time. While we highly recommend that you use some tools and protocols to organize conversations and to become efficient and productive, there is nothing particularly magical about the tools and protocols we offer here. We use them in our own work in a variety of settings, and we are constantly adapting them. They are intended to give you a toehold, a starting place, a way to do something tomorrow. We encourage you to adapt them for your own use, or if you have something that helps you do your work more strategically and effectively, use that instead (and even better, let us know what it is!).

We have tried to simplify without oversimplifying, to show some of the messiness without overwhelming readers with nuances, and to make the book relevant and applicable for leaders in a variety of contexts. A book is necessarily far more linear than is the work of a school system. While there is a logic to the sequence of chapters (e.g., take stock of where you are now; identify the problem before the solution; implement the solution), the work is not always sequential. We recommend that you read the book through once and then return to chapters as needed to go deeper in particular areas.

Chapter 1 meets school systems where they are—in the midst of doing their work, usually in the midst of dozens of initiatives competing for educators' time and attention. The chapter helps readers make sense of their existing work, introduces the elements of a strategy, and offers a way for systems to assess the extent to which they have a robust strategy.

Before leaping to help "fix" the strategy in whatever ways it needs fixing, systems need a strong foundation for strategic action, and the next three chapters of the book lay that foundation. Chapter 2 recognizes that education is a human enterprise that relies on adults working productively together. The chapter focuses on teams, a key component of a high-performing organization, and addresses the senior leadership team, which is central to the leadership of strategy, while laying out building blocks that are essential for high-functioning teams at all levels of the system. Chapter 3 takes up the question of how a school system identifies the right problems and opportunities to focus its strategy on, with particular attention to data. Of all the possible piles of data to mine, which are the most helpful when and why, and how does a system dig beyond glaring symptoms to deep causes? High-performing organizations do not, however, simply tackle problems at their roots. Thus, chapter 4 attends to the role of vision. While acknowledging that most systems already have a vision statement, the chapter focuses on how to ensure that the vision serves as a true "North Star" for the system, guiding and inspiring the work of the system, and clarifying why the system is doing its work and what it wants to make possible for all children.

With the vision, problems and opportunities, and teams in place, systems put it all together into a coherent strategy. Chapter 5 walks through a process for developing strategy that draws on expertise both inside and outside the system and helps a system do the challenging work of narrowing all the possible tasks into the few things it will do to best serve children. But having a strategy is not enough; systems need to execute the strategy effectively. Chapter 6 shows how to move to action and execute the strategy, including deciding what to start, continue, and (hardest of all) stop doing. The chapter shows the level of planning detail, as well as the stakeholder communication and learning loops required, to best support strategy implementation and adaptation.

While the book describes a number of specific activities that systems undertake in developing and executing strategy, we want to be clear that being strategic is not simply a matter of performing a set of tasks. It is not something that systems do. It is, rather, a habit that *people* infuse throughout their day-to-day activities. Managing the paradoxes of complexity versus simplicity and diving in versus stepping back is critical to being strategic. Our commitment to supporting individuals to be more strategic grows out of the reality that systems become more strategic and effective as the people who work in them become more strategic and effective.

To make this abstract idea of being strategic more concrete, we offer short "Managing the Paradoxes" interludes between chapters at three places in the book. These interludes highlight what the habit of being strategic looks like on a daily level. In these, we address readers at a more personal level, moving from the big, systems ideas of the preceding chapters to the small, real ways in which you can manage the paradoxes and cultivate the habit of being strategic. Perhaps you cannot change the whole system tomorrow, but you can do several things that will help you and your colleagues be more strategic and effective. Cultivating a strategic habit is like training a muscle or becoming fitter. It takes time, repetition, and commitment. We become more strategic through our daily decisions and actions. The "Managing the Paradoxes" interludes are about shaping up your strategic self.

The conclusion points out tensions in strategy that need to be balanced, and returns to the instructional core, the paradoxes, and the power of learning to deepen strategic thinking.

Appendix A summarizes the tools and protocols by chapter; appendix B presents descriptions and tips for some of the protocols. There is also a resource section of recommended further reading in appendix C.

The question that pervades this book is the one that Liz and Rachel both asked at our first meeting in the fall of 2001: *Why?* The aim of strategic thinking is to answer that question and to create a sense of purpose that can enable everyone in the system to develop a sense of efficacy, possibility, and commitment to contribute in positive ways. Organizational systems and structures without clarity of purpose and a sense of possibility provide an empty shell, a busy organization that lacks meaning. And we think the purpose for which school systems are organized is perhaps the noblest endeavor possible: enabling all young people to develop the knowledge, skills, and habits of mind that will ensure their success in a complex world. This book is a start on that journey.

CHAPTER 1

Strategy, Part 1

Making Sense of the Work Under Way

Strategy 101 is about choices: You can't be all things to all people.

—*Michael Porter*

Sonya, the superintendent of Moorwood Public Schools, held the glossy, colorful strategic plan in her hands, marveling that the six-month process had finally come to an end. The community meetings, the conversations within and outside the school system, all the efforts to define the most important work on behalf of student learning, to hear stakeholders' voices, to synthesize them and then set the direction for the system. Thumbing through the plan, Sonya was excited to review the final report. As she read each goal, she could feel the energy escaping from her body, like air from a balloon. She started to count each goal on her fingers. She felt some mixture of relief and horror when she got to the last goal and her last finger. Pulling her chair closer to her desk and feeling the tension rise in her body, she started counting: 10 major goal areas, 64 strategies, 198 initiatives.

Dropping the plan on her desk, Sonya leaned back in her chair and sighed, wondering to herself, "How in the world are we going to do all that?" Her second thought was, "Which of the things listed in the plan are the most important things to do to improve student learning?" Before Sonya could consider her last question, her assistant appeared in the doorway to remind her of her next meeting and to hand her messages from the school board president, the chief financial officer, and a community leader looking for answers. Sonya pushed herself up out of her chair, leaving the plan face down on her desk.

WHAT IS STRATEGY, AND WHY IS IT IMPORTANT?

Schools and school systems are noisy places. Crises, big and small, come one after another. Local, state and national politics (with all the interests they represent), add to the din. Many systems live in a persistently reactive mode to these external stimuli. We reassure ourselves that we are being responsive (usually a good thing), while in fact we are driven to distraction. We see it in the vignette above, where the superintendent spends an inordinate amount of time attending to the pressing interests of board members and various community leaders in a system that has just expended a great deal of effort on an unwieldy and not-at-all-strategic plan. It's reflected in the principal who spends all morning responding to the never-ending stream of requests, calls, and e-mails, never making it into classrooms to observe, although his morning schedule is blocked out for just that purpose. And it's reflected in the central office department that agrees to pilot a new student assessment simply because someone else is willing to pay for it, even though it is not the best tool for the system and will take instructional time away from students. We know there are compelling reasons for this behavior. Yet the results of all this distraction are predictable and unacceptable. Improvement efforts are fractured, disconnected, incompletely implemented, and never assessed.

Strategy is about filtering this noise. It's about deciding what the systems and the individuals in them must do on behalf of students and their learning and then putting that decision into action. It provides a focus based on data and beliefs about what will be most effective in helping students learn. By committing to and pursuing strategy, we have a calm center from which to act clearly and deliberately. Crises don't magically disappear, but we approach them differently and we don't bounce from one crisis to the next. The crises don't all get our immediate attention, because they don't all warrant it. We have work to do that is more important to ensure student learning.

Still, strategy is a tricky word. It is suggestive of something powerful and deliberate, and it can be just that when it helps an organization hold steady on a clear purpose. However, it can also be the catchphrase we attach to a multitude of well-intentioned but disjointed plans and initiatives. When invoked too loosely, it becomes just a word. For our purposes here, and indeed for the work of schools, we find our colleague Stacey Childress's definition very helpful. She explains strategy as "the set of actions an organization chooses to pursue in order to achieve its objectives. These deliberate actions are puzzle pieces that fit together to create a clear picture of how the people, activities, and resources of an organization can work effectively to accomplish a collective purpose."[1]

Developing strategy requires us to identify a few high-leverage ways to improve instruction and student learning. So, for example, a system might conclude that one of its few strategic objectives (ideally no more than five) will be this: Hire and retain effective educators. The specific "set of actions" directed at this goal might include initiatives such as these: work with institutions of higher education to tailor teacher and principal preparation programs and offer comprehensive induction programs for new teachers and principals. The articulated strategic objectives and the initiatives designed to accomplish them become the foci for the system's work, defining how policy is made, what is measured, and how staffing and financial resources are deployed.

Clearly, this is a complex, multistep process. In the next several chapters, we hope to provide you with a foundation for beginning or continuing this work in your system. This chapter is an introduction: what strategy is (and isn't), why it is important, and why school systems typically don't "do" strategy well. It is also about taking stock—what are we currently doing, and is there any discernable pattern to the individual pieces of work under way? Do they align, and if so, to what? By identifying and analyzing initiatives, we can unearth important information, both implicit and explicit, about the work and the choices it reflects. In this way, we may learn something about existing, emerging, or potential strategy in that system. Our goal in this chapter is to help you more deeply understand the relationship between strategic objectives and initiatives, and the power of strategy to focus and amplify a system's efforts to improve learning and teaching.

STRATEGIC PLANNING VERSUS STRATEGY

The word *strategy* is most commonly used in the context of strategic planning—an exercise of setting direction and prioritizing work that systems undertake every three to five years or with the arrival of each new superintendent. The vignette that opens this chapter, drawn from a real system strategic planning process, brings this dilemma into sharp focus: Too often, strategic planning is about creating a laundry list of goals and discrete tasks and repackaging programs to which the system has become attached or is already committed. Imagine being responsible for enacting the plan in the vignette. While everything on the list generally relates to students and their education, the sheer number of goals and initiatives proposed makes it impossible to work in concert toward their overall purpose. This lack of focus translates into dozens of disparate initiatives that do not fit together into a clear, deliberate, overall strategy. The distance between many of the initiatives and the work in classrooms makes it unclear how implementation will lead to improved outcomes for students. As a result, strategic planning in many systems tends to lead to one of two outcomes. Either the cumbersome plan sits on a shelf collecting dust, or the system functions much like the organizational equivalent of a chicken that has lost its head: Staff members run in a million directions, working hard rather than smart, exhausting themselves with only little pockets of success to show for it. Student learning suffers when the system is unable to be precise, agile, and intentional about giving students what they most need to succeed.

Figure 1.1 outlines some of the most salient differences between strategic planning as it is typically carried out in many school systems and strategy development.

Strategic planning is intended to be the vehicle for developing strategy. In high-performing organizations in education and in other sectors, it is. Yet, as the grid suggests, in many school systems strategic planning has devolved into a compliance activity, something done for the school board, or the state or the community. Systems march through the steps of planning, without a clear vision of why they are doing it, what they want to get out of it, or how to design the process to realize meaningful results. Planning is often approached as a community-building activity, which tends to be an attempt to respond to everyone's interests rather than an attempt to organize people on a common vision for the work. Both the compliance and the community-building orientations leave systems with plans that tend to be broad, shallow, and not very useful as in the vignette.

The static nature of many plans relates, in part, to issues of "planning fatigue" and a tendency to deemphasize implementation. After six months of strategic planning, there is a collective sigh of relief once the plan comes back from the printer. "Strategic planning" is checked off the organization's to-do list. While the strategic plan may be passed out at chamber of commerce luncheons and attached to every grant proposal submitted over the next five years, implementation is often reduced to mechanistically pursuing the work plans listed in the appendix with annual reports of accomplishments. The reality of how systems improve is much more dynamic, unlike the neat chart of roles and responsibilities published in the plan. Without a structure and various mechanisms in place for discussing strategy

FIGURE 1.1

STRATEGIC PLANNING VERSUS STRATEGY DEVELOPMENT: TYPICAL CHARACTERISTICS IN EDUCATION

Strategic planning	Effective strategy development
Status quo: tends to focus on organizing current work; often approached as a compliance activity	*Innovation:* draws on research and best practices and pursues new, promising ways of accelerating improvement; builds organizational conviction
Emphasis on external audience: written for external stakeholders and serves as the public document outlining the system's work	*Emphasis on internal audience:* developed to drive how the system focuses the work of its staff and deploys its resources
Broad and incremental: responds to a wide array of needs; there's something for everyone; focuses on slow and steady improvement	*Deep and intentional:* focuses on doing a few things well; aims for a mix of incremental improvement and growth realized in leaps and bounds
Discrete: includes a series of distinct initiatives that have limited relationship to one another and can each be pursued and measured independently	*Interdependent:* integrates a few key initiatives that require cross-functional team collaboration; when executed together, they yield powerful results
Easy fit: fits within the current organizational structure and ways of doing business	*Demands change:* requires organization to function differently to execute; the focus is on being intentional and working together to do something big that no single person or department can do alone
To-do list: lists initiatives and activities with timelines that, if tracked, are checked off as things "done"	*Ways of thinking and being:* develops the capacity of staff to think systemically, plan intentionally, track and evaluate work in light of data, reflect on experience to learn, and continuously look for ways to innovate and improve
Static: completed at a moment in time; revisited for the purpose of reporting on progress but seldom in response to new learning or data	*Dynamic:* developed on the basis of the best information available at that time; continually reconsidered and adapted in light of new learning and research, implementation experience, and qualitative and quantitative results

implementation, learning from it, and refining the strategy accordingly, the effects of the work are diminished and the plan becomes irrelevant. The answer is not to abandon strategic planning. Instead we must ensure that planning is driven by a clear understanding of strategy, is focused on strategy development, and is simply one step in building the system's capacity to act in a focused and coherent way to improve student learning.

WHY IS STRATEGY HARD?

Picture the school system that decides it's going to simultaneously implement new English language arts and math instructional materials K–12, as well as a new formative assessment system that includes organizing and reporting data to inform teachers' instruction. Moreover, a big high school initiative is under way that is about changing instructional methods from didactic to a more student-centered approach. Executing these initiatives is daunting both from the perspective of the central office staff responsible for designing and supporting them and for the teachers and principals who must implement them. It's not hard to imagine how this will go. Central office staff will be so pressed to get the initiatives rolled out to schools that the work will be siloed. Plans will be half-baked when they hit the schools, and the new materials and assessments will not be intentionally aligned to illustrate how the initiatives mutually reinforce one another and can be used together by teachers to guide instruction. At the high school level, the opportunity to weave the three initiatives together and show how the new instructional materials support student-centered pedagogy and how the assessments can be used in a way that engages students in monitoring their learning will likely be lost. Teachers will experience each initiative as a discrete thing to be done, not understanding the purpose behind each and the relationship between them. Their implementation of the initiatives will be similarly fragmented, creating a disjointed learning experience for students. In the end, student learning will suffer, which is the exact opposite of what the system intends.

Developing a tight, coherent strategy requires a clear vision for students and their learning and the few high-leverage things we can focus on that will get us there. As the image above illustrates, most school systems pursue more initiatives than any organization could ever hope to implement well. Even when the quantity of initiatives looks okay on paper, school systems tend not to sequence the work and not to clarify connections across initiatives, so that the intended coherence of the work is clear to people beyond the senior leadership team. Systems often layer initiatives on top of one another in part because people are not confident of the best thing to do. Many systems have limited data available about the effectiveness of work already under way and a disinclination to use the available data to systematically identify what work shows promise and should be scaled up or accelerated and what work should be stopped. (We delve into these issues of data more fully in the chapter 2).

Systems also tend to be fairly insular in thinking about improvement strategy, failing to tap the research and promising practices ongoing in other systems (traditional districts or charters), although these practices are already delivering strong results for students. When we do explore other promising practices, we often compromise our learning. We invoke the "those kids are different from ours" mantra, which immediately shuts down learning even when the practice itself has much to teach us. Conversely, we don't pay enough attention to the context and conditions—size of the system, the demographics of its students, its history, the capacity of teachers and principals, the organizational culture, the expectations of parents and the community—that helped make the initiative successful and would help us to determine how we might replicate the conditions or adapt the initiative to our own conditions.

The tendency to think of strategy as synonymous with strategic planning (something defined in a three- to five-year plan with little opportunity for revisiting or revising it) makes the work feel high-stakes, but for some misguided reasons. We think we need to make all the right decisions up front because we're going to invest heavily in them and not make any adjustments as we go. Once it's on paper, it's the plan. All of our decisions *are* high-stakes; they may or may not make a difference for children. That means the burden is on us to be as thoughtful and knowledgeable as we can be (an ongoing process we'll continue to explore throughout this book). The reality of improvement work is that even when we are very clear about what we are trying to achieve, have researched the best ways to go about it, and have chosen just a few things to do deeply and well, at the end of the day, we make our best bets. Inherent in making bets is the possibility that we will be wrong. Because the current approach to strategy provides little opportunity to redirect as a result of experimentation and learning, it makes perfect sense that systems hedge their bets, spreading resources thinly across a wide array of initiatives and, predictably enough, realizing weak returns.

STARTING WHERE YOU ARE

While there are multiple ways to develop strategy, in this chapter we start with what systems are already doing. Every school system we know is doing things. Those endeavors may not yet reflect a robust strategy, with the puzzle pieces fitting perfectly together, but examining the work currently under way will at a minimum make explicit the system's values and commitments. By understanding its present efforts, a school system will also determine whether it has any strategy—from a mere kernel to a full-blown, robust strategy—embedded in current activities. Currently, most school systems tend to fall into one of three categories with regard to strategy: In a relative few systems, there is a clear and deliberate relationship between a strategy and much of the system's work. The system is working to ensure the coherence of the strategy and pursues an iterative process of aligning activities and strategy, implementing, learning from the work, and refining the strategy according to work accomplished and organizational learning. Some systems have the beginnings of a strategy. They are beginning to focus their work on a few high-leverage things, but there are still lots of other activities under way that don't relate to the nascent strategy. Finally, many systems have no clear strategy at all. There are a variety of initiatives under way in the system, but the relationship of one initiative to another is vague. Further, there is no apparent overarching goal or strategic objective driving those initiatives. The system may or may not know what a strategy is, or that it needs to have one. The system probably has no idea what a system driven by a tightly focused strategy looks like. Whatever its current state, a system can benefit greatly by taking a close look at the programs and initiatives that comprise its daily work. This powerful process helps to assess the coherence, focus, and synergy of the system's strategy or implicit values and commitments, while also revealing the degree to which they are aligned with work currently under way.

We have developed a protocol and accompanying rubric to guide systems through this process. A senior leadership team can use the protocol to make sense of the work under way. Individual departments and schools can use it to understand how and how much their work reflects the system's work and to do a more fine-grained analysis of their own ongoing work. The process has the team brainstorm all of the initiatives under way in the system and then group initiatives that have a similar emphasis, for example, professional development or technology infrastructure. Once the initiatives have been grouped, the team uses a rubric (described later in the chapter) to assess the extent and quality of a system's strategy. This

FIGURE 1.2

FIRST STEP OF UNDERSTANDING YOUR SYSTEM'S CURRENT WORK: BRAINSTORM

Mapping curriculum to standards in all content areas, K–12	Adopting new instructional materials in math, K–12	Developing a system of formative assessments in English and math, K–5	Creating a data warehouse for all student and staff data, including assessment data
Adoption of English and math tutorial software	Redesigning how individual education plans are written and used to serve students with disabilities	Training all teachers in instructional strategies designed to support English language learners	Small schools for high schools

Revamping teacher hiring process	Upgrading the software used to track payroll, benefits, and earned time	Redesign of school budgeting process and timeline	Refining school improvement planning process	Creation of healthy school lunch offerings
Pilot of "workshop" model for literacy instruction, K–5, in 15% of schools	Developing new principal evaluation instrument	Introducing two-year new-teacher induction system	Developing scorecards to measure school and department performance and improvement	Middle school pedagogy initiative focused on math and science

Implementation of direct instruction pilot that involves 10% of schools representing K–8	Science technology, engineering, and math (STEM) initiative at the high school level	Upgrade to provide new computer labs in 40% of schools	Closing five schools
Collaboration with external partner on formative assessment system aligned to state assessment in English and math; currently serving 20% of schools	Conversion of 20% of elementary schools to K–8s	Upgrade schools' technology infrastructure to ensure Internet access in all classrooms	Developing professional learning communities (PLCs) among principals

Development of early childhood curriculum	School safety initiative	Character education training for all K–8 teachers	Creation of early childhood program to serve 600 children	Developing "green" curriculum for use in upper elementary grades

process is described in detail in "Making Sense of the Work Under Way Protocol," in appendix B. The full process takes three to four hours. To give you a sense of how it works, we will now walk through how the senior leadership team from the Moorwood Public Schools used the protocol. The superintendent, Sonya, arranged for an external facilitator to manage this process so that she (the superintendent) could fully participate.

1. Brainstorm

The team completed the first step, which asked team members to brainstorm all the initiatives under way in the system, write each one on a sticky note and post them on the wall (figure 1.2). An initiative is defined as something the system is doing on its own or in collaboration with partners and which is focused on improving some aspect of how the system functions. It may directly involve a set of schools or all schools. It might be a pilot program or a full-scale implementation. It may focus on some aspect of the central office's work. The team began this meeting by reading the sticky notes posted on the wall.

2. Sort

Once everyone had read the sticky notes, it was time to try to group them, putting like things together and categorizing them. Team members developed a rhythm as they quietly moved sticky notes around on the board. In less than ten minutes, the team had created eight clusters of sticky notes. Talking through the initiatives and how they were grouped together helped the team label the clusters. In the process of naming categories, several sticky notes moved from one cluster to another and others were listed in several categories to reflect that they related to more than one category. Two initiatives were dubbed "orphans," not fitting into any of the categories defined; those sticky notes were moved to the edge of the chart paper. The results of the team's work are shown in figure 1.3.

When the facilitator brought the group back together and asked what people noticed, the highlights from the conversation included these:

- We're doing so many things. They're all important, but we can't manage it all.
- According to this list, teachers are supposed to engage in forty-five hours of professional development this year. If we used all the contracted professional development time for system initiatives and gave schools none, we would still be ten hours short.

FIGURE 1.3

SECOND STEP OF UNDERSTANDING YOUR SYSTEM'S CURRENT WORK:
SORT THE BRAINSTORMED INITIATIVES

Instruction	Assessment	Curriculum and instructional materials
Science, technology, engineering, and math (STEM) initiative at the high school level Middle school pedagogy initiative focused on math and science Pilot of "workshop" model for literacy instruction, K–5, in 15% of schools Pilot of direct instruction model in low-performing elementary schools Redesign how individual education plans (IEPs) are written and used	Collaboration with external partner on formative assessment system aligned to state assessment in English and math; currently serving 20% of schools Creating a data warehouse for all student and staff data, including assessment data Developing a system of formative assessments in English and math, K–5 Developing scorecards to measure school and department performance and improvement	Adoption of English and math tutorial software Mapping curriculum to standards in all content areas, K–12 Adopting new instructional materials in math, K–12 Development of early childhood curriculum. Developing "green" curriculum for use in upper elementary grades
Professional development	*Technology*	*Operations*
Introducing two-year new-teacher induction system Training all teachers in instructional strategies that support English language learners Developing professional learning communities (PLCs) among principals Character education training for all K–8 teachers	Adoption of English and math tutorial software Upgrade to provide new computer labs in 40% of schools Upgrade schools' technology infrastructure to ensure Internet access in all classrooms	Upgrade schools' technology infrastructure to ensure Internet access in all classrooms Creating a data warehouse for all student and staff data, including assessment data Upgrading software used to track payroll, benefits, and earned time Revamping teacher hiring process Redesign of school budgeting process and timeline School safety initiative Creation of healthy school lunch offerings Closing five schools
Accountability	*School design*	*Early childhood*
Developing scorecards to measure school and department performance and improvement Developing new principal-evaluation instrument Refining school improvement planning process	Conversion of 20% of elementary schools to K–8s Conversion of two large high schools into small schools	Creation of early childhood program to serve 600 children

- We've got a couple of different formative assessment initiatives going on. Why? Is there a plan to pick one or the other or to integrate them? Are the people who are working on the formative assessments working with the scorecard people to make sure their data are included on the scorecard?
- Aren't direct instruction and workshop really different approaches to instruction? Why are we doing them both?
- We've got a coherence problem. Trying to make sense of all these initiatives is like trying to herd cats.
- It's reassuring to see how much we're focusing on curriculum, instruction, assessment, and teacher professional development, but there isn't much continuity in what we're doing across those areas. It's a bit schizophrenic.
- I agree we're doing too much, but there are some themes; it seems like we're focused on improving the instructional core through curricular, instructional, and assessment initiatives and that we're trying to use technology to support instruction, accountability, and operational functions.
- All this stuff is important, but it's not clear what is most important, which may mean that in the end, nothing is important.

3. Assess

Team members' comments reflected their initial analysis of the categories and initiatives. They were beginning to see that initiatives indicate something about the system's level of focus and the coherence of its work. This conversation led naturally into the third step of the protocol, which asks the team to assess the initiatives and their organization using the "signs of strategy" rubric in figure 1.4. This rubric is built upon four fundamental principles of effective strategy, which can be helpful in assessing an existing strategy, a strategy in development, or the work a system has under way. Using the rubric, participants rate the extent to which the categories and initiatives they identified earlier in the exercise reflect these principles of effective strategy on a four-point scale (4 = high; 1 = low). So, for example, a system with an effective, coherent strategy will score at least a 3 or 4 on all criteria; the work for this team will be to revisit the strategy to ensure it is achieving outcomes for students. A system with mostly 3s and 4s and one score of 1 or 2 is a system that has some very specific work to do to ensure the integrity of its strategy. If a system's scores are primarily 1s and 2s, this indicates that the system has a variety of initiatives under way but no overarching strategy. Those systems need to build a strategy that has integrity and is focused on the most important work of improving student learning.

FIGURE 1.4

THIRD STEP OF UNDERSTANDING YOUR SYSTEM'S CURRENT WORK: "SIGNS OF STRATEGY" RUBRIC

Principles of effective strategy	Level of impact (4 = high; 1 = low)			
	4	3	2	1
Instructional core	All strategic objectives* and initiatives target improving student learning and teaching quality. Operations areas are leveraged to support improving student learning and teaching quality.	Strategic objectives and initiatives focus primarily on improving student learning and teaching quality.	Some strategic objectives and initiatives focus on improving instruction.	Strategic objectives and initiatives focus primarily on operations and student support.
Focus, coherence, and synergy	Strategic objectives are tightly integrated, complementary, and high leverage, focusing on improving student learning and teaching quality.	There are three to five strategic objectives that are interrelated and focused on improving student learning and teaching quality.	There are more than five strategic objectives. Some are related. Others are in conflict or competition.	There are a lot of discrete initiatives.
Both visionary *and* problem solving	Pursuing the strategy addresses identified problems, leads to realizing the system's vision, and transforms student learning results.	Pursuing the strategy addresses identified problems and leads to realizing the system's vision.	Initiatives focus on solving identified problems without pursuing the vision, or are visionary but don't address identified problems.	The relationship between the strategy, the system's vision, and its current conditions and activities is unclear.
Ownership and enactment throughout the system	Everyone, from board members to community partners, understands the strategy and talks about how their work relates to it. Decision making at every level of the system is aligned to the strategy.	All department and school leaders can describe the strategy and their role in its implementation. Board members, families, and community partners know and talk about the strategy.	Key leaders in the system talk publicly about the strategy, but others in the system don't talk about or clearly understand the strategy.	There is no strategy, or there is a strategy but people in the system don't know about it.

*Strategic objectives are the main levers or key areas in which the system is placing its bets about how to achieve desired results. In the "Making Sense of Work Under Way Protocol" in appendix B, the categories that initiatives are grouped into can be considered the strategic objectives. You will further refine these throughout the process of developing strategy.

For this phase of the protocol, we suggest using the rubric to guide a discussion of the principles, one at a time, using evidence to guide the rating. We now rejoin Moorwood as it builds its understanding of the principles of effective strategy and works through the rubric.

Instructional Core?

The heart of a school system's work is often described as the instructional core, drawn as a triangle and symbolizing the complex interaction of teachers and students in the presence of content. Strategy and all its components must address the instructional core by supporting high-quality teaching of rigorous curriculum, answering the question "How will this improve the quality of student learning and teaching?" This is an easy test to apply to the part of the strategy that is clearly about teaching quality, student readiness to learn, curriculum, instruction, and assessment. Yet the question is fundamentally the same when looking at the operations side of the house. How can the design of the new building most effectively support student learning and improved teaching? How can new procurement practices make the process easier for principals and free up more time for supporting teachers and improved instruction? Every school system we know that is rapidly improving student learning places its bets on strategic objectives and initiatives with direct connections to the instructional core.

The Moorwood team gave itself a 2.5 on the instructional core, unable to agree on a score of 2 or 3. At first the team felt quite good about its ongoing work in relation to this principle. Four of the nine categories that the team came up with during the sorting step—instruction, assessment, curriculum and instructional materials, and professional development—related to instruction, and 50 percent of the initiatives fit into those four categories. When the team examined the noninstructionally focused categories and initiatives, it saw that some of the initiatives—e.g., data warehouse, upgrade school technology—supported instruction. Yet there were questions about both the potential for many of those initiatives to *actually* impact instruction and the extent to which they were deliberately designed to do so. For these reasons, the team settled on a 2.5, knowing it hadn't earned a score of 3 and thinking it had done better than a 2.

Focus, Coherence, and Synergy?

Individuals and organizations can only ensure deep, sustained attention on a few things at any given time. Therefore, effective strategy consists of a few, high-leverage ways to improve instruction and student learning and create strong coherence in the system's work. They are complementary and mutually reinforcing, creating a whole that is greater than the sum of its parts. A strategy of improving instruction, developing a student assessment system, and creating a comprehensive student support system is a good example of a strategy that is focused, coherent, and synergistic. A comprehensive assessment system provides teachers with valuable information about student learning; this information then informs how teachers use the curriculum, the instructional materials, and their training to maximum effect. The student support system adds to the sense of focus and coherence as it is entirely focused on students' physical, social, and emotional health and creating the conditions to support student learning. There are only three big ideas in this strategy. Each supports the other. To take one out of the equation would diminish the effectiveness of the other two.

The Moorwood team's conversation about the instructional core surfaced the issue of focus, so making sense of this principle was easier. The team quickly rated itself a 2 on focus, coherence, and synergy. The team members couldn't help but notice that within categories (particularly those related to instruction), there was a lack of coherence and alignment: competing instructional priorities, different assessment systems, and several math and science curriculum and instructional initiatives that were not integrated. The idea of synergy really captured the team's attention. The disparate math and science initiatives seemed like a missed opportunity for synergy, and the team talked about the effort it would take and what it would look like to integrate those initiatives.

Both Visionary *and* Problem Solving?

Picture a system that has trouble hiring teachers early and efficiently. Technology has not been used to its full potential to make the process fast and easy. Applicants are treated in a way that makes them feel unvalued. The system can't compete for the best teachers and ends up hurrying to fill positions in August with less-qualified teachers. This is a problem that needs to be fixed. At the same time, the system has a vision aimed at improving teaching quality, professionalism, and career opportunities. It includes an induction system for new teachers, differentiated treatment for high-performing teachers, and robust support and accountability for mediocre teachers.

The school system's vision can't be realized without fixing serious problems. But solving problems is helpful to the extent that it helps move toward the vision. A compelling vision suggests possibility, encourages innovation, and empowers people, things that are particularly important in school systems where expectations for students and adults in the system have been allowed to sink to a low level and mere survival seems like the goal for many of these systems.

Understanding that the goal is to be *both* visionary *and* solve problems was a new way for the Moorwood team to think about the work. The facilitator helped the team look closely at an individual initiative to make the principle more concrete. Looking at the developing formative assessment initiative, the team first identified the impetus for the initiative as the excessive time teachers spent analyzing the annual, summative state assessment, which they found pretty useless. Because of the delay between when students took the test and when results became available, teachers were looking at performance data for students they no longer had. Add to this the reality that the information provided by the summative data wasn't very fine-grained and was hard to use to guide daily instruction and differentiation. The team's initial consensus, therefore, was that the initiative was all about solving those problems.

Yet as the conversation continued, the focus shifted to how, given the need to ensure that all students finish high school college-ready, teachers need to know much more about what kids are learning, what they are struggling with, and how they learn best, and the teachers need to have this information much more quickly. Suddenly, team members started thinking about the assessments as a new tool in teachers' toolbox to support monitoring students' learning and adapt teaching in response to it. This shifted the teachers' focus from what they taught to what students learned, which felt kind of revolutionary to the team. With a better understanding of the principle, the team looked at a few more initiatives and realized that although the system often developed initiatives simply to address problems, the initiatives sometimes built visionary potential as they were implemented. Yet there wasn't a clear orientation toward trying to balance the two ideas. The team gave the system a score of 2.5 on the question of whether strategy is both problem solving and visionary, reflecting that it sometimes balanced both aspects, but that this balance has been more accidental than intentional.

Ownership and Enactment Throughout the System?
The fastest way to know if a system has a strategy is to ask members of the senior leadership team what the strategy is and ask them to give some examples of it in

action. The clarity and consistency of response (or lack thereof) is telling. You can assess how well the strategy is understood, owned, and driving practice by asking a teacher, a community partner, and a school board member what the strategy is, what it looks like in action, and how they support its implementation. Strategy is enacted when all the people throughout the organization, as well as outside partners, understand what it is, know what their responsibility for implementing it is, and carry it out.

The Moorwood team quickly realized that this fourth principle asks the question "To the extent that there is a strategy, does it primarily exist in the heads of a few of the most senior members of the system, or do staff members and partners understand it and have they internalized it and use it to guide their actions?" The team initially struggled to score this principle because the scores on the other principles prompted them to question the extent to which the system had a strategy to own or enact. The final assessment was that because the team itself wasn't clear on the strategy, it was unrealistic to think that anyone else in the system was. Having finished step 3 of the protocol, the team listed its scores on a piece of chart paper.

1. Instructional core: 2.5
2. Focus, coherence, and synergy: 2
3. Both visionary and problem solving: 2.5
4. Ownership and enactment throughout the system: 1

4. Synthesize

Using the rubric gave members an understanding of strategy and a language for talking about it. They were full of ideas about the kernel of a strategy that lay buried in their list of categories of work and initiatives. This last step of the protocol gave the team a chance to synthesize learning from the exercise and begin to think about what it suggested as good next steps. The score on instructional core suggested a place to start. The system's thinking about how to improve student learning and teaching was embedded in the categories and initiatives related to the instructional core. The team was clear that it needed to use data to inform this process. It was less clear regarding the most pressing problems it was trying to solve. The team members noted that the system's unintentional tendency to try to solve problems and pursue its vision was worth highlighting and making consistent and intentional. The team realized that the sheer number of categories and initiatives was a problem they would need to take on, figuring out what could be done to identify the most essential work, integrate it to maximize its impact, and eliminate nonessential work.

Stepping away from Moorwood's experience, let's look at this example in the context of where other school systems tend to fall on the continuum of not having a clear strategy to having one that is incredibly explicit, understood by everyone in the organization, and used to drive all of the system's work. Exploring the four fundamental principles of effective strategy (and the extent to which their work reflects them) is helpful to systems everywhere on the continuum. For systems with no strategy, the fundamental principles help define what strategy is, the role it plays in an organization, and how to go about developing it. For systems with the beginnings of a strategy, the principles illustrate the importance of focus and clarity, what makes a strategy effective, and how to align the system's work to the strategy. For systems that already have an explicit strategy, the four principles demonstrate how strategy evolves over time in response to organizational learning and progress made. These principles also help the system tune its strategy over time, as conditions and personnel change and strategy revisions may become necessary. As teams revisit this process multiple times, they deepen their understanding of both the principles and the system's facility with them.

Wherever a system falls on this continuum, there are deliberate steps senior leaders can take and conditions they can cultivate to develop effective strategy or refine existing strategy. It is the rare school system that starts from scratch. The entry points to strategy building are varied and context driven, but the necessity of strategy to the improvement of learning and teaching is absolute. Throughout the next several chapters, we will explore prerequisite steps—critical processes that provide the foundation for a system's strategy and contribute to its successful execution.

CHAPTER 2

Teams

Creating the Conditions for Success

> When we commit to bringing our deepest selves to the table
> we are transformed by the act of creating something that we
> cannot create alone.
> —*Peter Block*

It's thirty minutes into the weekly two-hour leadership team meeting of Moorwood Public Schools, and the members are still on the first agenda item. The conversation has devolved into a debate between José, the chief financial officer, and Derek, a regional superintendent who oversees principals, about why principals aren't following procurement procedures. Sonya, the superintendent, isn't sure how the conversation happened as the listed agenda item is "Budget planning for the upcoming fiscal year." Looking around the room, Sonya sees that the rest of the group has checked out: One person's fingers are dancing across his BlackBerry keyboard. Another is shuffling through a four-inch pile of mail. Another is trying to engage in the conversation. The chief financial officer, Victor, who brought a report on budget and spending trends for the group to discuss is leaning back in his chair with his arms crossed and lips pursed. Another member of the team pushes her chair back from the table and heads to the door without a word to the group. As she leaves, a member who had been missing in action slips through the door before it closes; she silently takes her seat at the meeting. She is thirty minutes late. Sonya resists the temptation to step in, take over the meeting, and snap the group to attention, but says to herself with resolve, "This cannot continue. We can and must do better."

This scenario, or some version of it, plays out every day in school systems across the country. Meetings like this can be somewhat painful for those involved in them. We know. We've been there. But do such meetings matter for the system and, more important, for the children the system serves? The short answer is yes. Every meeting is an opportunity to move the system's work forward or backward and to reinforce in positive or negative ways what the system is about (e.g., learning). Every time a team gathers, there is an opportunity for individuals to bring their deepest selves and to create something together that they cannot create alone. However, meetings in schools and the central office are often striking in their lack of clear purpose and direction, their emphasis on information sharing rather than knowledge building or problem solving, their plodding pace, the absence of norms of group interaction and meeting etiquette, and their general inability to accomplish the most important work before them.

WHY TEAMS MATTER

Working in teams is a twenty-first-century skill students need to be successful. It is also a skill teachers need to collaborate effectively with their peers, break down the isolation of teaching, and build their collective expertise and capacity to serve students well. The need for teaming runs up and down the system as principals engage school leadership teams in the work of school improvement. Central office departments create teams to do their work most effectively. The superintendent convenes a senior leadership team to shape and drive the direction of the system's work. Effective collaboration is critical to success at all levels of the organization. Yet the knowledge, skills, and dispositions required for collaboration are seldom taught. It is deeply ironic that a skill students need to ensure their future opportunities is one that the adults responsible for their education often do not possess and have not had the opportunity to learn.

Too often, team functioning is viewed as peripheral to improving instructional quality and learning for all students—something to be pursued, or not, depending on an organization's tolerance for such things. In reality, team functioning in a system has tremendous implications for that system's ability to organize and focus itself on the work of instructional improvement. Strategy will never be implemented nor vision realized without collaboration and teamwork. Strategy doesn't just happen. People working in teams make it happen.

The level of team functioning is a simple, predictive indicator of an organization's health.[1] In our experience, after observing a single senior leadership team meeting, we can predict, quite accurately, four things about the system as a whole: (1) how people throughout the system treat and interact with one another; (2) the level of focus and discipline brought to the work of instructional improvement; (3) the extent and quality of collaboration within the organization; and (4) the team's impact on the work of the system. The common issues of departments functioning as silos, the tyranny of the urgent over the important, and the like, are often reflected in how the senior leadership team functions. Addressing these issues at the senior leadership team level increases the likelihood that these issues can be addressed at other levels in the organization. Not addressing them at the senior level ensures that they will continue to drive the ineffective functioning of the system.

Every school system we know that is making great progress in outcomes for students has a high-functioning senior leadership team. The teams aren't perfect, and certainly, they have other strengths contributing to their success, but the teams are an essential element.

In the absence of a functional senior leadership team, there may be isolated pockets of teaming and collaboration, but there won't be a functioning *system* of collaboration and teamwork. Watching superintendents and principals drive their team meetings with little opportunity for team members to engage, collaborate, and problem-solve, one is not surprised when instruction is delivered in a similarly top-down, disengaging manner. Systemic improvement is not the work of a single, heroic leader, nor is it the work of a small group of senior leaders. For a system to experience improvement, everyone in the system must be engaged. This requires deliberate effort and support.

Public school systems invest roughly 80 percent of their budgets in people, making people the organization's greatest resource. Yet there is a fairly consistent lack of attention given to maximizing people's contribution to the work. This chapter focuses on the characteristics, or building blocks, of high-functioning teams, tools that facilitate this work, and some good habits that will help to sustain it. While this chapter is relevant for all kinds of teams, we concentrate on the work of a system's senior-most leadership team. This focus reflects the realities that systemic improvement requires the commitment and expertise of the senior leaders of the organization and that people watch and take their cues from what happens at the top of the organization.

BUILDING BLOCKS

What distinguishes a high-functioning team from a group of individuals who meet together regularly under the name of "team" is a sense of purpose and the commitment of the individuals on the team to focus on the greater good of the organization. This commitment means that organization-wide issues trump individual and departmental interests; that team members think critically, systemically, and strategically with the long-term health of the organization at the fore; that data drive decisions; and that the team commits itself to making tough calls when that is required. For these things to happen, the individuals on the team must trust one another, work well together, and hold one another accountable.

Embedded within the questions below are five key building blocks of effective team functioning. They are relevant regardless of the type of team or the level of the organization at which the team operates, and they can be used to diagnose and address problems with which an existing team is struggling. These questions can also guide the design and development of a new team.

- Is the team's *purpose* clear, challenging, and consequential?
- Are the *right people* on the team?
- Are the necessary *structures in place* to support a high-functioning team?
- Does the team have the *capacity* to function well?
- Is the team *accountable* for its processes and outcomes?[2]

1. IS THE TEAM'S PURPOSE CLEAR, CHALLENGING, AND CONSEQUENTIAL?

Have you ever found yourself on a team where (1) you weren't quite sure why you were there or what the work of the team was; (2) you thought the focus of the team's work was much too abstract with no concrete outcomes, too narrowly focused, or mired in details; or (3) you had a sneaking suspicion that the team was window dressing and that other people somewhere else were actually making the important decisions? You are in good company if you said yes to all three descriptors. Lack of clarity haunts teams and the individuals on them as people don't know what direction they are headed in and how they would know if the teams were effective. As a result, the teams often waste time focusing on inconsequential things or being driven by the most powerful or vocal members of the team.

When trying to provide a sense of clarity about purpose, a leader will often describe the leadership team as being responsible for realizing the vision and mission of the organization. The statement is both true and insufficient. Mission and vision are fairly abstract statements, not offering a team concrete images of what its work is when it gets together for two hours every Wednesday morning. The team, under the guidance of the superintendent, needs to craft a purpose that balances a powerful, inspiring vision with specifics about what the team is responsible for and what it is expected to accomplish. One of the tensions in defining the work of the team is the need to strike a balance between having the team be forward-looking, driving the organization to the future, and using the team to oversee the daily management of the system's work. Both need to be done. When the centrifugal force of daily operations squeezes out the work of championing vision and the strategy required to realize it, the team becomes more reactive than proactive and the energy and potential of the team are deflated by the relentlessness of managerial issues. To minimize the likelihood of this happening, the purpose of a team must be *clear, challenging, and consequential.*[3]

Clear means that team members can tell you in concrete terms what the purpose of the team is and what their roles and responsibilities to the team are. Saying that the team is responsible for ensuring that every student graduates with the skills required to enter the world of work or higher education doesn't provide a sense of what the team will actually do. Saying, instead, that a team is responsible for developing the improvement strategy for the system, ensuring coherence and aligning resources to the strategy, creating the conditions required for implementation, and tracking results is more concrete. It gives team members images of what their work will look like and what they will be expected to contribute. It also helps those not on the team to understand what the work of the leadership team is and what to expect from the team. This creates transparency and discourages people from wasting time and energy wondering what happens behind closed doors and who the real power brokers in the organization are.

Challenging means that the team's work isn't simple, technical work but strategic work where there is often no clear "right" answer. Everyone has to ask hard questions, bring their best thinking, and debate ideas and issues with the goal of making the best decisions for the organization. The painstaking task of balancing a system's budget isn't the work of a leadership team. Prioritizing initiatives for spending and making difficult decisions about what work is most central to the strategy (particularly critical in times of constrained resources) is the work of a leadership team. Think about your most rewarding team experiences at work, in your community, or on a playing field—facing a good challenge as a group was probably part of what made the team experience meaningful and memorable.

Consequential means that the team makes decisions about important things. The goal of the team is not to share updates across departments, provide advice to the superintendent, or coordinate projects. Rather, this team focuses at the level of strategy—for example, deciding on the most effective approach to building teachers' instructional skills or deciding to partner with charter management organizations to improve the quality of the educational opportunities for families and to accelerate improvement in the district. The team then delegates the execution of that work and tracks the results. The team also decides what the organization will start doing, stop doing, and do differently in light of current conditions and the system's vision and strategy.

Defining or Redefining Purpose

Whenever possible, the superintendent should set the purpose of a newly formed senior leadership team *before* convening that team. In setting the purpose, the superintendent needs to be very clear and honest about what role he or she wants the team to play. What authority will he or she give the team, and what authority will be reserved for the superintendent? Is this leader prepared to buffer the team from the many pressures that can distract a superintendent and leadership team from focusing on the work of improving instruction? If not, what support can he or she create to help with this? Communicating the answers to these questions (and many others) is a critical part of setting the purpose of the team and creating clear, shared expectations. The team has the best chance of doing meaningful work if the superintendent's vision for the team includes taking on substantial work related to leading the organization toward its vision. Individual team members need that sense of purpose to propel them and the team as a whole forward. They also need to feel a part of something bigger and more powerful than their individual responsibilities to convince them that they should let the interests of the whole system supersede their individual departmental interests.

Below are a series of questions to guide a superintendent or team leader who is thinking about the work of an existing leadership team or who is considering developing such a team:

- What is your charge to the team? Concretely, what do you see the team spending its time doing?
- Is the team's purpose clear, challenging, and consequential?
- How much authority are you prepared to give the team? (What decisions will the team be responsible for making? When will you look for guidance from the team but make decisions on your own?)
- Could others in the organization do this work? If so, why is the team necessary?
- How will the team work with the rest of the system?
- Where does your picture of the team's work fall on the continuum—from keeping the trains running on time to driving strategy development and realizing the system's vision?
- Where might the team's work get bogged down? How can you safeguard against that?

Being clear about purpose guides the superintendent's choice of team members, who are selected on the basis of their ability to help the team fulfill its purpose. Clarity of purpose also helps team members understand what they are being asked to do. It is likely that the purpose of the team will evolve according to the developmental stage of the team, where the system is in the process of developing and implementing an improvement strategy, and so on. Thinking about this at the front end so the people recruited onto the team are those who can add value as the purpose evolves saves a superintendent from the pain and discontinuity of having to ease people off and on the team.

For a team that already exists, it is important to answer the question "What is the purpose of this team?" Asking team members this question individually can be enlightening. If there are eight team members and more than five purposes articulated, there is a problem of purpose. For existing teams suffering from a lack of a common sense of purpose, repurposing can be very effective. The work of repurposing can be the sole domain of the superintendent or can be something the team is intentionally asked to engage in as a way to build a sense of ownership and commitment. In the process, it is quite likely that the composition of the team will be reconsidered with the goal of reflecting the redefined focus of the team and the knowledge, skills, and dispositions required of its members.

2. ARE THE RIGHT PEOPLE ON THE TEAM?

Who should be on the team? Often, team slots are allocated according to job title rather than expertise, skill sets, and overall team composition. The job title approach makes sense on a practical and political level, but lacks the intentionality and orientation toward purpose that a team needs if it's going to effectively drive the system's work. A better approach is to ask, "Who should be on the team to help it fulfill its purpose?" The chief operating officer and the chief academic officer should be on the team not because they're near the top of the organizational chart, but because their work is so central to the mission or healthy functioning of the system, or both, and they have the power to realize or squash ideas at the point of implementation.

A seat on a senior leadership team is generally seen as an indicator of a person's power. As a result, people have a vested interest in being on the team and often assume, on the basis of their position as a senior staff person, that their title ensures them a seat at the table. The usual approach of assembling a team of the people in the eight most senior staff positions reinforces the perception that the team is first and foremost about power and that members of the team are there to represent every major department or division. On high-functioning teams, the focus is on ensuring the health and success of the overall organization rather than its individual departments.

The team must be small enough to be nimble and include the decision makers who are able to drive systemic improvement. Common wisdom is that senior leadership teams should be lean, with fewer than ten members often thought to be optimal even in large systems. Ensuring that the "right people" are on the team involves thinking practically, politically, holistically, and a bit creatively—all in the midst of expectations about team membership that are often more about power than they are about purpose.

With this in mind, we can consider a number of things in developing a senior team. Figure 2.1 lists important characteristics of a good member of the team. Members who help the team fulfill its purpose are curious and think systemically and strategically. This means that team members can think about an idea or issue from all sides and aren't easily married to a position. They inquire with the goal of understanding rather than advocating for a particular position. They can see the implications of decisions for all the different stakeholders in the organization and for how the organization functions in both the short and the long term. They are

---

FIGURE 2.1

SENIOR TEAM MEMBERSHIP: CHARACTERISTICS FOR CONSIDERATION

Big-picture thinker: Looks at problems and potential solutions from all sides; sees how decisions about one aspect of the system affect other areas and must be considered holistically and over the long term; thinks about the best solution to a problem, taking into account issues of substance, finances, capacity, politics, and so on.

Teaching and learning knowledge: Has deep understanding of the instructional core and the interplay of its components: teachers, students, and content.

Team player: Puts the overall vision and health of the system above departmental interests; supports others; likes being part of a team and the sense of belonging it offers; will roll up sleeves and get things done.

Fun: Has perspective and sense of humor and can maintain both in stressful times; sees the lighter side of things sometimes.

Truth speaker: Speaks up if the person has concerns, disagrees, or thinks the team is missing important information.

---

comfortable and thrive in the expanse of gray that connects black and white and don't assume there are right ways and a wrong ways.

A favorite chief financial officer (CFO) of ours embodies this way of thinking. He is a quiet soul who watches and listens intently as his leadership team colleagues debate an initiative under consideration. Whether the topic is expanding instructional coaching from literacy to math or devoting significant resources to new teacher induction, just as the momentum of the group's enthusiasm compromises its ability to think critically, he quietly asks questions like, "In what ways is the work of improving math instruction similar to or different from what we are trying to do in literacy, and to what extent do we think instructional coaching will help us accomplish it?" Every time he asks a question like this, you can hear a pin drop as team members stop in their tracks, knowing that his question is pushing them to think harder, more critically.

In addition to thinking systemically and strategically, strong team members understand that the success of the team requires team members to leave their individual interests at the door and come to the table thinking about the organization as a whole and what will ensure its growth and overall health. This means that individual team members think about decisions from the perspective of what will accelerate the system's rate of improvement and opportunities and outcomes for children rather than the perspective of what this means for their division. People who come to their work with a strong team orientation naturally think this way. It is important to know that this skill can also be taught and nurtured in people who don't lead with it but show great promise in other key areas. We will address capacity building of this sort shortly.

In this list of requirements for team composition, the trick is identifying people with all the attributes. Life in school systems is rarely so simple. Specifically, the case of the key decision maker who doesn't think systemically or strategically or isn't a team player can pose real challenges. This manifests itself in several ways: an inability to see the big picture and a tendency to perseverate on details; a preference to go it alone and a failure to understand or believe in the wisdom of teams; or an ego that makes it hard to imagine that he or she isn't always right. This behavior can quickly impede the development of trust in the group or erode that which already exists, undermining the team's ability to function well. If key decision makers can't think strategically and systemically or can't commit and contribute to a team, then this raises the question of whether they should be in such important roles. This dilemma is one of the great leadership challenges superintendents face. How it is addressed affects the functioning of the team and signals what is valued as well as what will be tolerated in the organization.

Selecting or Adjusting Team Membership

The superintendent makes the final decisions about who is on the senior leadership team. That means he or she invites people to serve on the team, gives people feedback on how they are contributing to the team, and decides when the team would benefit from reconstitution. Deciding whom to ask to serve on the team requires a good sense of potential members' expertise, skills, and ability to play well with others. When a superintendent is new, due diligence and triangulating data sources to make sure a potential team member gets strong marks from more than one source can be helpful.

When a superintendent is reassessing an existing team that is not functioning well, he or she must do a gut check about team members. One of the hardest jobs for a superintendent who is dissatisfied with the leadership team is to figure out the extent to which the problem stems from the people on the team or their skills, dispositions, or interpersonal skills. Taking on challenging team members is essential, difficult, sometimes costly, and a key measure of a leader's commitment and courage. Everyone on the team knows who the difficult team members are in the same way teachers in a school always know who their poor-performing colleagues are. Ruth Wageman and her colleagues' research suggests that CEOs are slow to address poor team performers and only do so after team functioning has been severely compromised.[4] This is a cautionary tale to encourage superintendents to make this hard call at the front end, when they have the opportunity to decide the membership of a team, or to name the problem as soon as it becomes apparent. When taking action against a disruptive or poor performer, a leader may not get a public pat on the back, but he or she can almost hear the collective sigh of relief. Conversely, when a disruptive or poor performer is allowed to continually behave in an unproductive manner without consequence, other team members get frustrated, questioning why they are working so hard when expectations for performance seem to be quite low. Over time, if these concerns are not addressed, the effectiveness of the team is compromised and the leader's credibility is called into question.

Figure 2.2 is an example of a matrix that Sonya, the Moorwood Schools' superintendent used to evaluate her leadership team members. This populated example illustrates the superintendent's analysis of her existing team—Sonya's attempt to be deliberate about membership, to consider who on her team may not belong there, and to think about areas where the team or individuals need development.

All team members in this example are mere mortals with strengths and weaknesses. A no in a single characteristic does not necessarily mean somebody isn't fit for the team, but it does identify areas where they can improve and where other members might bring balance. The question is not necessarily what each individual brings, but how all the individuals complement one another to fulfill the team's purpose. On a holistic level, the team of people Sonya is sure she wants to keep is strong on big-picture thinking and has a slight majority of people with teaching and learning expertise, a team orientation, and the abilities to have fun and speak the truth. She is aware that only a slim majority of members are strong in the skills that will have the greatest impact on the team's work (a team orientation, a fun attitude, and the ability to be honest). This may need to be an area for team training and something she will need to attend to. The team's strength in big-picture thinking is exciting to Sonya, but she also understands the importance of balancing this with concrete thinking and action that responds to the on-the-ground reality faced by students, teachers, and schools. Only one person on the team with teaching and

FIGURE 2.2

SONYA'S CHART FOR COMPARING POTENTIAL TEAM MEMBERS

Potential team member	Title	Big-picture thinker	Teaching and learning knowledge	Team player	Fun	Truth speaker	Include on team?
Sonya Shaw	Superintendent	Y	Y	Y	N	Y	Y
Patrick Leary	Chief Academic Officer	Y	Y	Y	N	Y	Y
Derek Jones	Regional Superintendent	Y	Y	?	?	?	Y
Victor Ponte	Chief Financial Officer	Y	N	Y	N	Y	Y
Betty Scott	Chief of Staff	Y	N	Y	Y	Y	Y
Iris Watkins	Director of Accountability	N	Y	Y	Y	N	Y
José Vega	Chief Operating Officer	Y	N	N	Y	N	Y
Claudia Torres	Director of School Innovation	Y	Y	N	N	N	?
Maria Savance	Regional Superintendent	N	Y	Y	?	N	N
Fred Stone	Regional Superintendent	N	Y	N	Y	Y	N
Jane Bennett	Director of Assessment	Y	N	N	N	N	N

learning expertise works directly with schools and principals, which means the team will have to work hard to make sure that this person isn't the only one sharing the needs and interests of principals. As the superintendent considers other possible team members, she might look to fill those gaps but overall she is pleased to see that team members collectively constitute a strong team and provide a nice complement to her own skills.

Derek Jones is the only regional superintendent of three listed to be a clear yes for the team. He is new in the job, but has already demonstrated his knowledge of teaching and learning and his ability to consider the big picture. Because he is new, people can't assess his team skills, his capacity for fun, or his ability to speak the truth, and it's clear he is just beginning to learn the system. Those feel like risks worth taking, particularly when he is compared with his two other regional superintendent colleagues. He seems to have the broadest skill set, and there is a commitment to having at least one regional superintendent on the team because their perspective as the direct supervisors of principals is critical.

José, the chief operating officer, poses a challenge. His scores indicate he's not a team player and disinclined to speak up if he has a concern or disagrees. That combination is particularly problematic as it suggests he won't be forthright and then will do what he wants. Because the academic work must be preeminent, it is critical that the person in charge of all the nonacademic departments is fully on board with supporting that work. Given that he is the COO, this is a real issue the superintendent needs to wrestle with to figure out if he can be supported to change or if he may not be the right person for the job. Avoiding the personnel issue by simply leaving him off the team won't work, as he's a key decision maker in the organization. Sonya decides to keep him on the team and to work with him directly to build his team orientation and willingness to speak up. She reminds herself that he is fun and brings energy and enthusiasm to teams, which can be a real contribution to this team.

Other team members get a yes or no vote according to their mix of skills and dispositions. Claudia Torres, the director of school innovation, has ratings worth considering. She is strong on big-picture thinking and teaching and learning, but weak in team orientation and the ability to speak the truth. On the one hand, she is managing a critical and growing area of district work—new school development and school transformations—which is clearly part of the strategy. On the other hand, her tendencies to go it alone and not attend to process have already been noticed by other leaders in the system. The concern is about whether she might jeopardize the team's level of functioning. At the end of the analysis, the superintendent has six clear yes votes for team membership and one decision to make. She is also left thinking about who on the team can bring the assessment perspective and if one regional superintendent (a new one, at that) brings enough of the principals' perspective to the table. Her instinct is probably yes, but there may need to be some adjustments.

3. ARE THE NECESSARY STRUCTURES IN PLACE TO SUPPORT A HIGH-FUNCTIONING TEAM?

Structure supports the rhythm of work in high-functioning teams and creates room for them to be creative and innovate. People on the team know what is expected of them. The flow of meetings is consistent and familiar. There is a clear process for making decisions. Everyone leaves meetings clear about decisions made, actions to be taken, and their individual responsibilities. The team knows how to assess its effectiveness and does so regularly. Two key structures that support high functioning are norms and meeting agendas.

Norms

Norms are a set of agreements that define how team members will behave when they meet. One high-functioning senior leadership team we know of meets at a long, oval table each week, and there is a glass jar in the middle of the table. On the rare occasion when a team member is late to the meeting, the person puts a dollar—the cost of breaking the norm of coming to the meeting on time—in the jar. At one meeting, a team member was driven to critique an idea that had been introduced, but he did not provide an alternative (one of the team's norms); he started his comments saying, "I know this is going to cost me five dollars, but I have to say this." This team has well-established norms, and individual members of the team

---

FIGURE 2.3

**TYPICAL NORMS OF BEHAVIOR AT MEETINGS—SET BY A TEAM
EARLY IN THE STAGE OF DEVELOPING TRUST**

- Begin and end on time.
- Refrain from using BlackBerries during meetings.
- Assume good intentions.
- Be succinct, concrete, and explicit when speaking.
- Stay on topic, and stick to the meeting objectives.
- Before speaking, ask yourself, "Is what I'm about to say going to add value to the work at hand and the team?" or "Am I asking for help?"
- Think about the organization's overall growth and progress rather than the growth and progress of specific departments.
- Listen to understand, and ask if you don't understand.
- Wait until the person speaking is finished before talking.

FIGURE 2.4

TYPICAL NORMS OF BEHAVIOR AT MEETINGS—SET BY THE SAME TEAM
ONCE TRUST WAS DEVELOPED

- *Demonstrate integrity:* Be transparent: Say what you mean, and mean what you say; say the same things outside the meetings that you say in the meetings. Be reliable: Do what you say you will do; provide honest feedback.

- *Be trustworthy:* Assume good intentions; listen to understand, and ask for clarification when it's needed; communicate clearly.

- *Be a team player:* Support colleagues in your words, thoughts, and deeds; focus on the good of the whole over the good of your department or division; offer your time and expertise when it will add value; ask for help when you need it.

- *Be engaged:* Prepare for meetings as needed; attend meetings (no substitutes); ask questions to push the team's thinking and learning; speak up when the team is not functioning well, and commit to helping it get back on track.

- *Be efficient:* Start and end the meeting on time; have a timed agenda at every meeting, with decision points defined; provide materials related to agenda items and decisions in advance of the meeting for review; have a timekeeper.

- *Be accountable:* Abide by decisions once they are made; communicate the work and decisions of the team to your stakeholders accurately; commit to doing whatever it takes to bring the team's decisions and commitments to fruition; assess the work of the team and the individuals on it; track outcomes and results.

---

have internalized them and monitor their own behavior. In addition to reinforcing expectations, it's fun for the team; the members laugh about who has a running tab and what they'll do with the money once it amounts to a meaningful sum.

The key to developing norms is describing the preferred behavior in simple terms that help people know what it looks like. The two sample lists in figures 2.3 and 2.4 reflect different approaches to norm setting. The first list describes behaviors very concretely; the other names values and then describes what they look like in action. The first example comes from a team that was early in the process of building trust. Members had developed bad habits, including a way of communicating whereby everyone added their own two cents without any effort to build on ideas and move the discussion forward. The team devoted thirty to forty-five minutes to developing norms, with a primary focus on curbing unproductive behaviors.

The second example reflects a longer conversation by the same team, which focused more broadly upon values of the organization and how to ensure they are reflected in the norms.

Given that there is a common set of issues norms address, it is reasonable to ask if a team should simply adopt or tweak a set of norms introduced to the group from another source rather than take the time to develop its own norms. People who have been part of building a team's norms often describe it as both painful and incredibly important. It forces a team to think about the team's behaviors, describe what the work looks like when it goes well (or not), and to name the team's bad habits. Norm building also lets the team surface its core values and can be an important team-building activity. Finally, and perhaps most important, teams are generally much more invested in implementing norms they helped develop. It's also worth noting that norms need to be revisited periodically to see how they fit once they're put into practice and whether they need to be revised as the team and its work evolves.

Establishing and Modeling Norms

The role of the superintendent in developing and implementing norms is about signaling that this work is a priority, pushing the team to address the most important issues about their process, modeling how to follow the norms and reinforcing them by recognizing when people follow the norms as well as when they don't. Developing norms, whether the group is new or more established, can be sensitive. Simply asking, "What were the bad habits of a low-performing team you have seen in action that you want to make sure we avoid?" often helps the team get started. If team members are slow to respond, the superintendent can suggest a norm or two, giving people permission to talk about negatives. The corollary is also useful: "What norms will help you and the team as a whole do our best work and fulfill our purpose?" Brainstorming on sticky notes can be helpful for generating ideas quickly and for providing the "cover" of anonymity in dysfunctional systems. Once the ideas start flowing, team leaders and the superintendent can facilitate and strategically suggest norms that have been overlooked. Once the norms are developed, the superintendent must be vigilant about modeling them, acknowledging others who follow them, and calling out those who do not. Such regular maintenance reinforces the norms and signals that disregard is unacceptable.

Meeting Agendas

A productive and satisfying meeting begins with a well-designed agenda. The agenda signals priorities for the meeting and expectations for what will be accomplished. Therefore, it should be developed with an eye to focusing the team on the most important work of systemic improvement and organizing the meeting to focus on a few top priorities with clarity about outcomes, decision points, next steps, and responsibilities. Agendas are to meetings what lesson plans are to instruction. Just as it is easy to identify a lesson that has not been well planned, it is also easy to figure out if a meeting agenda has been patched together at the last minute. An agenda doesn't provide an ironclad guarantee that the meeting will be a success. Unexpected things may arise in a meeting, just as they may in the classroom, requiring a shift in direction. But we all know what a wasted opportunity teaching without planning can be and how painful it can be for everyone involved; the same holds true for meetings.

Let's consider two examples of agendas. The first one is a reasonable representation of what many meeting agendas look like. The second agenda reflects a more strategic approach to meeting planning.

Looking closely at the first, more typical agenda, we can see a number of things that stand out (figure 2.5). The late afternoon timing of the meeting makes it unlikely that people will come to the meeting fresh and able to do their best work. The first agenda items are informational, while the most substantive items are at the end of the agenda. Note the absence of time allotments per item for this two-hour meeting and the meaty nature of a couple of the items (e.g., student performance data, budget, contract negotiations), suggesting that either the team won't get through the agenda or it will superficially cover each item without the opportunity to explore important issues deeply.

In this first agenda, the purpose of each agenda item and any expectations for action are unclear. The first two agenda items could be easily addressed by handing out quick updates and having people read them and follow up with questions as necessary. If the eight departments represented at the meeting really do updates, they will likely take anywhere from twenty-five to forty minutes (three to five minutes per department) total. The third and fourth agenda items either are purely informational or might require a decision about attempting to incorporate best practices from high-performing schools into the system's overall improvement strategy. It is not clear with any of the agenda items if there are decisions to be made or outcomes to be realized. As a result, the meeting participants do not know

---

FIGURE 2.5

TYPICAL SENIOR LEADERSHIP TEAM MEETING AGENDA

Senior Leadership Team Meeting
3:00–5:00 p.m.

Agenda

1. Updates from departments

2. Presentation of new district promotional materials, including video for families

3. Presentation of best practices used in three schools with strong achievement results

4. Review of just-released state assessment data

5. Discussion of budget projections for upcoming year

6. Setting priorities for upcoming teachers' contract negotiations

---

what is expected of them in terms of preparing for, participating in, and following up after the meeting.

The second agenda (figure 2.6) differs from the first in several notable ways. Devoting 75 percent of the meeting time to two agenda items and giving half of the meeting time to just one agenda item signals an emphasis on deep exploration and analysis. Being a contributing participant in the meeting requires advanced preparation and a level of engagement that is quite different from the first meeting. Participants are expected to read materials in advance and think critically about them. The questions listed under the first agenda item emphasize building understanding as a precursor to making decisions. The listing of "outcome/decision points" makes it very clear what the outcomes are for each agenda item and what decisions the team needs to make. The "outcome/decision points" listed under the second agenda item illustrate a clear connection between the first and second agenda items and a systems approach to the leadership team's work. That is, budget planning is driven by student achievement results and priorities identified for improving instruction and student learning results. The agenda reflects the themes of clarity, challenge, and consequence—themes that give a team a sense of purpose. The agenda items are mission critical and of such importance that this is the only team that can address them.

FIGURE 2.6

MORE STRATEGIC SENIOR LEADERSHIP TEAM MEETING AGENDA

Senior Leadership Team Meeting

9:00–11:00 a.m.

Agenda

1. How are we doing: discussion of state assessment data (60 minutes)

   Outcome/decision points: team identifies performance results that require deeper analysis and program areas for review

   Prep for discussion: review data analysis provided in meeting prep packet; bring responses to the following questions to the meeting:

   - What clarifying questions do you have to make sure you understand the data?
   - What three findings from the data are most striking to you? Why?
   - What questions do the data raise for you about the improvement strategy the system is pursuing?
   - What additional data would you like to see to get a clearer picture?

2. Aligning resources to instructional priorities: starting the conversation (30 minutes)

   Outcome/decision points: team understanding of budget outlook for coming year, anticipated fixed costs, and comparative spending over the past three years; agreement about how to use findings and priorities from agenda item 1 to inform budget planning

   Prep for discussion: review budget report provided in prep packet

3. Next steps and assignments (20 minutes)

4. Meeting debrief (10 minutes)

   - Highs and lows
   - Recommendations for improvements

Who Drafts the Agenda?

The superintendent plays an important role in ensuring that leadership team meeting agendas are well constructed and carefully focused on the most important work of the system. Depending on the size of the system and the style of the superintendent, this may be something the superintendent does himself or herself, or it may be something delegated to a competent and trusted staff person, most commonly a chief of staff or chief operating or administrative officer. Regardless of who is overseeing agenda development, it is essential that the person focuses on agenda items that are mission critical, brings data to inform conversations whenever possible, allows time for deep discussion and debate, is clear about decision points or products of the work, coordinates with key staff to get premeeting readings and briefings out to team members in advance of the meeting, and tracks the next steps and the follow-up. This requires that the person chosen to do this work has the right skill set, has scheduled time devoted to this work, and meets with the superintendent regularly. The superintendent must signal to the person and the rest of the team the importance of this work and the superintendent's authorization of that staff person to do the work on his or her behalf.

4. DOES THE TEAM HAVE THE CAPACITY TO FUNCTION WELL?

Developing and implementing norms for how the team will work together and carefully crafting agendas are two basic structures that can go a long way toward ensuring the effectiveness of teams. With this foundation in place, it is likely that team members will need to learn ways of being part of a team that may be unfamiliar to them. High-functioning teams exhibit a high level of trust, a willingness to be vulnerable, and comfort with conflict, three things that are not commonly observed in teams. They are critical because trust makes conflict possible, and conflict makes commitment possible.[5] The team's ability to debate issues and respectfully hear and consider different perspectives is what allows team members to commit to the work of the team even when a member may not agree with the team's decision.

Building Trust

There are lots of ways to build a new or existing team's sense of trust. At the most basic level, trust is built as we get to know one another better and understand where we are each coming from: what matters most to us, how we think, what our pet peeves or places of sensitivity are, and so on. It is amazing how often, in the name of getting down to the work, we forget that a group of individuals will be hard-pressed to do good work together if they have not had the opportunity to get to know one another.

Trust can be a big and daunting concept. Yet it is built through an infinite series of interactions, some of which can be orchestrated. Creating simple, purposeful ways for team members to get to know one another at both a personal and a professional level can be invaluable. It becomes much harder to label someone "difficult" or "wrong" or personalize disagreements once we know something important and personal about the person. By getting to know one another personally, team members tend to feel a greater sense of connection, empathy, and concern for the person, which makes them more committed to working together and struggling together through the work when it gets hard.

One simple way to build trust is to be deliberate about it

Devote time on the agenda to helping people get to know one another. Each individual question below (and lots more you'll dream up) can be used to guide a time of team sharing and team building.

- What made you choose education as your profession?
- What was your experience as a student, and how does it inform the work you do now?
- What was your most defining experience as a student or a learner?
- When did you know you would be involved in education?
- Who was the most influential educator for you as a student? Why?
- Who are the children in your life, and what do you hope we create for them?

It's also okay to ask questions that aren't about who we are at work. One senior team we know asked each person to share something about themselves—something outside work—that other people on the team were unlikely to know. They thus found out that the deputy superintendent liked racing cars, someone else was an expert guitarist, and the superintendent cooked to relax. Connecting as humans, not just as educators, is part of what helps us know and be known and to support one another, particularly when the work is hard and the conversation is heated and when everything seems urgent.

Another way to build trust that moves from personal experiences to something that might best be described as personal "wiring" involves using one of the many leadership or work styles inventories (e.g., Myers Briggs, DiSC) that exist. These tools explain how each of us is inclined to work and lead in a particular way. Having team members take the assessment, bring the results to a meeting, and participate in a facilitated introduction to the framework of the tool, the meaning of different results, and the implications for teamwork can be incredibly helpful. If approached in a lighthearted way and with a clear understanding that there is no right way to be, this can also be quite entertaining as people have *aha*s about why their teammate always asks that same question, why certain habits of a teammate drive another batty, and how to rely on certain people's strengths to guide the team in particular circumstances.

Building trust through vulnerability

Expressing vulnerability is one of the most powerful ways to build trust and one of the strongest indicators of the level of trust that exists in a team. A style inventory like those described above begins to get at this as people share their strengths and places where they may be less adept. As teams build from such a foundation, the most powerful moments of trust building happen when people express uncertainty about what to do next or ask for help. The vulnerability (and courage) exhibited when someone tells colleagues they don't know what to do or how to do something can accelerate the development of trust. The superintendent can model this kind of behavior and the appropriate, constructive responses to it with profound effect. Because he or she is the person in the room with the greatest positional authority, the risk the superintendent takes (no matter how great it feels) is the lowest of anyone in the room. In addition to signaling that this behavior is acceptable, the superintendent creates the opportunity for the team to respond to this uncertainty or request for help, building its skills of acting in supportive and trusting ways and advising him or her.

Developing comfort with conflict

As trust is built, a team's tolerance for conflict grows. To be sure, conflict can and does occur in a context of low trust. However, in that case conflict is created to separate and protect people and avoid the work at hand. Conflict that occurs in a team environment of trust can help to focus the team on doing the best work possible. In high-functioning teams, there is a dynamic tension between trust and conflict. These teams have confidence in their members' ability to manage conflict. They know that a good, meaty conflict, when handled well, builds greater trust. And they know that to make good decisions, they will need to turn ideas inside out, disagree and hash through things. For some people, this kind of conflict is seen as a negative and something to be avoided. If teams have done some sort of leadership survey together, the team members may already know something about their colleagues' approach to conflict, which can help in building this team capacity. Culture can also play a role in how we experience conflict. In some cultures, conflict is as common and innocuous as a cup of coffee, while in other cultures, it is nearly nonexistent and something to be avoided at all costs.

Clear norms for engaging in these conversations that separate people from their ideas and build everyone's comfort with conflict are essential. Because working in this way may be unfamiliar to team members, it is important to give them images of what these habits look like in action, to make it clear what behavior is preferred, and to provide opportunities to build these capacities. This is another place where the superintendent or team facilitator can work to build this capacity of the team through example by strategically surfacing conflicts that have been simmering just beneath the surface in the group, coaching team members to raise contentious issues, and recognizing team members who try to productively raise points of conflict. Leading this work requires that the leader is comfortable with conflict and has the ability to manage it; this may prove to be a place where the superintendent himself or herself needs to grow.

5. IS THE TEAM ACCOUNTABLE FOR ITS PROCESSES AND OUTCOMES?

At the end of the day, the makeup of a team, its meeting structure, and the skills and capacities of its members should all contribute not only to the team's level of functioning but also to the outcomes it is able to realize. By outcomes, we mean such things as completing the agenda in the allotted time, the quality of decision making, collaboration within the team and with departments managed by team members, and the effect of the system's work (guided by the leadership team's decisions) on student learning. A team needs quick and easy ways to assess its performance as well as more occasional, in-depth reviews of its work and processes. The quickest way to check on team functioning is to spend five minutes assessing it at the end of a staff meeting. A process that some call pluses and deltas and others call cherries and pits consists of a quick whip around the table; everyone says something they liked about the meeting and something they think can be improved. Though simple, this quick assessment reminds the team of the importance of functioning well and gives everyone the opportunity to comment on the team's process. Revisiting

FIGURE 2.7

QUICK CHECK ON TEAM FUNCTIONING

	Yes	No
Purpose and clarity		
The purpose of the team is clear.		
Members of the team understand their role on the team.		
The team's decision-making authority is clear.		
The work of the team is challenging.		
The team's decisions are consequential.		
The right people		
Key decision makers are on the team.		
The team includes people who are systemic thinkers and team players.		
The team includes people knowledgeable about teaching and learning.		
The superintendent periodically assesses the strengths and weaknesses of the team and makes adjustments when they are needed.		
Structures		
The team has clear norms for behavior and adheres to them.		
There is a clear agenda for every meeting, and the team follows the agenda.		
The agenda allots an appropriate amount of time for each item and sets goals.		
The superintendent sets the agenda or designates the person who does.		
Capacity		
The team devotes time toward building trust.		
Team members demonstrate trust in one another.		
Team members feel free to express vulnerability.		
Team members display comfort with conflict.		
Accountability		
The team regularly assesses its performance.		
The team conducts occasional in-depth reviews of its work and processes.		

norms affords another opportunity to assess team functioning and to see how it could be improved. Senior leadership retreats are a more occasional way teams can take time to think more deeply about both their process and their success in achieving meeting objectives, preparing for meetings, completing follow-up after meetings, and sharing responsibility for the team's success. Particularly when held off-site, retreats are also good opportunities to build relationships between team members as the setting and pace often encourage less formality.

Figure 2.7 presents a quick-check tool to evaluate current team functioning—strengths and opportunities for development. The tool is based upon, and in some cases elaborates upon, the five building blocks we have discussed in this chapter. While some of the questions in figure 2.7 are directly intended for a system's senior leadership team, most of the assessment is applicable for teams at any level in the system. The tool can be completed by individual team members to understand individual perceptions of the team's level of function or can be used by the full team to help it assess and discuss its level of functioning.

Regardless of where they sit in an organization, teams are a powerful tool for leveraging the collective wisdom and expertise of individuals and ensuring a level of coherence and alignment that can't be realized when everyone is off doing their own thing. The power of teams has tremendous potential at the highest levels of the system because that is where the strategy for the system is set, making the stakes particularly high. Finding the time and energy to build and maintain high-functioning teams is undoubtedly challenging, but also a necessary investment in the success of systemic instructional improvement.

Finding the Parts in the Whole

Every whole is made up of parts. Making sense of the system's work requires considering the collective whole of the work while examining specific pieces of the work to understand the nuances that can strengthen the system's efforts. Similarly, in the highest-performing teams and systems, there is a strong whole, the "we," that is purposeful, focused, and committed to a collective goal. Yet the individuals who make up the team, and the ways they routinely act and speak is what moves the system closer to that collective goal. The process of taking stock of your system's initiatives and building a high-functioning senior leadership team presents multiple opportunities to be strategic (and multiple opportunities to be "unstrategic"). Being strategic requires that you discern both the whole and its parts. This requires deftly balancing complexity and simplicity, and diving in and stepping back. This is a bit like doing the tango while carrying fine china. Here are a few ideas for how to dance gracefully while holding on to the plates that matter.

DIVING IN VERSUS STEPPING BACK

Engage fully. A strong leadership team is composed of people with different expertise, experience, and perspectives. What they (and you) bring can be leveraged to make the team and the system more effective, or it can become an obstruction, depending upon how each individual engages with the work. Fully engaging means taking that deep breath, regularly and intentionally recommitting oneself to the purpose of the work and all that it entails. Most meetings and team interactions provide plenty of decision points—is this a time to dive in or step back? How do you step back without disengaging, dive in without hitting your nose on the bottom of the pool or swimming solo? Here are a few ideas:

- In meetings, ask questions that build understanding and that ensure that the conversations dig down to the meatiest issues.
- Show courage by talking about things that may be uncomfortable. Talk honestly about what is not working; approach it as a way to help the system get smarter rather than as a judgment of something (or someone) as a success or failure.
- Listen hard to understand the meaning beneath people's words so you can respond in a way that is productive and supportive.
- Pick one thing you could change about your behavior that would help the team: Come to the meetings on time; ensure that your remarks build on the comments of others; don't disengage when a comment rubs you the wrong way.

Help the team. Teams, like classrooms, are composed of individuals with different learning styles and temperaments. Understanding your team's processing style and group dynamics will enable you to help it function well. Inevitably, during any group process some people will want to get on with it and make decisions while others will want to continue to explore and consider. Some people will figure out what they think by talking; others will want to think before talking. The big-picture folks may be ready to move on when others want more specifics. This rich mix of preferences is simultaneously a team's greatest strength and—ever so maddeningly—its potential greatest weakness. You can help the team by diving in to get to know your colleagues' styles, and stepping back to think about what *you* are doing that is helping or hindering the team. When the going gets rough—when, for example, the person who is the polar opposite of you (i.e., the one who pushes your buttons and is, much as you hate to admit it, the one whom the team most needs to balance *you* out) says or does something that drums on your very last nerve—try to ask yourself what you could do that would most help the team. Stay silent? Ask a question? Offer a smile? The way a team is structured can support this kind of reflection in action. Setting a team goal at the beginning of a meeting—starting on time, being clear about next steps at the end of the meeting—and checking in on how well the team attended to it is one way to build the team's level of consciousness and commitment. Taking time to check in at the end of meetings to evaluate how things went using a simple plus/delta process is an even quicker and more informal way to improve reflection, investment, and performance.

Remember children. Some of the best education leaders we know simply won't entertain issues that don't focus on children. These leaders are tenacious in this commitment, standing up to their most powerful stakeholders when they have to. It works because it's hard to argue with the logic of focusing on what's best for children. A focus on children helps everyone step back from the work—it's not about any of us, but about children—and helps everyone dive in; children are the reason we do this work. They are why we persist in challenging times, why we are, at the end of a long workday, the luckiest of adults. Think and talk about what it would look like if everyone in the system thought about their work in terms of how it directly supports students and their learning. Would the system do different things? Would it do the same things differently? Probably it's some of both. Budget crises, tough contract negotiations, ugly school board politics, bad press, and the like, all have the potential to distract from serving children well. In the face of each problem, one question helps focus complex systems and teams in all of their complex humanity: *What is best for children?* One leader we know said it was easy to figure out her system's strategy because she and her staff just kept asking, "What's best for kids?" In truth, it was a bit more complex than that, but the question did drive their strategic improvement work and every meeting. *What is best for children?* Ask it whenever a decision is made. Ask it before entertaining an agenda item. Ask it when someone or something distracts you. When people come to expect the question from you, they will also begin to ask it of themselves.

COMPLEXITY VERSUS SIMPLICITY

Acknowledge imperfection. The Moorwood team's struggle to place itself somewhere on the continuum between problem solving and vision pursuing illustrates that things aren't always neat and clear. We're good at some things some of the time and not so good at some things at other times. It's okay to say the system was really focused and had great coherence and alignment in one initiative while it fell down in other areas. That's so often true. What's most interesting and helpful is to figure out what can be learned from this dichotomy of focus. Here are some ways to do so:

- Unpack successes to understand the elements that make them work. Figure out what contributes to the failures the system experiences; failures offer tremendous opportunity for learning and are important markers along the road to success. Do this regularly so it becomes familiar and less personal.

- Look for common themes among the successes and among the failures whenever possible. Use this information to generate key conditions for success and hazards to avoid that can guide future work and build the system's capacity.

Avoid generalizations. A chief academic officer participating with his colleagues in making sense of work under way stopped the action at one point. Barely able to hide his frustration, he commented, "We keep painting with a broad brush. We're making comments like, 'All of the teachers . . .' 'None of the schools are . . .' 'The principals think . . .' It's not true. They're not monoliths. We can't talk in generalities." This CAO was pointing to the learning opportunities missed when we plaster over variation in the system. Generalizations are tidy and can make conversations more comfortable, but they don't help us to understand what is most needed in the system and to learn from the variations and exceptions. When tempted to oversimplify and generalize, remember to dig deeper to understand the nuances of why a project works in some settings better than it does in others. Use data to guide your analysis. Look closely. Ask questions. Wonder.

Wear two hats. Most people define themselves and their role primarily by the position they hold, their direct reports, and the work of the department(s) they oversee. But, when acting as a leader in an organization, a person is also (and many would say, first and foremost) responsible for the whole of the system. People who serve on the system's leadership team feel these dual responsibilities most keenly. Sometimes, the duties are in conflict. What you think is best for the part of the system you oversee may not be best when the totality of the system is considered. Sometimes, it will be very tempting and simply seem easier and a better service to your division to advocate for your piece of the pie. Hold this tension and choose purposefully.

Try to figure out when addressing your division's needs is in the best interest of the whole system and its overall health and when it is more about short-term interests. Be an advocate for your department, the system, and, most important, the children in the system. When you ask and answer, "What's best for children?" you embrace your role and get some distance on it; you hold the nuance and strive for simplicity. And you move closer to serving all children well.

CHAPTER 3

Data

Identifying Problems and Opportunities

A problem is nothing more than an opportunity in work clothes.

—*Michael Michalko*

Betty, the Moorwood Public Schools chief of staff, launched into the "Vital Signs" section of the agenda. "You've all read the quarterly numbers on attendance and dropouts, which we've said are two of our indicators of how things are going. What did you think?" José, the chief operating officer, said, "Well, we're trending slightly down on dropouts and slightly up on attendance, which seems like a good thing, but we've still got big problems, especially at the high school level." Betty added, "As a parent, I have to tell you that the start time is a huge problem—teenagers just aren't awake at seven thirty. I know we've got bus issues, but the youngest children should start school early, and the older students should start later. We do the opposite. Why is that?" José said, "Well, there are extracurriculars for the older students, and high school students can choose to attend any school in the district, so that means we've got a lot of transportation needs. We've raised these issues before, and if we want to go down that road, we've got to realize that it's not going to be popular with lots of parents and students."

"My classrooms visits are quite illuminating," said Derek, a new regional superintendent. "The principals have been talking a good game in our monthly meetings, but when we get into classrooms, teachers are asking low-level questions and students are bored. The level of rigor is way too low. No wonder our test scores look the way they do, and no wonder high school students don't want to come to school. Frankly, I wouldn't want to, either."

"We've been doing professional development about 'rigor' and 'questioning' for two years now, but you wouldn't know it. It's time to try something new," said Iris, the director of accountability. "We have got to move these test scores now, or we're going to be in trouble with the state. Maybe we should be expanding our after-school programs so that more students get extra support, or maybe we should put in some software for high school students to do tutorials."

"I don't want to just add another thing," said Sonya, the superintendent. "I think part of our problem is that we have too much going on, as we saw when we mapped all our initiatives. We do need to move test scores, but the only way we're going to do that is by figuring out what's really happening, including what we're doing to contribute to the problem. Why are we having attendance problems in high school? Why does rigor continue to be low? Why is the dropout rate dropping a bit? Let's spend some time trying to understand the answers to those questions."

The Moorwood senior leadership team members are doing many things right. They've identified some key indicators to track, they've integrated the use of data into their meetings, and they're willing to challenge each others' ideas. For all that, their response reflex is still quick to surface in conversation. Solutions are suggested (later start time, after-school programs, software, etc.) before the problem is fully articulated and understood. Is the problem that students aren't awake enough to learn? That the professional development is ineffective? That students are bored? Some combination of these things? Something else entirely? Is there anything to be learned from the slight improvements in dropout rates and attendance?

In our heartfelt urgency to improve student outcomes now, we educators tend not to ask these sorts of questions, which invariably take precious time to answer and, maddeningly, often lead to more questions. We want the quickest, simplest way of understanding what's going on so that we can "fix" it. Unfortunately, most of the problems worth solving in classrooms are complex and multidimensional and unlikely to respond to simple solutions. Still, we press on. Trying to be data-driven, we focus on the obvious and the immediate. We usually look at one type of data—often, state test scores—as our measure of success or failure. We respond to perceived problems by adopting new programs as if to show ourselves and others that we really are trying to do something. We add work onto an already overburdened system, hoping this new thing will—finally!—do the trick.

Alas, this approach is not working well in our school systems. Too often, we do not have a rich understanding of what the real problems are. Test scores might signal that something is wrong, but they say little about why something is wrong or what might be done about it. And we seldom examine a range of potential solutions that might get at the heart of the issue and lead to real improvement. Instead of being data-driven, we are driven to distraction. We rush to a rapid response—Let's open school later! Let's implement a new math program!—that is too often superficial, inadequate, and ineffective and that leads to frustration and cynicism. Instead, we need to take a strategic approach in identifying problems and opportunities so that we can spend our time, our people, and our dollars on solutions that will really help children learn more every day in classrooms.

This chapter examines ways to use a broad range of data to assess a system's needs and priorities. We describe various forms of data and their uses to help district leaders discern what data (out of all the overwhelming possibilities) to choose for what purpose. We address how to dig beneath a superficial level to deepen understanding, hone in on the system's problems, and uncover opportunities to help the system move closer to its vision for children.

LEAVING THINKTOWN

To understand the challenges in using data effectively and the perils of inappropriate data use, consider a midsized district that we'll call Thinktown. Leaders in Thinktown knew they had a problem: Math scores were low, and achievement gaps were wide. The senior leadership team was very thoughtful, spent a lot of time figuring out its strategy, and had a multicolor graphic to show for it. And yet, one year later, it wasn't getting the traction it wanted. Math performance did not improve, and achievement gaps did not close. Moreover, few in the district could explain what the strategy was or why the district had chosen it.

Why? It turned out that Thinktown had relied on an all-too-typical process for dealing with perceived problems. The district's new director of innovation had led an effort to improve high school math performance in his previous district, so the leadership team agreed to adopt that strategy in Thinktown. This way of responding to the problem, while rational, is ineffective, because it stands on a weak "why" foundation. The system knew little about the cause of the lagging scores. Then it directed a resource to the problem in hopes that this would lead to improvement.

But nobody knew why the scores were low, which made it impossible to direct the resource at the source of the problem.

This approach is also dangerous, because it damages the ability of people in the system to work effectively. The work required of adults and children to make real progress in the instructional core is demanding. There has to be a compelling reason to engage in it and sustain it when it proves challenging. If the reason is because some senior person in the system said so or the system has a person who can lead the work, few people are likely to follow with enthusiasm.

The fact that few people in Thinktown could even articulate the strategy or its rationale a year after implementation signals that there is something wrong with the way district leaders analyzed the problem and developed the strategy. For teachers and school administrators, the strategy amounted to "improve test scores." It had no meaning. Without a centering "why," people defaulted to doing their daily work, which contained a long list of things that seemed more urgent than and quite distinct from the math strategy.

CULTIVATING THE HABIT OF USING EVIDENCE

Part of Thinktown's challenge was that most team members couldn't remember any of the evidence that had led the team to identify the problem or to adopt the strategy. In fact, it was unclear if the strategy had used evidence at all. The senior leadership team members had not developed the habit of using evidence to help them think about actions.

This lack of discipline around using evidence is still surprisingly common among central office staff and senior leadership teams. Nevertheless, education as a sector has traveled a long way from ten to fifteen years ago, when the systematic use of data, especially data related to student learning, was the exception rather than the rule.[1] This attitude is changing, in part because district data systems are more sophisticated now and allow district leaders to examine and analyze a broad range of data more easily than ever before. And it is changing because evidence is mounting that districts that are effective in using data are successful at improving student results.

In such systems, the habit of using evidence is well ingrained throughout the system at every level and in every department. Evidence is used to assess the effectiveness of work under way and to figure out how to improve it. Teachers meet together to discuss student work and the results of common assessments and to decide how to adjust their instructional practice accordingly. School leadership teams examine multiple forms of data—state test scores; formative assessments; student, parent, and teacher surveys; classroom observations—to design a schoolwide improvement strategy and to monitor and refine the strategy. Principal supervisors visit classrooms with principals and discuss what they see and how that connects to the next steps. Human resources tracks teacher retention and turnover, surveys departing teachers to understand why they are leaving, and matches information about teacher preparation to data about teacher success (e.g., student performance data, teacher evaluation data, tenure) to see if any teacher preparation institutions or programs are regularly producing more effective teachers. The special education department tracks patterns in identification (e.g., African American boys disproportionately identified with behavior disabilities, Latino students underidentified compared with their peers), and the distribution of students with various disabilities. The system's senior leadership team, meanwhile, regularly reviews multiple forms of data to design, monitor, and refine its strategy.

In successful systems, data are everywhere—in the hallways of schools, in the senior leadership team's meeting room, on the system's Web site. Data are constantly referred to in conversation—"What's the evidence? What do the data say? According to the data . . . "

School systems do not wake up one day using evidence, even with the arrival of a new superintendent. It is a habit that must be cultivated and reinforced over time. Identifying specific problems and opportunities to focus on is part of that habit and helps keep the process of using data from becoming overwhelming, especially for people who are relatively new to it.

Developing the habit requires, first, reconceptualizing what problems are. Many educators we know don't like the word *problem*. To them, it sounds negative and possibly personal, as if there is a personal failing implied by the word. The common reality that those farthest from the perceived problem are often the ones who identify it adds to educators' trepidation. Perhaps they have resisted looking at data because they fear that someone might accuse them of causing the problem. Other educators we know embrace the word *problem*. To them, it sounds like a challenge, the equivalent of a Sunday crossword puzzle. A problem well solved helps children and brings personal satisfaction all at the same time.

What accounts for the difference? In the latter group, everyone in the system is involved in a continual process of identifying and responding to problems. Suddenly, problems become more of a mechanism for focusing the work rather than focusing blame. Then, when it comes to being strategic and to designing, implementing, and refining a strategy for improvement, everyone is involved in identifying opportunities.

In practice, the distinction between problems and opportunities is not as sharp as the words imply. As the opening quote to this chapter suggests, the two are intertwined. At one level, problems are opportunities that require rolling up sleeves and getting to work. Problems and opportunities are two sides of the same coin, and some people will be more motivated and responsive to one framing than the other. At another level, as we discussed in chapter 1, a school system needs to hold both a problem-solving and a vision-pursuing stance. If the focus is always on problems, and not on opportunities, the system is going to constantly be in a mode of "fixing" things, which tends to orient people reactively and generates a different sort of energy and focus than does seeking opportunities to move toward the vision. Conversely, if the focus is always on opportunities, the system runs the risk of ignoring or refusing to discuss very real problems that require attention. In school systems that are making progress for children, it's okay—indeed expected—to talk about both problems and opportunities. Which problems and opportunities, when attended to, will help us move toward our vision for children?

DATA AND WHAT IT IS GOOD FOR

Types of Data: What You Count, Hear, and See

School systems, like most organizations, rely heavily on quantifiable data. However, if you want to improve outcomes, numbers alone will probably not provide all the information you need, particularly in the very human endeavor of teaching and learning. To use a medical analogy, a doctor will use numbers (blood pressure, temperature) as one form of data when trying to diagnose a problem. The doctor will also have a conversation with you—What's going on? How long has it been going on? Where does it hurt? How severe is the pain? The doctor will also look at you—What additional information does observation provide? The doctor will use this combination of information to diagnose the problem and make a prescription for improvement. Sometimes the doctor will rely more on one form of data than another; that is likely to vary from one case to the next. Similarly, a coach trying to improve a team's performance will look at statistics, listen to how the team members talk about and understand problems and potential improvements, and observe the team in action. In both instances, there are three types of data in use: what you count, what you hear, and what you see.

What You Count

Numbers are often the most accessible form of data. They are relatively easy to scan, discuss, monitor, and use to assess progress, especially at scale. The most visible form of quantitative data in education is test scores. Despite the criticism that often surrounds tests, test scores do provide useful information. They tell us the extent to which all our fourth-graders aren't as proficient in math as we'd like and that we can currently predict, with an unacceptable degree of accuracy, which groups of fourth-graders are more likely to be proficient, according to their income levels, race or ethnicity, and disability. Yet test scores also have limitations, particularly as currently implemented in the United States. For example, most states, such as our home state of Massachusetts, measure "improvement" by comparing this year's fourth-graders to last year's, rather than tracking students' actual improvement over time.[2] One of the fun and challenging facts of education is that this year's fourth-graders really aren't just like last year's fourth-graders. With a big enough sample size—that is, a large system or a state or a country—this might be okay because the differences would average out, but the accountability stakes are attached to *schools*, many of which have one or two classes of fourth-graders. Because of this, test scores do not provide a full or completely accurate picture of a school's performance.

Other types of quantitative data provide useful information that can augment test scores to inform scans of system health. Attendance and graduation rates indicate if all students are remaining in school and showing up for class. Operations data show the extent to which business operations are running efficiently. Initiative tracking also often includes numbers for both process and outcomes—How many people have received training in the new assessment system? What percent of eighth-graders are enrolled in Algebra 1? How many days from application to hire for a teacher?

Quantitative data are most useful when reported in context. One important piece of contextual information is how the numbers have changed over time. By comparing the current state with baseline evidence, school systems can determine whether things are improving, and at what rate. This information helps systems make their best guess about where to target their strategy and invest their resources.

Similarly, comparative information helps systems determine if their performance is "good enough." Here, scans of the external environment are crucial. How does our performance compare with similar districts? With the state average? With the highest-performing systems? How does our performance compare nationally and internationally? What does U.S. performance internationally tell us about problems and opportunities in our own system?

Education as a sector is slowly coming around to the concept of benchmarks, which are used in other sectors as another way to count. In some cases, districts are implementing benchmark assessments to measure student academic progress during the year, to determine if they are on course toward proficiency on the end-of-year test. In other cases, systems look at external markers—How do our per-pupil expenditures, energy bills per square foot, transportation, professional development dollars per teacher, average teacher salary, and so forth, compare with other systems? School systems are using this information to identify problems and opportunities for greater efficiency and creativity. Currently, a lack of comparable data makes the benchmark concept difficult, but there is progress being made in this area.[3]

What You Hear

Hearing from the people closest to the core work provides an important source of information. Surveys and focus groups provide opportunities to gather information in a more formal way, while conversations provide informal opportunities. Many systems are beginning to include some combination of student, parent, and teacher surveys as part of their general data checks, and partners are often helpful in designing, collecting, and analyzing the surveys.[4] Surveys, focus groups, and conversations can also be important when a system takes on new work. They can surface problems early on in implementation and provide an understanding of what's working about an initiative and what needs to be adjusted. When systems want to better understand the work of their schools that get consistently strong student achievement results, surveys and focus groups can help to describe innovations that might not be obvious to people farther away from the work. Surveys, focus groups, and forums can provide helpful scans of the community and partners—What's important to them? What are they concerned about? What are they proud of? What opportunities do they see? Surveys and focus groups do not have to be elaborate to be helpful—What's going well? What's not going well? What suggestions for improvement do people have? Conversations with peers in formal networks (e.g., superintendents' networks) and conferences can also provide some deeper understanding of problems and help to identify opportunities.

What You See

Because much of the instructional core is about the interactions of teachers and students in the presence of content, the best way to understand what's happening in the instructional core is to observe it. Compared with quantitative data and surveys, observations of classrooms are less common as a regular source of data. This is not surprising. Classroom observation takes longer than looking at numbers, dashboard graphics, and survey results. The evidence is not easily captured in numbers. In fact, three people can observe the same classroom and make sense of it in three entirely different ways. Moreover, many educators, particularly those with little background in education, aren't always sure what to look for in classrooms or what to do with what they see.

As imperfect as classroom observations are, they are essential. Too often, "data"-based conversations at all levels of the system are plagued with little knowledge of what is actually happening in classrooms. Little wonder systems tend not to focus on things directly affecting the instructional core. For example, the No Child Left Behind legislation requires systems to measure whether teachers are "highly qualified," meaning whether they hold certification in the subject they teach and demonstrate competency in that subject. "Highly qualified" is not a proxy for "effective," and yet we track credentials rather than looking at instructional practice in classrooms to see whether teachers are engaging students and helping them learn. Similarly, we can measure student attendance, so we'll track that rather than looking at students' experience in classrooms. Yet we know students' experience in the classroom informs whether they think it's worth their while to come to school.

Systems have to embrace the messy work of classroom observations. Our advice? Take your senior leadership team on a field trip once a quarter. Spend a day (or perhaps two or three mornings) visiting two or three schools. Choose schools that are all at the same level, or maybe a fast-improving, a medium-improving, and a stuck school. Or maybe choose the three highest-performing schools in the system. Divide into groups of four or five people, and visit four classrooms for twenty minutes each. Invite the principal and a couple of people from the school leadership team to join you. In classrooms, ask yourself this question: "If students in this classroom did exactly what the teacher asked them to do, what would they know and be able to do?"[5] Talk with students. Ask several students this question: "What are you doing, and why are you doing it?" Write down the answers to these questions. After observing in classrooms, discuss the answers with colleagues. Incorporate these data into your regular review and analysis of key data. When observing a new program, tailor the questions. And, to place observations in context and to learn about different practices, take the opportunity to observe classrooms outside the system. For example, when traveling to a conference, see if you can visit a couple of schools while you are there.

What's more important—data you can count, hear, or see? Many people prefer one kind of data over another. When we're working with people about using data, we often ask about their favorite kind of data as an icebreaker. Some people will take great comfort in numbers, while others will find what they observe or hear more compelling. (One educator summarized his favorite kind of data as "anything that shows improvement.") Indeed, systems often have preferences that reflect what the external environment or senior leadership values (hence the heavy focus on state test scores). But a school system trying to identify problems and opportunities needs all three kinds of data—counting, hearing, and seeing. Together, these three sources provide a full and accurate picture of a system's performance that a single source cannot offer.

What Data to Look At?

There is no shortage of data in school systems. The sheer piles make it hard to find the "right" data (if it exists) and overwhelm or exhaust many efforts to use data to identify problems and opportunities. The coy but true answer to the question of what data to look at is that it depends on what you want to know. One of the reasons educators are often overwhelmed by data is that they come to data with a sense that they *should* be looking at this information. They are less clear about why they're looking at data and what they want to know. This uncertainty stems from the pattern of focusing on finding answers rather than on figuring out the right questions. Another reason educators are often overwhelmed by data is that they haven't decided which data are most helpful in informing them about the state of their vision and strategy, and so they don't know how to discriminate between various sources of data and to focus on a few key indicators.

In this chapter, we focus on data needed for identifying problems and opportunities. In particular, we focus on regular scans of three categories of information: system, initiative, and external. System data speak to the overall health of your organization. Initiative data speak to how particular initiatives are going and whether they're producing the hoped-for short and long-term results. External data speak to what is happening beyond the walls of your own system—What are other systems and sectors doing? What does research say? What are the policy trends?

Regular Scans of Key Indicators

To revisit our medical analogy, in a visit to the doctor, you can be sure that no matter what problem has landed you there, someone will check your temperature, blood pressure, and pulse, and the doctor will reference that information as part of the diagnosis. In longer-term stays in a hospital, these same vital signs are monitored regularly, sometimes as critical indicators, and sometimes as more general indicators of a patient's health. Similarly, businesses identify key indicators such as profits, customer satisfaction, and growth rates and monitor them as signs of the business's health. Some key indicators are core to the enterprise and will always need monitoring. Some may be particular to an organization in light of its needs and values, in much the same way that a patient with diabetes may monitor blood sugar and one with asthma may monitor peak oxygen flow. Similarly, in education, some data collected and analyzed are the same across school systems. Other data differ, reflecting the different priorities of each system.

The current trend toward dashboards and scorecards in education is essentially an exercise in deciding which data are most essential to monitor—in other words, what are the system's key indicators? To some extent, every system must decide for itself what key indicators to watch. The process of deciding key indicators develops some ownership and understanding of them and surfaces what the system values. Monitoring parental satisfaction, for examples, signals something different from monitoring four-year-college attendance and attrition rates (not that the two are mutually exclusive—a system might monitor both, or might care a lot about one, and not so much about the other). Even so, some types of data are critical to the core enterprise of student learning, like evidence of what the students are actually learning. Enough systems are now using dashboards and scorecards that a school system doesn't have to start from scratch to get ideas about what to pay attention to and to match data sources with its own goals and aspirations. See, for example, Further Resources in appendix C for resources about where to access sample dashboards and scorecards.

Performance data provide general pictures of the system's overall health. These data are usually most helpful as red flags, identifying problems that require closer analysis, and are often particularly useful when tracked over time. Most school systems focus on performance measures in the areas of student achievement (e.g., standardized test scores, perhaps disaggregated by poverty, race-ethnicity, language, or disability), student attainment (e.g., graduation rates, dropout rates, college-going rates, annual retention rates), and operations (e.g., financial audits, safety audits, on-time rates for buses, school staffing). Systems further add to and refine their lists of key indicators on the basis of their strategy for improvement, a topic we will discuss more in chapter 6.

Though currently less common in practice, initiative data, or more fine-grained data about particular initiatives that are more specifically tied to a system's strategy, serve an important role. First, they help us understand what is contributing to the system data—Is the new policy to add Advanced Placement offerings affecting course enrollments and grades? Sometimes they provide an important early-warning system about problems—Before the state test happens, do we already have evidence that the new math curriculum may require more professional development than we expected, and if we don't do something soon, might test scores in fact drop rather than increase? Sometimes the initiative data provide hopeful information that may augment system data—Before the system data on dropout are tallied, has the number of students passing all their classes in the second quarter of ninth grade increased? These data usually include a combination of process and outcome data to track the implementation of the initiative as well as the result. Thus, they help a system adjust in a more nimble and nuanced fashion than if the system relied entirely on the system data. Second, initiative data offer more information to understand where the opportunities inside the system might be. In what schools do initiatives take off and why? How are people adapting the initiatives on the ground, and what can be learned and enacted from their innovations?

Scans outside one's own system are the third type of key indicator data. Like initiative data, these are less commonly employed than performance data. We tend to be so focused on what's happening in our own system that we don't make time for quick, regular scans of the external environment. These external scans are particularly helpful for identifying opportunities—Where are other systems and countries that we haven't thought about, or aren't currently paying attention to, having success? What does research say that informs how we think about new possibilities (e.g., the increasing evidence about the link between physical exercise and academic achievement for students)? Where might a policy change or conversation open a new window of opportunity, like the president's discussing performance pay and teacher

union leaders' agreeing to talk about it? These scans also help leadership teams identify and understand problems—perhaps other people are struggling with the same
challenges. Understanding what they're doing and learning will help systems avoid
learning all the same lessons and is likely to accelerate progress based on that learning. There are several periodic (daily, weekly, monthly) summaries of essential news,
research, and reports that can help systems efficiently scan the external environment
(see Further Resources in appendix C for some of our recommendations).

In our experience, the limiting factor is not the availability of the summaries, but
the time to read them. External scans are seldom urgent; there are always a hundred
other things that must be attended to immediately. But scanning the external environment may very well be more important than any of those tasks on the to-do list.
Figure out a small, regular habit that you can keep, and expand from there: Spend
the first ten minutes of every day scanning the newspaper; spend twenty minutes
on Friday afternoon reading through one summary; divide multiple information
sources across a leadership team, and ask everyone to read for fifteen minutes a
week; carry the sources with you electronically or in paper format, and read them
while waiting in line somewhere. These are just some ideas.

While the senior leadership team in a school system will have an overall set of
key indicators for the system, each department should also have its own key indicators that are at a more fine-grained level more particular to their part of the enterprise (and aligned to the overall system's strategy). At every level of the system,
departments (and schools and classrooms) are asking, "What data do we want to
monitor regularly to tell us how effectively we're touching whatever part of the ele-
phant we're responsible for (producing student learning, supporting students with
disabilities, providing efficient and effective transportation and food service, generating a rich pool of potential teachers and principals)"? They should also be asking,
"How will we assess how things are going? Who's closest to the work, and what can
we learn from them (e.g., the bus drivers, the cafeteria workers, the HR employees)? Who is supposed to be served by the work, and what can we learn from them
(e.g., the students, the parents, the principals, the teachers)?" And they should also
ask, "What might we observe in action to understand the realities on the ground
(e.g., ride a bus, eat lunch in a cafeteria, attend an HR recruiting session, go to a
staff meeting)?" Because education is a human endeavor, much of the enterprise
involves interactions of one kind or another—interactions in classrooms, in department meetings, in the course of doing the work. Seeing those interactions will give

educators a kind of information that numbers and reports about the interactions just won't.

HOW TO IDENTIFY PROBLEMS AND OPPORTUNITIES

Even after the data are narrowed down to a set of key indicators, the volume of information can still seem quite overwhelming. Yet the value of the key indicators is that they can alert system leaders to the most glaring problems. These problems are often quite severe, and most systems have them. They don't require an elaborate understanding of the initial *what* to suggest a strategy. But they offer a juicy place to dive in and a productive way of doing so.

Using data often leads to more questions than answers. While some people find this aspect of the process fun, other people find it frustrating. This iterative process of inquiry can feel like a circular road to nowhere. The trick is to ask key questions and to dig deeper, pursuing a line of inquiry until it leads to an actionable place (a place where you can either take some action or decide not to take action). A question is key if the process of asking it and searching for the answer helps the system unlock something it needs to understand in order to serve children better. These questions often emerge in response to something that bubbles up in the vital signs check—Why are math scores dropping from elementary to middle schools? Why are parents so much more satisfied in this school than in that school? Why does all that professional development we're doing not seem to translate into classroom practice? Why are teachers asking students to do work three grade levels below standard? Why does the classroom practice of teachers in the same building look so different? Why do some schools have such high teacher turnover? Notice that the questions all start with "why"—a critical word in probing for understanding.

The point is not just to arrive at an actionable place, but also to have conversations along the way that build understanding and shared ownership of the problem or opportunity, which in turn will make action more likely to happen with some success. For this reason, we use protocols, or semistructured conversations, to support dialogue and the efficient use of ever-precious time. The trick when you are looking at data, which protocols can help with, is to move back and forth from a wide view (looking at lots of data) to a narrow view (picking a few things). The dance can look a bit like the diagram in figure 3.1.

In moving to strategic action, we articulate four steps that help you move through this wide-narrow iteration:

FIGURE 3.1

IDENTIFYING PROBLEMS AND OPPORTUNITIES:
NARROWING AND WIDENING YOUR VIEWPOINTS ON THE DATA

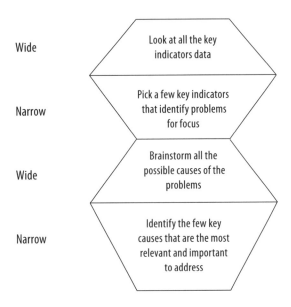

Wide — Look at all the key indicators data

Narrow — Pick a few key indicators that identify problems for focus

Wide — Brainstorm all the possible causes of the problems

Narrow — Identify the few key causes that are the most relevant and important to address

Synthesize: Scan your vital-signs data, and identify a few issues (symptoms) to investigate that, if addressed, would affect the instructional core.

Generate: Brainstorm hypotheses about why those few symptoms exist.

Focus: Narrow to a few hypotheses, using impact and instructional core as main criteria, and dig into root causes.

Vet: Confirm the identified root causes, and check actionability.

The rest of the chapter takes you through these four steps. We focus on using them to identify problems, but a similar approach can also help in an analysis of potential opportunities.

1. Synthesize

After a scan of key indicators data and the identification of a few issues, the first question to ask is this: Out of all the potential problems to focus on, which are the most critical to address? In this *synthesize* step, you take the available information and choose a few problems to dive into. How to choose among the possibilities? Think impact and instructional core. Which issues are close to the instructional core and, if acted upon, would have an impact on student learning? While some judgments will involve a certain amount of strategic thinking, we find that many problems that look different on the surface have similar roots. We thus recommend not getting too hung up on which issues to choose. There will be opportunities later in the process to think very systematically about the most strategic routes to pursue. For now, choose issues that are compelling and that are about student learning.

For example, an examination of key indicators might elicit the following reactions:

> Wow! This is a *big* problem. This is unacceptable! I can't believe that 45 percent of all our eighth-graders aren't proficient in math and that 62 percent of our African American and 54 percent of our Latino eighth-graders aren't proficient in math.

> Third-graders' ability to read at the end of third grade seems greatly influenced by which classroom they're in.

> The performance of students with disabilities seems greatly influenced by which school they're in.

> Our students are scoring low on open-ended questions, and the level of questions in classrooms appears to be quite low.

The next step is to choose no more than three of these issues that are most compelling, and take them through the generate-focus-vet process.

2. Generate

Problems have causes and symptoms. We often mix these two things up. For example, attendance issues and a rising dropout rate are symptoms of a problem. They are observable, measurable manifestations of a deeper problem. We don't yet know what the causes of that problem are. If we try to address the symptoms without getting to the root causes of the problem, we will put all of our energy and resources into getting students to come to school, but we'll neither properly understand why they aren't coming to school nor address the root causes. We won't be any smarter about what we need to do in school to engage the students. As a result, our efforts may provide a short-term fix, but they will not be effective in the long term or responsive to the changing conditions.

A simple metaphor for a problem is a tree growing in nature. All the parts above ground—bark, branches, leaves—are symptoms of the problem. They are observable. Everything below ground—the root system—is a cause of the problem. The roots are not observable, and we must do some digging to examine and understand them. Some trees have root balls, where all the roots come together; this is akin to a problem that has a single root cause. Other trees have a complex system of runners or multiple roots that are similar to a problem with several root causes.

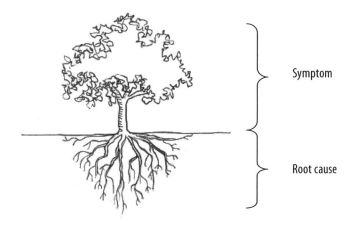

Source: Image used with permission of the University of Minnesota, www.sustland.umn.edu/implement/planting.html.

Identifying the root of the problem requires a level of disciplined inquiry that digs beneath the symptoms of problems to understand what is really going on. It also requires that we use data and analysis to ensure that we are basing our root-cause analysis on facts rather than best guesses or assumptions. We all have ideas about why there is an attendance and dropout problem in high schools, but developing a strategic response to that pressing issue according to our personal perspectives and assumptions runs the likely risk that we won't actually address the central problem and will waste time, money, and effort with limited results. It's a bit like plucking a dandelion without taking out the roots—it's just going to grow back unless you address the roots.

In the *generate* step of the process, we begin digging into root causes by brainstorming possible hypotheses, preferably with a group that brings varied perspectives to the issue. The most important thing is to generate a great variety of ideas about the causes of the problem. Engaging a group that reflects different perspectives on, and experiences of, the issue helps ensure that the level of analysis will be both broad and deep and that the focus won't be too narrow or premature. The example of student attendance and dropout from the opening vignette illustrates the limitations of quick and narrow focusing. In that example, if the Moorwood leadership team remained content to limit its focus on the school start time or bus routes, it would overlook deeper roots of student disengagement, such as the quality of students' experiences once at school and the students' possible role in a problem that is manifesting as poor attendance and dropout symptoms. As we will see shortly, the Moorwood team realized during the course of the root-cause analysis that attendance and dropout are caused by multiple factors, of which the early start time and long transportation routes are a real but incomplete part. School systems tend to focus on fixing these sorts of technical issues and not examining the dimensions of the problem that have to do with learning—which is more complex to both understand and address.

A quick way to generate lots of ideas, hear multiple voices, and surface hypotheses about the causes of a problem is to use the *affinity protocol* (see appendix B). The most important rule of brainstorming is that every idea is honored. The goal is to think expansively and generate a lot of ideas; the focus will be narrowed later.

One of the values of brainstorming is that it brings out people's beliefs. For example, a common reaction to problems is blaming the students themselves. This reaction reveals something about the assumptions of people who leap to that conclusion. When they blame others for the problem, it signals their sense of disempowerment and how little control they think they have over improving the conditions in schools and student achievement. These are valuable data because they tell us something about the culture of the organization and the beliefs of individuals. These data inform how we think about the extent of the culture change we face and the most appropriate roles of specific individuals in the work of improvement.

For an example of what this process might look like, let's consider the experience of Moorwood Public Schools. In the *synthesize* step, the senior leadership team identified a compelling symptom: *Student performance consistently lags behind state standards. When student achievement results are disaggregated by race and ethnicity, there is a significant achievement gap.* They invited several people to join them for root-cause analysis, particularly because the senior leadership team has few people

FIGURE 3.2

RESULTS FROM MOORWOOD LEADERS' GROUP BRAINSTORMING ABOUT ROOT CAUSES (HYPOTHESES RECORDED RANDOMLY AS THEY ARE SUGGESTED)

Lack of resources	Inconsistent quality and low rigor of instruction	Students starting kindergarten already behind

Teacher quality	Low expectations of, and accountability for, adults	Circumstances in students' lives make it impossible to learn	Adult beliefs about students' abilities to learn at high levels

Physical school environment doesn't support learning	Parents aren't doing their part	Principals don't know how to lead instructional improvement

Students are disengaged	Not enough time on learning	Lack of assessments that inform instruction

with a background or direct responsibilities for teaching and learning. Included were several principal supervisors, principals, instructional coaches, and teachers to join them for an afternoon session of analysis. The group generated dozens of hypotheses and grouped them into the categories shown in figure 3.2. The group then applied a "sphere of control" check to the categories, meaning the group decided whether a category was something the school system had control over. Since the item about circumstances in students' lives lies outside the school system's sphere of control, it was removed from further consideration.

3. Focus

After a broad set of hypotheses and a narrower set of categories about the possible causes of the problem are generated, the next step is to further narrow the focus to identify a few key hypotheses into which the team will dig. As with the initial step, *synthesizing*, the key question to answer in deciding what hypotheses to focus on is this: Which of these hypotheses, if acted upon, would have the most impact on the instructional core? Much of the power of this process lies in the discussion that group members will have as they work to come to agreement about which hypotheses to focus on. Some issues are easy to cite—for example, the quality and rigor of instruction, which relates directly to the instructional core, or the physical school environment, which doesn't directly support learning and thus is far from the instructional core. The most interesting and important discussions will relate to the hypotheses that are less clear-cut in terms of their relationship to the instructional core and their potential impact—for example, expectations and accountability for adults, the use of principals as instructional leaders, and the lack of enough time for learning.

When the group from the Moorwood Public Schools had a conversation about impact and instructional core, it decided to focus on four hypotheses: the lack of assessments that inform instruction, the quality and rigor of instruction, the adults' beliefs in the students' ability to learn, and teacher quality. Before investing further time and energy in digging into these hypotheses, the team members stepped back from their work to check their hypotheses against evidence. This step ensures that the hypotheses they chose are valid and worthy of further examination. Sometimes, conversations can become un-tethered from evidence, and the process of checking in helps re-tether the conversation to data. The key question is, What's the evidence that support this hypothesis? Answering and tracking the answers to this question becomes part of the storyline that explains why attending to this hypothesis is important.

The Moorwood group used a graphic organizer to track its answers (figure 3.3). Looking at the available evidence, the group felt confident about three of its hypotheses, but wasn't as sure about the fourth. The group assigned a subgroup the task of further analysis of teacher quality, which they revised to be teaching quality, but felt confident enough in the hypothesis to pursue digging into all four.

Having prioritized and verified the hypotheses about the causes of the problem, the group then needed to examine them more closely to move beyond symptoms

FIGURE 3.3

MOORWOOD GROUP HYPOTHESES (NARROWED)

Hypothesis	Evidence
Quality and rigor of instruction is inconsistent	■ Low-level questioning by teachers that focuses on recall ■ Classroom observations K–12: significant variations in classes within the same grade and school and across schools
Assessments aren't used to inform instruction	■ Lack of formative assessments in high school math, science, or social studies ■ Elementary math assessments that provide a score for students but no additional information to teachers about the skills students have mastered or not mastered ■ Survey of teachers indicating that some K–3 teachers are using literacy assessment data to drive instruction and others are unsure how to use the data ■ Reports from literacy coaches (grades 4–12) that literacy formative assessments don't provide teachers with data they can immediately use to inform their instruction
Adults have limiting beliefs about students' ability to learn	■ School climate survey data in which teachers indicate their preference to teach the "top" students and teachers' belief that many students can't meet the state standards ■ Student survey data indicating that students think they perform best in classes where teachers explain things if they don't understand and in which expectations are high* ■ Classroom observations (K–12) of the interactions and the language that teachers use when working with students; observations indicating different expectations for different students as well as some teaching effectively designed to meet the learning needs of different students
Teaching quality is poor	■ Attrition rate of new teachers close to 50 percent at the end of three years ■ Hiring novice teachers to fill 20 percent of teaching positions every year ■ School-level analysis of teaching quality (as defined by value-added student performance results, National Board Certification, local district distinctions, graduate credits) indicating lowest-quality teaching is concentrated in low-performing schools

*See, for example, research by Ronald Ferguson and the Tripod Project: Ronald F. Ferguson, "Helping Students of Color Meet High Standards," in *Everyday Anti-Racism: Getting Real About Race in School,* ed. Mica Pollock (Cambridge, MA: Harvard Education Press, 2008), 78–81.

of the problem to deep root causes. This is done through a simple exercise of asking why repeatedly to dig beneath the surface to the root causes. Our favorite protocol for this endeavor, called *5 Whys*, is a key tool in the improvement arsenal of many school systems as well as organizations outside education, like Toyota.[6] It's called 5 Whys because you keep asking why until you reach something that feels like a deep, actionable root. Experience suggests that it often takes five why questions to get to that place, but it can take more or fewer. The Moorwood group came up with the analytical chart in figure 3.4 when using the 5 Whys protocol for its four high-priority hypotheses.

4. Vet

In the final step of the process, the group must step back from its work to see whether the root causes it has identified make sense, have potential to impact the instructional core if acted upon, and have an evidentiary basis. Sometimes, this may require additional data collection or simply conversation. Sometimes, the group may want to understand some nuances of the issue before proceeding. The root cause can sound generic, as if something looks the same across the system, when in fact there may be distinctions worth noting.

In the Moorwood example, when people looked at the roots, they felt solid about most of them. But some areas warranted further discussion. The second hypothesis in figure 3.4 ("assessments aren't used to inform instruction") felt like a real root cause, but several people in the group hypothesized that teachers might not know how to use the assessments even if these tools were more informative, given the lack of assessments in the system historically. The question was asked: Why would people know how to use them? The research was clear that teachers had to use assessments to inform instruction on a daily basis if the assessments were going to lead to improved outcomes for students. So the group wanted to make sure that it addressed both the quality of the assessments and the training and support that teachers would need to use the assessments effectively.

One of the people in the group disputed the "low teaching quality" hypothesis. Professional development for new teachers was up to individual schools, and some schools were better at it than others. Was the variation in teacher quality an HR Department function or a Teaching and Learning Department function? Representatives from each department took the lead on getting a few people from their departments to gather evidence of the current new-teacher programs in the system and which ones seemed effective (based on both retention and new-teacher input).

FIGURE 3.4

MOORWOOD GROUPS USES 5 WHYS PROTOCOL TO FURTHER FOCUS HYPOTHESES

	Hypothesis 1: Quality and rigor of instruction is inconsistent	Hypothesis 2: Assessments aren't used to inform instruction	Hypothesis 3: Adults have limiting beliefs about students' ability to learn	Hypothesis 4: Teaching quality is poor	
				Whys by hiring practices	Whys by new teacher suport
Why 1	There are no common instructional expectations guiding teacher practice or teacher evaluation.	Many assessments in use do not provide teachers with specific enough information about what the students know and what they are struggling with to inform instruction.	Many students are struggling to learn at high levels.	The district is unable to recruit or retain its fair share of high-quality teachers.	
Why 2	The district does not have teaching competencies or standards for teacher practice.	The assessments in use in the district focus on measuring student learning, providing simply a score for each student and grade-level benchmarks.	Students are not being taught higher-order thinking skills.	The district is not seen as a desirable place to teach, because of arcane hiring practices.	There is limited support for new teachers.
Why 3	The district doesn't have a shared vision of high quality instruction.	When the districts selected assessments, few available assessments provided instructional suggestions.	Curriculum materials and instruction focus on basic skills.	Hiring is done after many neighboring communities hire. And the hiring process is not customer focused.	There is limited mentoring and no targeted professional development for new teachers.
Why 4	People in the system don't talk together about instruction.	Instructional focus is a more recent development in assessments.	The district is using low-level curriculum and instructional materials.	HR and principals focus on getting teachers hired by the first day of school and don't cultivate strong applicants.	
Why 5	People in the system have different ideas about what good instruction looks like and don't know how to talk about those differences productively.			HR and principals don't understand that early hiring leads to higher quality hires and that strong teachers are highly sought after.	

When someone else wondered whether early hiring actually leads to higher-quality hires, a couple of people were charged with gathering relevant research and seeing whether there were patterns within the system of hiring fills and vacancies. Were some schools better at hiring earlier, or was it a problem that plagued the whole system? If there was variation, why, and did it seem at all connected with student performance?

The hypothesis regarding adults' beliefs about students' ability to learn required some rethinking. One group member suggested that adding the root cause "using low-level curricular materials" was both plausible and a way to "let us off the hook." The argument was that this framing didn't help the system own a problem critical to closing the achievement gap, a key part of the symptom that initiated the analysis. It was too easy to blame the problem on curricular materials, and there was clearly more going on. Someone suggested revisiting the 5 Whys to see if breaking the analysis into parallel tracks, as the group had done with the fourth hypothesis, might be helpful. The group took on the challenge and further refined the hypothesis (figure 3.5). With this important refinement made, the group decided to pause, confident it had strong root causes.

The vetting process addresses the inescapable bias described in the Talmud: "We see things as we are, not as they are." Continual loops back to evidence and

FIGURE 3.5

REFINING THE "WHYS" ABOUT HYPOTHESIS 3 AT MOORWOOD

Hypothesis 3: Adults have limiting beliefs about students' ability to learn	
Many students are struggling to learn at high levels	
Students are not being taught higher-order thinking skills.	Students are bringing other issues into the classroom that distract them from learning.
Curriculum materials and instruction focus on basic skills.	District isn't providing enough social and emotional support to students.
District is using low-level curriculum and instructional materials.	District hasn't built a comprehensive student support infrastructure.
	District doesn't know what a comprehensive student support system looks like and how to build it.

continual questions about why help us surface and dig through the assumptions and beliefs that inevitably inform the way we see and respond to evidence.

At this point in the process, the group has dug deeply into what is currently happening, identified key learning issues it wants to address, and developed some nuanced understanding of why those challenges persist and how the system is contributing to them. This understanding puts the team well on the path to figuring out how the system should respond to the challenges. Now the team needs to step back from the data about the current work in the system to look forward and envision what it wants the system to make possible for all students.

CHAPTER 4

Vision

Keeping the End in Mind

Every great advance . . . has issued from a new audacity of the imagination.

—*John Dewey*

The state test scores were in. The Moorwood senior leadership team members looked at how their schools had performed, and were both pleased and dismayed at what they saw. "We've got several schools that are really making progress," said José Vega, the chief operating officer. "Yes, but we've also got good schools that are in trouble," said Betty Scott, chief of staff. "I'm so tired of No Child Left Behind—it punishes good schools because of the underperformance of a few failing students." In the awkward pause that ensued, Sonya, the superintendent, counted silently to herself to help her resist responding first. Would someone else on the team respond to Betty? As Sonya's silent count reached "ten one thousand" (which seemed more like ten minutes than ten seconds), Patrick Leary, the chief academic officer, jumped in. "I'm the first to admit it's not perfect legislation, but how can we call schools 'good' if they have students who are failing? I think part of our problem is we talk about 'good' schools and 'bad' schools, when what we should be doing is talking about how effective all schools are in educating all children. Underperforming students aren't the problem—they're the reason we're here." Patrick had surfaced the issues of race and equity that had forced Sonya to count to ten. Now she drew the team's attention to the big picture, reminding the members, "We need to reflect on our student performance results in the context of what we have said we want to accomplish and make possible for all students."

This vignette reminds us that knowing what we are working toward—our vision for our work—is critical to knowing how to interpret and respond to student achievement results. Similarly, having a clear vision for a system's work is essential to having a strong strategy for reaching our goals. Vision also inspires people and helps everyone look beyond the reactive "got-to-fix-this-problem" mind-set to something bigger and more powerful that sustains people in their daily efforts.

The vignette also illustrates the power of a vision for all students and shows how tackling head-on the issues of race, achievement, and equity can focus a leadership team on what is really important. While many people aren't quite as blunt as Betty, we hear variations of her comment frequently. The message is the same—"Except for *those* students, we're doing great. We're not really responsible for why *those* students are underachieving." This message reflects a narrow and exclusionary vision that lets systems abdicate their responsibility for *all* children. A system's vision and the strategy it develops to achieve it must reflect a commitment to *all* students.

It is not good enough to orient a system's vision solely on solving the problems identified through state tests and NCLB targets—too often that results in seeing children, especially particular groups of children, as the problem, and reinforces school systems' reactive tendencies. A system must be pursuing a vision, orienting itself to the future and a yet-unrealized picture of what's possible for children. Being vision-pursuing gives our work meaning, answers the question of *why*. "Why?" is the companion question to "What do we want to do?" and "How are we going to do it?" The latter two are key questions of strategy development and execution and are answered elsewhere in this book. "Why?" is the motivating question whose answer helps us repeatedly recenter, refocus, recommit, and, sometimes, get out of bed in the morning when the going is very tough.

The vision paints a vivid picture of the future while acknowledging the past and present. Developing such a powerful vision that drives extraordinary effort and achievement requires imagination. Two key components of imagination are image and belief—a picture and the ability to see and believe in that picture. John Kotter, a leading authority on leadership and change, defines vision as "a picture of the future with some implicit or explicit commentary on why people should strive to create that future."[1] Developing a vision requires asking and answering these questions: What do we want for our children? Does that aspiration apply to all of our children, or just some? When the vision is clear, everyone in the system gives the same responses to these important questions.

Vision is most powerful when it is shared. Yet in practice, vision is rather flat in many organizations—quite literally flat in text that has been carefully crafted by a few people and that exists only on paper. But it is not enough for a few people to be the "imaginers." The foundation of shared, purposeful action is shared belief, and most of us have to be able to "see" something in order to believe it. Too often, we assume that we're all on the same page about what the vision is and what it means, but as soon as we start digging, we see that we're in entirely different books.

Without collective clarity, ownership, and energy guided by the vision, the "system" is an assortment of individual agendas, pockets of excellence and mediocrity, and a beehive of activity that is producing little honey. The vision shapes what the system is focused on and how it is organized. If we are trying to keep children safe, out of trouble, and able to read a newspaper, we should go about that differently than if we are trying to help children be able to find, parse, and analyze information; work in teams; and be ready to succeed in college and beyond. If we are trying to help some children succeed in college, we'll go about that differently than if we are trying to help all children be prepared for college without remediation.

Even so, to be honest, the two of us roll our eyes when we hear the word *vision*. We've sat in too many meetings full of wordsmithing and debate about where the commas should go in the vision statement, and we've then seen little correlation between the vision statement and how the system and the people in it choose to invest their time and energy on a regular basis. We're not asking you to revise your vision statement. We are asking you to consider whether your vision is vibrant enough to guide your strategy. If not, what kinds of conversations do you need to have to help people develop a shared and compelling answer to the question "Why?" Why do we want to do this work? Why must we do this work?

In this chapter, we breathe some life into the word *vision* and encourage you to think with "audacity of the imagination" about what is possible for students, adults, and the systems that support them. This is what drives a system's strategy to succeed and to improve. We suggest processes for visioning and re-visioning—processes that are driven by a sense of urgency and that provide powerful and inspiring images of what is possible, make explicit the values of the organization, and require participants to consider what they will contribute to the enterprise.

In cultivating strategy for a school system, we encourage assessing the present, imagining the future, and learning from the past. Assessing the present helps us look at the state of the system's vision currently and determine the extent to which it needs to be reconsidered and how that might best be done. Imagining the future lets us step away from the present to envision what could be possible and what we want to create for children. Learning from the past reminds us of the evolution of the vision for American education and helps us makes a proactive decision about our vision, guided by history and context.

ASSESSING THE PRESENT

What is the current state of your system's vision? How do you know whether your vision needs some revision, and if so, what kinds of revision? A robust vision applies to *all* students and is multidimensional, clear, shared, enacted, and audacious. A vision is multidimensional when it includes aspirations for students beyond test scores, including goals for their individual success, their contribution to the community and democracy, and for their health and happiness (i.e., good living, citizenship, and life), all appropriate for the twenty-first century. A vision is clear when you can picture it when you read it or hear it. A vision is shared when a variety of stakeholders answer consistently when asked what success looks like for students. A vision is enacted when it guides everyday decisions and when you can see it whenever you walk into schools. A vision is audacious when it dares to imagine the seemingly unimaginable. This last characteristic is perhaps most striking in the systems and schools that surprise even the most hopeful among us with what they are able to do. People in these systems are driven by an audacious vision of the possible, one that is both inspired and inspiring to people inside and outside the system.

The tool in figure 4.1 can help assess a system's vision. It can be used within the senior leadership team or across multiple stakeholder groups. If the latter, the data can be disaggregated by stakeholder groups to see if different stakeholders have different perceptions of the vision. What areas are consistent across groups, and where are there contrasts? What does that tell you about your vision and your system?

Creating or refining a vision is an opportunity to help people become clear on what is necessary and possible, to believe in and own the vision, and to generate urgency for acting on the vision. It doesn't matter how eloquent the vision is or if it scores a 5 on "all-encompassing," "multidimensional," and "clear" if it is not also shared and enacted. The vision of a few does not equal the success of all students. Similarly, it's not all that helpful for students if a vision is shared and enacted, but is limited in imagination, only imagines a future for some students, or best prepares students for the past rather than the future.

FIGURE 4.1

VISION ASSESSMENT TOOL: SIX ESSENTIALS OF THE VISION

On a scale of 1 to 5, with 5 being high, how would you rate the following?					
	1	2	3	4	5
All-encompassing Does our vision apply to all students, or some? If some, who's included and who's not? 1 = none, 5 = all					
Multidimensional Does our vision include aspirations for students beyond test scores? 1 = all about proficiency on test scores, 5 = addresses aspirations beyond tests					
Clear Is our vision clear? When you read it or hear it, can you picture it? 1 = unclear, 5 = very clear					
Shared Is our vision shared by stakeholders, including students, parents, teachers, board, central office staff, and community? 1 = resides in 1 person or small group, 5 = shared by all stakeholders					
Enacted Does our vision guide our decisions and our actions on a large (annual, systemwide) and small (daily, individual) basis? 1 = only on paper, 5 = lived consistently throughout system					
Audacious How bold is our vision? How "impossible" is it? 1 = not bold, 5 = very bold; seems impossible, yet worth striving for					

The Moorwood senior leadership team's experience shows how the assessment process can lead to a broader look at what the system is aiming to accomplish. The team began its assessment of its vision by having individual members of the team complete the vision assessment tool and make a visual of the results. The results of the assessment are presented in figure 4.2.

Let's look at Moorwood's vision statement that the team was assessing: "Ensure our students meet the state academic performance expectations and graduate from high school able to choose college or career and be successful. Our graduates are

FIGURE 4.2

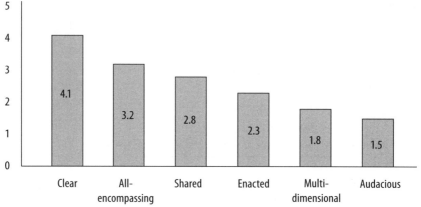

MOORWOOD RESULTS OF THE VISION ASSESSMENT TOOL

curious learners who know how to think critically, analyze information, and apply their knowledge in different settings to create things and make new knowledge. They are also good people, capable of empathy, and prepared to be citizens in a diverse democracy."

As the senior leadership team discussed the results of its assessment, team members were struck by their agreement that the vision appeared to be fairly clear, but that it was not well shared or enacted, and that it was viewed as one-dimensional and not bold. The low scores on multidimensional and audacious were not too surprising to them, given their recent focus on improving student achievement—a focus that was tied mostly to the state tests. The irony is that the educators' official vision statement suggests that they want to do something for children greater than helping them pass tests.

The team agreed that the vision statement wasn't the problem. The problem was that the system was actually focusing on a small slice of the vision. It was so focused on fixing test scores that it had largely ignored students' social and emotional needs and their learning in areas not tested. The leaders didn't know what the vision they had adopted looked like in action.

They decided that they needed ideas of what excellence and success look like, and to challenge their own notions of what is possible. They needed to see audacious new possibilities for how they could bring to life the entirety of what the vision statement set forth. They didn't want to spend a lot of time on this visioning process because they felt an urgency to define a strategy. Yet they knew that having a clear vision would ensure they developed a strategy aligned to it that would make achieving the vision possible.

IMAGINING THE FUTURE

In the 1980s, education philosopher Mortimer Adler and colleagues framed the "three callings for which schooling should prepare all Americans": "(a) to earn a decent livelihood, (b) to be a good citizen of the nation and the world, and (c) to make a good life for one's self."[2] Much current rhetoric focuses on the first of these callings, with a particular emphasis on so-called twenty-first-century skills. It's clear that a high school diploma is no longer a guarantee of a decent livelihood. What's less clear is what precisely those twenty-first-century skills are (and whether they're at the expense of or in combination with "basic" skills) and what responsibility schools have on the "citizenship" and "good life" fronts.

Economists Richard Murnane and Frank Levy define the skills needed for today's economy as "expert thinking" and "complex communication."[3] Tasks that can be done by rules are best done by computers; people are best at tasks like interpreting a law and arguing a case, teaching, and caring for an elder, which require analysis, improvisation, and flexibility. What kinds of tasks do our schools give students? Mostly ones that can be done by following a set of rules or procedures. This prepares them for work that is largely done by computers or pays low wages—certainly not enough to earn a decent livelihood. The first step of visioning or re-visioning, then, is to imagine what we want students to know and be able to do in the economy and society of the twenty-first century they will be entering, and how we want them to be able to function in that world.

There are a variety of ways to imagine the future. One school district we know spent several months engaging multiple stakeholders inside and outside the school system in conversations about twenty-first-century skills as they revised their vision and strategy to be more focused on preparing students for success beyond high school. They gathered a large group of community stakeholders as well as district personnel and invited a university professor to talk about the changing economy and what that meant for the knowledge and skills that students needed. They then had a community dialogue about how they would define *twenty-first-century skills* and worked within their district to further hone that definition as part of their strategy. The product of these conversations was this vision statement: "Graduates will be fully prepared for college and career by having twenty-first-century skills, high aspirations, and excellence in teaching and learning." They defined a list of measureable goals, from grade one through high school, that would show that students were progressing toward this vision, what the system called its commitment to providing a "Bridge to Success."[4]

Another district used text-based protocols to guide a discussion of several articles and reports about skills that students need for work and college. We've also seen districts use videos to show how the world is changing and to show what students want for their future and what students think school needs to do to help them reach that future. These are most powerful when the video portrays the district's own students—a project that students have both interest and talent in producing. (See Further Resources in appendix C for sample articles and Web sites.) The combination of data, images, and stories can help make a vague term like *twenty-first-century skills* more concrete and can help develop shared understanding.

The practice of looking forward as part of visioning can also take the form of looking into the future while acknowledging the past and present. People often need structure and help being creative (a counterintuitive but common duo—structure and creativity), and some practices can enable people to be imaginative, to go beyond the current reality, and to picture the future. One district, which we'll call "Cityside," used a protocol called Back to the Future with its senior leadership cabinet to refine its broad vision and to articulate more detailed visions around several areas that had emerged after many months of analysis and dialogue as potential focal points in the district's strategy.[5] This approach comes out of the National School Reform Network and carefully uses verb tenses to help people imagine their future as the present and their present as the past (see "Back to the Future Protocol" in appendix B for a modified version of the protocol). Cityside's senior leadership cabinet members began to refine their vision by stating the future they expected and their goals for the re-visioning process (figure 4.3).

They then divided into small groups in three key strategic areas they had identified: resource allocation, human capital, and accountability, and went through the protocol for each of their areas. There was great energy in the room when people described their future in the present tense—it sounded attainable and real. As they had fun with it, they became bolder and more creative in their imagining. They enjoyed describing their actual present as the past—something that they were looking back on with delight. Describing the (hypothetical) path they took to get from

---

FIGURE 4.3

**CITYSIDE SCHOOL DISTRICT GOES BACK TO THE FUTURE
TO CLARIFY ITS VISION OF THE FUTURE**

2015: The "Cityside miracle" is complete.

- Cityside students K–12 are outperforming peers across all socioeconomic, racial, and other lines.

- The superintendent is sick of going on Oprah. . . .

How did we get here?

Goals:

- Expand and clarify the vision of what Cityside is really trying to accomplish.

- Identify opportunities and avenues for focused improvement.

- Guide purposeful actions and reduce wasted efforts.

---

past to future was aimed not to define action steps to follow up on, but to help them see that the future was attainable, that there were pathways between here and there. When the group had completed the protocol, one participant laughingly said, "I like the future. I don't want to come back to the present."

Another way to imagine the future is to visit schools or systems that provide vivid pictures of what great education looks like. Vague talk about twenty-first-century skills becomes very concrete when you see middle school students working in teams to develop proposals for new bus routes for their city from population density projections, an analysis and mapping of current transportation routes and usage, and interviewing residents in underserved neighborhoods. Visits help people think more broadly about what is possible, see vision in action, distill from observations the beliefs of a system, and be inspired by possibility.

We know that system leaders and staff don't have free time to be traipsing all over looking at other schools and systems. There is much to be learned from visiting your system's schools that are most effectively serving all their children. Find examples of places that are successfully living part or all of your vision or are simply doing outstanding things for children, and visit them. If you venture beyond your system, we encourage looking at traditional school district schools as well as charter and private schools. As with other visioning exercises, visits may be something the senior leadership team does, but the system will probably get further down the road of a shared vision if people beyond the senior leadership team are involved.

Brainstorm all the places the group might visit, grouping them by what you think you might learn and why you should go there. Choosing at least one site from each category, or one from each high-priority category, will provide a broad perspective. Depending on the size of the group and the number of sites, you might divide into small groups and reconvene as a larger group, which puts some responsibility on each group for gathering and relaying information. Be really clear about the purpose for the visits and the process for reporting back, or it will be hard for the system to learn together. It's helpful if you agree on a protocol that everyone will use (see figure 4.4 for an example of a protocol to follow during school visits). Encourage people to bring back photos and other evidence to share.

School visits proved a powerful tool in informing the Moorwood team's review of its vision. Constrained for time, the team focused on several Moorwood schools that seemed to be living all aspects of the system's stated vision, as well as two local schools outside the system—one charter and one private—that also seemed to be having success with all students on both academics and other fronts, like community service, arts, and college-going rates. The team wanted to see what classrooms look like in those schools. Armed with a list of questions (similar to those in the sample visitation protocol), the team divided into small groups, with each member of the senior leadership team going with a group of central office staff and principals. Each group visited one school.

When the groups returned from their visits, they met to share what they saw. They were excited. In classrooms, they saw fourth-grade students doing things that ninth-grade students in their own system do. Over and over, they heard people talking about using data to help them figure out what to do next. They shared images of what "curious learners" look like and how they saw people applying and creating knowledge. They also discussed what life in these organizations looked like for the adults who work in them and why the places they visited felt like good places to be. Some members of the team were fired up, inspired by what they saw, ready to figure out how to build that sense of possibility. Others, though, were overwhelmed by the distance between their own system's current conditions and what they saw. They cautioned the team against reaching too far too fast. The conversation got pretty heated as the two different interpretations of the observations surfaced. Team members stuck with the conversation through some hard spots, ultimately uncovering

---

FIGURE 4.4

SAMPLE VISITATION PROTOCOL FOR USE IN SCHOOL VISITS

Things to observe:

- What does it look like when you first walk into the organization's building? What do you notice?
- What's the nature of the relationship between children and adults in the building?
- What's the nature of the relationship between adults in the building?
- What kinds of talk do you hear? Give examples.
- What kinds of tasks are students engaged in?
- Report on your general observations.

Things to ask:

- What does it mean to be successful in this school? What does a successful leader, teacher, or student do?
- What happens if you're not successful?
    - To whom are you accountable for what?
    - What kind of support is available to you?
- How do people learn how to do their work better?
- Who is best served in this organization? Who is least served?

Things to collect:

- Printed vision or mission statements
- Photos of people at work and of the physical environment
- Examples of work

Things to think about and discuss in the visitation team:

- If students in this school did exactly what teachers asked them to do, what do you predict students would be able to do?
- What would it feel like to be part of this school?

Other takeaways: record any other observations that are not specifically included in this protocol.

that the tension reflected the anxiety people felt about not knowing how to realize the vision the system adopted two years before. The team had to acknowledge the huge piece of work that lay before it. But it felt hopeful as the members saw the words of their vision statement start to take on new meaning.

UNDERSTANDING THE PAST

Though it is increasingly hard to recall, in American education, we have not always defined success in terms of test scores. And we have not always expected all children to learn. In fact, these ideas are a relatively recent development, and speak more to our past than to our future. Amid the pressure of AYP (Adequate Yearly Progress) and NCLB, it can be hard to get perspective and to imagine a different way that schooling might be. Understanding a bit of the history of schooling in America can help us see how we are trying to do something awesome that we have never tried to do before: namely, educate *all* children to high levels. It also reminds us that we have stopped trying to do many important things that we used to value. In trying to imagine a different way that schooling might be, it is helpful to understand what schooling has been.

How have Americans envisioned successful schooling in the past? Historian Patricia Albjerg Graham divides the last hundred years into four periods and suggests that in each period, schools and educators have been responsive to what larger society wants for children, albeit perhaps more slowly than society might like.[6] Graham describes the four periods as those of *assimilation, adjustment, access,* and *achievement.* Assimilation was the first part of the twentieth century, in which schools' primary role was to take large numbers of immigrant and farming children and turn them into English-speaking and English-reading Americans. Few children attended school beyond eighth grade, and the nation's best schools were in the cities. During the adjustment period, from 1920 to 1954, schools for children who were more affluent focused on making sure children were well adjusted for life and happy, with little worry about what children knew or were able to do. Schools for less affluent children continued to focus on the basics of reading and writing. The *Brown vs. Board of Education* decision in 1954 ushered in a period of access to education for many groups who had been denied all or part of that education, including African Americans, students with disabilities, and girls.

The vitriolic *Nation at Risk* report in 1983 warned of a "rising tide of mediocrity" and raised alarm bells about the poor preparation students had for both work and democracy. The period since then has been focused on achievement as usually measured by annual, largely multiple-choice tests with little emphasis on the democratic focus of the early twentieth century or the focus on the "whole" child of the mid-twentieth century. The "standards-based reform" that began to get traction in the mid to late 1990s introduced the still-radical notion that schools ought to educate *all* children to high standards and that, indeed, there are some things that all children ought to know and be able to do.

It is not that American schools are worse than they used to be. In fact, the only comparable national data about learning that we have, the National Assessment of Educational Progress (NAEP), shows that average reading and math scores are higher today for both the general population and for subgroups of students than they were thirty years ago. But these achievement levels are not good enough to meet new demands. Many school systems use this kind of historical context and data as a way of giving people perspective and of addressing the personal/not personal paradox: Current failure is not about us ("The world has changed! Schools aren't worse than they used to be!") and is about us ("We can and must do something now! The current state of learning in our schools is not good enough!"). We're trying to do something that has never been done before in American education—educate all children to high levels. If that sounds inspiring and terrifying to you, you're in good company. The trick is to not let the terrifying (or the cynicism that says it cannot be done) overwhelm the inspiring.

If the historical trend holds, we will be moving to a new phase soon, one that is more than a reauthorization of No Child Left Behind.[7] What will it look like? Who will define it? How do you organize a system on a vision that is forward looking and depicts new possibilities for the children and thus for the adults in the system?

TIPS FOR VISIONING AND RE-VISIONING

Considering the present, past, and future is key to ensuring a robust and compelling vision. As you examine and reexamine the vision of your school system, keep several things in mind to make the process a valuable learning experience for the people involved and to produce a stronger vision. The tips below suggest some important things to consider as you proceed.

Focus on excellence. No *but*s. Expect to hear "but that wouldn't work here." Maybe not; the goal is not replication. You're trying to paint a picture. You want to know what learning and teaching look like when they're great.

Pay attention to process. Use protocols to structure conversations and to enable a variety of voices to be heard in a safe setting. Be purposeful about who is involved in the visioning process, ensuring that people who are key to bringing the vision to life are involved in the process (this means teachers, among others!). Include skeptics and people who initially have a different vision.

Balance internal and external voices. Both internal and external partners must be on board with the vision, and both internal and external partners have ideas to contribute to the conversation. Be careful about allowing any constituency to dominate, and ask who is absent from the dialogue. External partners shouldn't dictate everything (e.g., business partners articulating the vision based on their hiring needs), but they have a unique and important perspective. Parents, an oft-overlooked or underrepresented constituency, are important for both informing the vision (the system is trying to serve their children, after all) and owning it so that they support it beyond the school walls.

Get into classrooms. You'll hear this idea more than one time in this book because the system's work is learning and classrooms are often the richest data source about that work. The best place to see how the vision is lived is in classrooms, and the best way to get a picture of what is possible is by visiting classrooms where students are learning and doing things beyond expectations.

When the conversation gets emotional, you're making progress.[8] The more clear and open people are about purpose, the more they lay bare what they value and why they come to work every day. Some people will cry, some will speak angrily, some will whisper. Some will speak with an intensity that frightens others. Some will tell their own stories that bring others to tears. Some will tell stories that others can scarcely imagine. When people are honest, they will disagree sometimes. They will not all value the same things, they will not all hope for the same things, and they will not all believe in the same possibilities for all children, much like Betty and Patrick in the vignette at the beginning of this chapter. When they are willing to say this to each other, they're moving closer to a shared vision. Leaders play a key role in sharing their values and vision and in carrying on when the conversation gets messy and hard and uncomfortable.

Apply vision and purpose on a daily basis. In regular endeavors, like meetings and conversations, ask, "What's our purpose? What are we trying to do here? How will we know if we're successful?" Remind people about the vision. Ask, "How will this help us prepare all students for success in work and college, or prepare them to be curious learners, or prepare them to be good people [whatever your vision is]"?

In most systems, like Moorwood, there is already a vision in place, at least on paper. How do you convince people to reexamine the vision if you think it is not powerful enough to inspire and guide the work? New leadership often brings an opportunity to reexamine the vision. In the case of existing leadership, you often need to convince people that the current vision is not sufficient by making a case on pragmatic or moral grounds. —For example, a pragmatic argument is that students need to be more proficient at reading, math, and problem solving when they graduate because they're not ready for a twenty-first-century world and won't be able to make a living. The moral side of the argument is that it's not okay that our students living in poverty are dropping out at three times the rate of their peers. In many systems, urgency far outstrips time. You could spend a meeting re-visioning, or you could spend many months. You could involve ten people or hundreds. Students need improved opportunities to learn now. Yet you don't want to move so quickly that your strategy for improving learning and teaching will later fall apart when you try to implement it. It is worth spending some time on vision, even if it is just one meeting. It is worth nurturing the imagination of people in the system.

Refining the vision is not necessarily about fine-tuning the language of the vision. That can be a long and painful process that doesn't ever really affect the experiences and outcomes of students in the system. Instead, the focus is on how to get people to share a vision and how to make it both tied to the reality of the twenty-first century and filled with pictures of success and possibility. In our experience, it is these areas where school systems struggle the most. Engaging in the conversations and exercises described in this chapter may seem to yield similar language to the vision statement the system started with. Perhaps the system started the re-visioning process with something like "We will prepare all students for twenty-first-century success and support them to be lifelong learners, contributors to the community, and prepared for college and career." Perhaps after one or more conversations, the vision statement language has changed to convey the shared vision. Or maybe the vision statement language hasn't changed at all. What has changed is the meaning that the sentence carries, and for whom. Now there are the pictures and stories that go with the words and that are shared more broadly within and outside the system. Discussion and action have transformed the sentences from lofty language to an audacious vision that can drive action that will transform the system and student learning. And the focus is on how we are beginning to enact that vision on a daily basis.

And, of course, the process is continual. The meaning—and the words, pictures, and stories—will continue to evolve as people in the system try to enact the vision, as their understanding of what is possible changes, and as the world continues to change. Pausing to periodically assess how multidimensional, clear, shared, enacted, and audacious the system's vision is, and whether it is all those things for *all* students, will help the system move closer to both articulating and realizing a bold vision worthy of the students it serves.

Embracing Reality and
Moving Beyond It

At the simplest level, using data lends itself to stepping back, getting perspective, and separating ourselves from our practice. And yet, using data rarely leads to action if it does not also become personalized and personal. Vision invites us to dive in, commit, become excited about audacious possibility. But visionary action without analysis and reflection often ignores learning. Data and vision are deceptively simple concepts—if we just use data, we'll figure out the right answers. If we say, "All children will learn at high levels," everyone in the system will believe it and make it happen. And yet, as soon as you start using data you realize they generate more questions than answers, and as soon as you move beneath the language of the vision you realize that not everyone understands the words or enacts their understanding in the same way. Below are a few suggestions for how to dive in and step back from data and vision, how to manage the complexity and simplicity of them, and how to help others do the same.

DIVING IN VERSUS STEPPING BACK

Personalize. Putting faces, stories, and names with numbers and lofty vision statements makes the successes and challenges that the system faces real, concrete, and compelling. Personalizing helps people answer the "why" question—"*Why* do I/we need to do something here?"—so essential to motivating them to head into unchartered waters. There are multiple ways to personalize the work, even while stepping back. Here are some examples:

- Post photographs of children and examples of their work and art on central office walls to remind people who don't see children every day why they're doing this work.
- Hear from students in their own voices. One system asked students to make a video of their peers talking about how challenging their classes are and what they would like their classes to look like (students made and produced the video themselves). The leadership team then viewed the video as it discussed the issue of academic rigor.
- Invite students to share their talents (sing, play instruments, dance, etc.) during meals or breaks of professional development days, board meetings, or strategic planning sessions. The performances will remind adults of whom they are serving and create a mood conducive to learning.

The same principles apply to personalizing data about adults: Tell the story of a new teacher's experience, read quotes from the principals' survey, include photographs of real people when you're sharing numbers. Sharing names of schools and people who are performing well or struggling can be a delicate dance and countercultural in some places. Yet every fast-improving system we know has moved beyond anonymity, mostly by putting names to data and focusing the conversation on describing the evidence, learning from one another, and helping children rather than placing blame. These systems have managed to personalize data without the information being personal, the ultimate act of simultaneously diving in and stepping back. They use data and vision to create urgency while supporting people's agency in taking individual and collective action.

Generate images. For many systems, it is quite powerful when their leaders have the opportunity to see clear images of what it looks like when kids are learning or when an organization is functioning well. These images help people answer the questions of *what* and *how*—what does it look like, and how do you do that work? Many people need pictures of the *what* and *how* in order to believe that the vision is possible and to have the confidence to dive in. The images often highlight the most important work in which the system needs to engage for improvement. Sometimes these things can be seen within the system; other times it's helpful to look outside. Visits to high-performing schools can be illuminating if you dive into these visits. Notice how you feel when you first walk in the door. See how the secretary greets visitors. Notice what's on the walls. Take pictures to remind you of what is most striking. Talk to children. Observe a faculty meeting or teacher team meetings. What do they show you about high-functioning teams? Visit other systems or departments that function well. Talk to staff about how *they* work. Look at the tools *their* team uses to guide and assess its work. Observe meetings and the interaction of staff more generally. Then step back and think about how to apply the images in your own system.

Encourage audacity. In their busy day-to-day lives, school systems are barraged with strong external messages about appropriate improvement measures and targets. It is easy to react to the external environment rather than setting internal aspirations and goals. Audacity, however, rarely emerges from reaction. Instead, you have to create space and time for people to be audacious, to generate bold ideas, actions, and targets, helping people see and feel that the collective risk (and the risk for individual children) in not dreaming outweighs the risk of potential failure involved with dreaming. Measures and targets help us step back and know whether we've been successful. Setting our own targets helps us take ownership of hitting them. We've seen school systems get perspective on their own data by using data from other systems—both U.S. and international—to show what students are capable of and to encourage their own system to set the bar higher and dream bigger for students. One system we know held a "Dream Day" to which it invited parents, teachers, community members, and others to articulate their dreams for children. When people in your system start talking about proficiency scores as floors rather than ceilings, you know you're making progress.

COMPLEXITY VERSUS SIMPLICITY

Ask children. If you really want to know how things are going for children, what they aspire to, what they need, and how to help them, ask them. Children are absolutely the best source of information about what is happening in the instructional core and what they need to succeed. Give them a survey, meet with them in focus groups, invite them to serve on an advisory panel, eat lunch with them in the cafeteria (even better, take them out to lunch, a favorite tactic of several of our colleagues), talk with them in classrooms and hallways. They're usually very honest, and it's just plain fun to talk with them. Yes, they'll give you contradictory messages, and yes, talking with them will add to the complexity of your work—but it will also make the work simpler. When you're getting overwhelmed with data, when the vision seems too flat and lifeless, children's voices will provide clarity.

Go beyond test scores. While 100 percent proficiency for all children is an ambitious goal, it's not audacious enough. Children are more than test scores and AYP statistics. Going beyond test scores means holding the whole of the child. Describe what you hope for children as humans, as citizens, as learners. Engage stakeholders in articulating hopes to build a collective commitment that extends beyond test scores. It's more complicated to organize a system that supports children as learners, citizens, and humans than one that supports children as high test scores. That's okay because it is also much more rewarding for teachers and honors their capacity to shape the lives of children.

Keep it simple. One of the skills of successful system leaders is that they use language to describe things in plain terms while holding complexity in their heads. They use stories, metaphors, and tag lines to share their vision and ideas. One leader we know used the metaphor of a Rubik's cube to talk with principals about their work, and how they had to hold multiple pieces simultaneously because each time they made a move, it moved other pieces. Montgomery County Public Schools uses the tagline "Raise the Bar, Close the Gap" to concisely capture its strategy to raise achievement for all students, while closing racial/ethnic achievement gaps. The superintendent, union president, and other senior leaders continually reinforce what it means and they use data to show why it's necessary and how the system is making progress on it. Strategic leaders capture complexity in ways people can hang onto without oversimplifying. They reinforce the nuances with their talk and actions.

Digging deeply into data, considering their implications for you and for the system, and not getting overwhelmed by them is delicate work. Crafting and living a vision that is audacious without doubting the possibility of reaching the vision is a dance. Both require some artistry. Sometimes leaders focus more on one part of the paradox—it's more important to personalize than to step back, or more important to keep it simple to communicate than to convey the complexity. Other times balancing the paradoxes is key. All of the time, strategic leaders think and act purposefully.

CHAPTER 5

Strategy, Part 2

Pulling It All Together

We can't solve problems by using the same kind of thinking
we used when we created them.

—Albert Einstein

Sonya, the superintendent of the Moorwood Public Schools, and her senior leadership team sat around the conference table. The team had spent the last several meetings designing the system's strategy, and had chart papers and stacks of paper on the table to show for it. Patrick, chief academic officer, said, "Okay, we're clear about what problems we need to solve, so let's get to solving them. I think we've done enough talking. It's time to do something."

José, the chief operating officer, replied, "Do we know what to do?"

"I think it's a matter of really doing what we say we're going to do instead of getting distracted by a thousand things," Betty, the chief of staff, said. "I think it's more than an alignment issue. Presumably, if we knew what to do to solve the problem, we'd already be doing it. No doubt we have some implementation issues, too, but I think we need to figure out the right thing to do. Just doing things doesn't seem to produce the best results."

Sonya added, "The board wants to see our strategic plan at the next meeting. I've been stalling them as long as I can to give us space to be thoughtful, but we do need to show them something at the next board meeting."

This senior leadership team is at a critical juncture. The members have taken stock of where they are now and envisioned where they want to go. They are less clear about what to do next—is it a matter of figuring out the right thing to do? Of aligning the things they're already doing? Of better implementation and follow-through? They are under some internal and external pressure to do *something*. How will they traverse this daunting space between current conditions in their system (where their data tell them they are now) and their vision of where they should be?

Earlier in this book, we introduced strategy, describing what it is (and isn't), why it is so important, and why school systems struggle to do it well. That introduction also addressed the important first step of taking stock of work under way, which the Moorwood senior leadership team has already done. At long last, they (and we) are ready to dive into the work of putting it all together and designing a focused, context-driven strategy that can produce significant improvement in student learning. This work is cumulative, building on each of the big ideas introduced in this book so far—the instructional core, the extent to which work under way in the system reflects the beginning of a strategy, what it takes for a leadership team to drive this work, data and the opportunities and challenges they present, and vision and purpose.

This chapter is about deciding where you're going to place your bets to best help children, how to move closer to your vision, and (most exciting to the action-oriented among us) what you're going to *do*. We'll discuss theory of action first: Why place your bets *here* rather than *there*, and what results do you expect? Next, we'll explore the relationship between strategy and theory of action: How will your proposal get you where you want to go? We will then return to the Moorwood superintendent and her senior leadership team as they mine the work outlined in the previous chapters to design their theory of action and strategy.

THEORY OF ACTION

A *theory of action* describes the beliefs that undergird an organization's strategy and links the strategy to the organization's vision; "a theory of action can be thought of as the storyline that makes a vision and strategy concrete."[1] It is a hypothesis using an *if-then* statement to articulate what will be achieved and how, in the broadest sense, it will be achieved. The power of a theory of action is that the theory helps an organization be explicit about why it is doing something and how it expects that those actions will lead to improved outcomes, such as student achievement. When the leadership team develops the theory of action, it must test its reasoning, surface its assumptions, and make its intentions clear. Doing these things may challenge fundamental beliefs about how the organization will improve or highlight assumptions that need to be challenged.

Here is an example of a theory of action used in a real school system: "If we provide teachers with a prescribed set of curriculum and instructional materials that define what is taught, pacing guides that define when things are taught, training and support to implement the materials and hold teachers and principals accountable for implementation, then student achievement will rise."

This theory of action is firmly focused on the instructional core, signaling the belief that teaching children is the most important work in the system and everything should be organized in support of that. It reflects a belief that to ensure consistency, the system must be clear about what it wants teachers to teach. It also suggests that it is the system's responsibility to support teachers to implement new materials and meet expectations. This theory of action assumes that the combination of clear expectations, support, and accountability will lead to improved student learning. It also assumes that teachers won't provide excellent instruction at scale without the system's intervention.

Another system's theory of action focuses on nurturing innovation: "If we provide schools that meet certain performance guidelines freedom and flexibility from system policies and expectations to make choices about curriculum, instruction and assessment and support innovation, then schools will develop innovations that will accelerate student achievement and inform the work of other schools and the system as a whole."

Underlying this theory of action is a belief that once schools reach a certain level of performance, they know what to do to improve student achievement and do not need direction from the system. In fact, they will pursue innovations that can inform the system. There is also an assumption that successful innovations in one school can be scaled up and effective in other schools or across the system as a whole. This theory of action assumes that principals are strong instructional leaders able to drive improvement in their schools and that central office staff can work to support schools, abandoning the compliance role that many central offices assume.

There is no one right theory of action. A theory of action that leads to amazing student results in one system may be an unmitigated disaster in another. Even within the same system, a theory of action is constantly revised as the system learns which assumptions hold under what conditions and adapts the theory of action accordingly. Context matters. Designing or choosing a theory of action requires careful consideration of the goal, organizational capacity and prevailing culture, and the extent to which actively changing either the capacity or the culture is warranted. Ultimately, theory of action is about intentionality, one of the core ingredients of being strategic.

RELATIONSHIP BETWEEN THEORY OF ACTION AND STRATEGY

Which comes first, theory of action or strategy? The answer is largely driven by context—what is already in place and the location of pressure points for improvement. Some systems articulate their theory of action and then design an aligned strategy. Others may do the reverse, designing the strategy and the theory of action simultaneously. Quite often, a system develops a theory of action after realizing that its work is fragmented and incoherent. Developing a theory of action can help a system build and tell the storyline—how will doing X lead to improvement in the instructional core? How will doing X move us closer to our vision for children?

As is probably clear by now, one size does not fit all in this work. We don't recommend that you pick a strategy or a theory of action because someone else has done it. Conversation and adaptation are crucial, in part because context matters. In order for a strategy and theory of action to work in a specific system, it must be tailored to fit that system. Further, it is in the conversations that people in the system begin to understand the what, why, and how behind the strategy and theory of action. This understanding is critical to successful implementation. Even so, we also recommend that you learn from the work of others and not waste valuable time dreaming things that have already been dreamt. Some common threads in the strategies and theories of action have emerged from the work of school systems. These can provide guidance to a leadership team as it embarks on this work and thinks about where to focus energy and resources for the greatest effect. Recall that a system's strategy comprises a small set of strategic objectives on which are aligned a set of initiatives deliberately chosen to achieve those objectives. Figure 5.1 lists some common theories of action and related strategic objectives that may be useful. Note that they all focus on the instructional core.

These examples provide a sense of the range of approaches and the importance of thinking about this work in context. Different systems need different things to

FIGURE 5.1

SAMPLE THEORIES OF ACTION AND STRATEGIC OBJECTIVES

Theory of Action	Strategic Objectives
Human capital: If we find the best and brightest educators to lead our schools, give these leaders and their teachers the tools to do their jobs well, and make the leaders responsible for the success or failure of students, then they will create excellent schools that ensure high levels of student performance for all students.	■ *Leadership:* system-driven principal preparation program, three-year new-principal induction system; performance management; and pay for performance ■ *Empowerment:* curriculum, instructional materials, assessments ■ *Accountability:* school, department, and system scorecards and dashboards; performance management; and pay for performance
Managed instruction: If we set clear, high expectations for student learning; provide uniform curricula, instructional materials, and lesson plans; and hold schools accountable for implementation, then student performance will improve.	■ Develop K–12 curriculum aligned to state standards and assessments ■ Adopt direct instruction model and aligned instructional materials ■ Organize all professional development on direct instruction and adopted materials ■ Create implementation monitoring system to be used by principals and principal supervisors ■ Align teacher, principal, and school accountability measures to direct instruction implementation and student outcome measures
Empowerment and accountability: If we become a data-driven system that collects, analyzes, and uses data to track the learning and performance of students and adults in the system and to inform teaching and the support and accountability systems, then we will see teaching and learning improve and realize better outcomes for students.	■ Develop an information management system that can provide timely, relevant, user-friendly data to teachers, schools. and departments ■ Build the capacity of teachers and principals to use a variety of student performance data to inform instruction and school programming ■ Build an employee performance management and compensation system that incentivizes performance according to measureable outcomes ■ Introduce systemwide, departmental, and school-specific scorecards and dashboards to measure outcomes and build a performance culture
Mix of managed instruction, human capital and autonomy and accountability: If we provide excellent instruction, attract and develop talented people, expand options and opportunities for students, manage performance, and align resources with priorities, then we will ensure that every child in every school—African American, Hispanic, Asian, and white—is on track at every stage in his or her career as a student in this school system to graduate prepared for success in postsecondary education and employment.	■ *Instructional excellence:* curriculum, instructional materials, a model of effective teaching, and assessments ■ *Talent attraction and development:* hiring the most effective teachers and principals and retaining them ■ *Expanding educational options and opportunities:* longer school day and year, preK, school choice ■ *Performance management:* performance standards for staff, strong system of supervision and evaluation, performance incentives ■ *Resource alignment:* directing existing dollars and raising additional ones to support the strategies

serve students effectively. Designing a theory of action and strategy is iterative work requiring deep engagement. The conversations this work facilitates are invaluable in building common understanding and commitment. They are driven by the senior-most level of the organization but need to happen at all levels. Hearing the voices of on-the-ground implementers will make the decisions reality-based and more likely to succeed. Balancing these voices with the vision-holding responsibility of the senior leadership team will ensure a balance of current reality and aspirations for the future.

DESIGNING A STRATEGY AND A THEORY OF ACTION

Designing a strategy and theory of action draws on the work of assessing current conditions, analyzing data, and developing a vision. The steps (synthesize, generate, place bets, vet) echo the steps used in chapter 3 and are useful for strategic thinking in a variety of contexts. In designing a strategy and theory of action, a leadership team could follow these steps:

1. *Synthesize:* Pull together all of the team's work from the earlier chapters in the book—work that defines the system's vision, its problems of practice and their root causes, and its analysis of its current work. Look at all of this information together, and see what it suggests about where and how the system should focus its energy to improve instruction, accelerate student learning, and realize its vision.
2. *Generate ideas:* Step back from the work the team has done in the system, and explore more broadly the ideas about how to most effectively address the areas of focus identified in the *synthesize* step.
3. *Place bets:* Decide on the few high-leverage things the system is going to focus on deeply to accelerate progress, and decide how it will do so. Determine the theory of action underlying the emergent strategy. Consider strategic initiatives, ease and impact, synergy, and pacing and sequencing.
4. *Vet:* Vet the strategy to ensure that it has integrity, and check the beliefs and assumptions underlying the theory of action.

The theory of action explains the beliefs that drive the strategy; articulating it after naming the strategic objectives allows you to check your assumptions and reasoning and make sure your strategy will actually get the results you aspire to before expending time and energy determining the strategic initiatives. In the final step of vetting, you return to the theory of action to check your reasoning and make sure that the strategy, strategic initiatives, and theory of action are consistent and coherent. We recommend developing strategy first to acknowledge the action orientation of most school systems, and then doing theory of action to provide an underlying *why*. It is often easier to start by talking concretely about what we think are the most high-leverage things we can do to address the instructional core and improve student outcomes. Nevertheless, some people prefer to develop the theory of action first, and if that works better for you and your system, by all means do so. Ultimately, you need both a theory of action and a strategy, and you need to look at them together. The sequence of designing them is up to you.

To better understand the four steps for designing a strategy, we will now consider the Moorwood team's experience.

1. Synthesize

The first step is to look through the various data and evidence collected through the preliminary steps in the strategy design process. That information includes all the data related to current conditions and the vision, which describes the system's aspirations for children. For Moorwood, this synthesis looked like the various elements in figure 5.2.

With all the charts posted on the wall, it was time for the team to engage some of the skills it hopes to develop in students: curiosity, creativity, and critical and analytic thinking.

It engaged in an hour-long conversation that surfaced some important learning. There were several big areas of focus in the conversation. First, the connection between three findings: (1) inconsistent rigor and quality of instruction; (2) the different ideas that people in the system have about what good instruction looks like; and (3) all the different initiatives under curriculum and instructional materials and instruction. The team realized that the system hasn't decided what it values in instruction. As a result, the system is sending mixed signals and is overwhelming teachers with the sheer number of initiatives. Consequently, teachers don't know what is the most important and are trying to address everything, which makes it impossible for them to do anything very well.

Second, the team realized, the system doesn't organize for success. A close analysis of the formative assessment development, the data warehouse, and the scorecard

FIGURE 5.2

SYNTHESIS OF MOORWOOD'S VISION, ROOT CAUSE ANALYSIS, AND INITIATIVES UNDER WAY

Vision

Ensure that our students meet the state academic performance expectations and graduate from high school able to choose college or career and be successful. Our graduates are curious learners who know how to think critically, analyze information, and apply their knowledge in different settings to create things and make new knowledge. They are also good people, capable of empathy, and prepared to be citizens in a diverse democracy.

Key symptoms

Student performance consistently lags behind state standards. When student achievement results are disaggregated by race and ethnicity, there is a significant achievement gap.

Hypotheses	Root causes	Evidence
Quality and rigor of instruction is inconsistent.	People in the system have different ideas about what good instruction looks like.	■ Low-level questioning by teachers that focuses on recall ■ Classroom observations, K–12, showing significant variations in classes within the same grade, within the school, and across schools
Assessments aren't used to inform instruction.	There is limited availability of assessments that can truly inform instruction, and teachers don't know how to translate assessment information into instructional objectives and practices.	■ No formative assessments in high school math, science, or social studies ■ Elementary math assessments with a score for students but no additional information to teachers about the skills students have mastered or not mastered ■ Survey of teachers indicating some K–3 teachers are using literacy assessment data to drive instruction and others are unsure how to use the data ■ Literacy coaches' reports, 4–12, that literacy formative assessments don't provide teachers with data they can immediately use to inform their instruction
Adults have limiting beliefs about students' ability to learn.	District is using low-level curriculum and instructional materials that are limiting what students are asked to do. System doesn't know what a comprehensive student support system looks like and how to build it.	■ School climate survey data in which teachers indicate their preference to teach the "top" students and their belief that many students can't meet the state standards ■ Student survey data indicating that students think they perform best in classes where teachers explain things if they don't understand and in which expectations are high ■ Classroom observations, K–12, of the language teachers use when working with students and how teachers interact with different students: different expectations for different students; some observations also indicating strong teaching designed to meet the learning needs of different students
Teaching quality is poor.	Training and development for teachers is insufficient; HR and principals don't understand that earlier hiring yields higher-quality teachers.	■ Attrition rate of new teachers close to 50% at the end of three years ■ Hiring novice teachers to fill 20% of teaching positions every year ■ Analysis of teacher quality (as defined by value-added student performance results, national board certification, local district distinctions, graduate credits) by school, indicating lowest-quality teachers are concentrated in low-performing schools

FIGURE 5.2, continued

*Current initiatives under way**

Instruction

Science, technology, engineering, and math (STEM) initiative at the high school level

Middle school pedagogy initiative focused on math and science

Pilot of "workshop" model for literacy instruction, K–5, in 15% of schools

Pilot of direct instruction model in low-performing elementary schools.

Redesign how individual education plans (IEPs) are written and used to meet the educational needs of students with disabilities

Professional development

Introducing two-year new-teacher induction system

Training all teachers in instructional strategies that support English language learners

Developing professional learning communities (PLCs) among principals

Character education training for all K–8 teachers

Accountability

Developing scorecards to measure school and department performance and improvement

Developing new principal evaluation instrument

Assessment

Collaboration with external partner on formative assessment system aligned to state assessment in English and math; currently serving 20% of schools

Creating a data warehouse for all student and staff data, including assessment data

Developing a system of formative assessments in English and math, K–5

Developing scorecards to measure school and department performance and improvement

Early childhood

Creation of early childhood program to serve 600 children

Technology

Adoption of English and math tutorial software

Upgrade to provide new computer labs in 40% of schools

Upgrade schools' technology infrastructure to ensure Internet access in all classrooms

School design

Conversion of 20% of elementary schools to K–8s

Conversion of the large high schools into small schools

Curriculum and instructional materials

Adoption of English and math tutorial software

Mapping curriculum to standards in all content areas, K–12

Adopting new instructional materials in math, K–12

Development of early childhood curriculum.

Developing "green" curriculum for use in upper elementary grades

Operations

Upgrade schools' technology infrastructure to ensure Internet access in all classrooms

Creating a data warehouse for all student and staff data, including assessment data

Upgrading software used to track payroll, benefits, and earned time

Revamping teacher hiring process

Redesign of school budgeting process and timeline

School safety initiative

Creation of healthy school lunch offerings

* Italics indicate that the initiative is listed in more than one category because of its focus.

(continued on next page)

FIGURE 5.2, continued

Analysis of initiatives

- We're doing too much; we're headed in too many directions, and as a result, we're not doing anything as well or as deeply as we need to if we want to make real gains.
- We're trying to focus on the instructional core, but the plethora of initiatives doesn't signal the one or two most important things to focus on.
- We avoid making tough decisions.
- We tend to react, trying to solve problems of the past; sometimes we try to think about how to do that in a way that moves us toward the future and our vision, but that's not consistent.
- Our strategy may have something to do with using the curriculum, instruction, and assessment initiatives to improve instruction and leveraging technology to support that work as well as operations functions and accountability.
- When we engage in work that requires cross-functional teams and cross-departmental communication and collaboration, we don't know how to do it, we don't have norms for our work, and our outcomes are inconsistent.
- Our ability to refine our work in action is not consistent.
- We align our resources to support discrete initiatives rather than to drive strategy execution.

Overall scores on "signs of strategy" rubric:

Core	2.5
Focus	2
Visionary and problem-solving	2.5
Ownership and enactment	1

---

indicated that these initiatives should be tightly integrated, but the four departments working on them—research and assessment, information services, teaching and learning, and school accountability—are not working in concert. Each department sees the initiatives differently and wants to get something different out of them. And schools are left in the middle, managing the "noise" of different central office interests and expectations.

Third, it's not easy to focus, prioritize, and create more clarity for schools. Because all the Moorwood initiatives were developed in response to a need, it is hard to figure out what is most important. Should the system stop doing some things even if it means it loses the money that supported that work? Does it make sense to choose one or two content areas to focus on and to stop or slow down other work? Can the system afford to slow down, given the students' needs, or is the pace compromising the effectiveness of the work such that there is no other choice but to slow down?

The team was far from clear about what to do at the end of the discussion. The facilitator reminded the group that it was exactly where it needed to be: wrestling with big, important issues. The goal of the first conversation was to surface the issues, not resolve them. The team's conversation focused on curriculum and instruction, defining effective teaching, and the assessment work, suggesting that they are areas of concern and import that warrant further discussion. The facilitator suggested that these priorities might provide a good starting point to inform the next step in the process.

2. Generate Ideas

This stage in the strategy design process asks teams to step back from their own work to learn from the promising work of other individuals, schools, and systems. In this step, teams generate a list of key questions to investigate and potential data sources, and then go gather information. This is a good opportunity to involve staff members at multiple levels of the organization (beyond the senior leadership team), which will help to build learning and ownership of the resulting strategy across the system.

The focus is on in-depth learning from inside and outside the system on a few particular issues, as identified in the synthesis step above (e.g., how central office departments collaborate to create coherent support for schools, clarity of instructional expectations). How have other people made progress on these issues? What are the right buttons to push and doors to walk through? Often, teams will also do scans that are more generic, investigating what high-performing systems are doing in case there are other promising areas that pertain to the needs of their own system, but may have been missed during the internal analysis. The Moorwood team generated such a list of questions and investigators, as well as a list of potential data sources, as shown in figure 5.3.

Note that the membership for each investigating group includes at least one member of the senior leadership team for convening and communication purposes. These people were assigned particular tasks because of their expertise and responsibility in the system. Other leaders in the system who do not participate on the leadership team were included because of their involvement and expertise in the

FIGURE 5.3

KEY QUESTIONS, INVESTIGATORS, AND POTENTIAL DATA SOURCES

Questions	Investigators	Potential data sources
How do systems ensure consistent rigor and quality of instruction? What kind of curricular and instructional materials are high-performing systems using?	CAO; deputy superintendent; two members of teaching and learning department; one principal; one instructional coach; and one teacher	■ A newly released book about three systems that went from the lowest quartile in student performance in their states to the highest in three years ■ Creighton Public Schools, a system with a similar demographic in the same state that has 90% of its ninth grades at proficiency along with really strong college enrollment and retention rates ■ The highest-performing schools in the system to see how they're organizing their work ■ Review of what was learned from the school and system visits done during "visioning" ■ Research on high-performing and strong growth in achievement systems nationally ■ Literature on aligned instructional systems ■ The literacy overhaul the system did ten years ago ■ Review of some frameworks of effective instruction, e.g., Danielson, Marzano
How do systems make useful assessments available and help teachers know how to use the data from them to inform instruction?	Head of research, assessment, and evaluation department; head of information services; chief accountability officer; CAO; and three teachers (elementary, middle, and high school)	
What does a comprehensive student support system look like?	Chief of staff; heads of special education, early childhood, and English language learning departments; student discipline or student support officer from high school; and two principals	
What are the hiring practices of high-performing systems? What does new teacher support look like in high-performing systems?	Head of HR; members of HR department; one principal; one instructional coach; one new teacher; and CAO (for new-teacher support)	
How do central office departments in high-performing systems collaborate to support schools?	COO and team from operations department; deputy superintendent; CFO	
What are high-performing systems doing to improve student performance? (Focus on above questions and other ideas that seem essential, particularly those that accelerate achievement for some student populations.)	Superintendent; board member; key local partners; deputy superintendent; and principal	

Abbreviations: CAO, chief academic officer; CFO, chief financial officer; COO, chief operating officer; HR, human resources.

issues that surfaced during the analysis (see chapter 2 for more information about designing effective teams). For example, it was critical that the group investigating the assessment question included members of the four departments involved who hadn't been coordinating. Similarly, it was critical to involve teachers in that group since the senior leadership team was concerned about teachers actually using the assessments.

As the senior leadership team reconvened a month after receiving the synthesis assignment, the buzz in the room was powerful. Each team had developed a poster board to share the highlights of its learning. Team members took a "gallery tour," moving from one poster to the next, reading with curiosity, making notes of things that caught their attention or imagination. The team's discussion surfaced common themes about the work of high-performing systems, and many of these themes were new to the Moorwood team. One such revelation was the dogged, focused determination of these other systems regarding teaching quality. Most of the systems the groups visited or read about have well-aligned standards, curricula aligned to the standards, assessments that provide teachers a feedback loop on student learning and the effectiveness of teaching, and intensive professional development. Leaders in other systems talked about walking away from grants and donors whose interests would distract the system from its focus. The visits and reading also highlighted the extent to which some facilities and human resources departments are organized to support instruction, so much so that even school maintenance people can speak to how their work supports student learning.

As the gallery tour and debrief continued, the team noticed something else from their research: the high priority consistently placed on the hiring and retaining of top talent in high-performing systems. Just as students were held to high standards, so too were teachers and principals.

The group's research into comprehensive student support reinforced the idea that it is important, but didn't provide a clear picture of what it would look like. There weren't many models of systems providing comprehensive student support, though there were some examples of schools both inside and outside the system doing so. It looked as though some other countries might serve as good models for the system in thinking about student support, but the group hadn't had time to delve deeply into what was happening beyond the United States.

The visits to high- and low-performing schools within the system also yielded important lessons. When the group visited schools that were improving their results for students versus schools that weren't, it came to a few conclusions, which they shared with the team: Leadership matters. In both kinds of schools, the principal was the driving force for better or worse. The high-improving schools had a culture of collaboration and learning among the adults—a culture that mirrored the experience of students. The culture in low-improving schools was consistently one of hopelessness and low expectations for teachers and students. The principal blamed the teachers. The teachers blamed the students, creating a vicious cycle.

By the end of this discussion, the team had honed in on some things it knew needed to be addressed in the strategy. These conclusions were based on the team's synthesis of conditions in the system and what it had learned from other places.

3. Place Bets

Armed with a synthesis of your system's data and with ideas from the research of successful systems, you can now decide what your system's strategy for improving student learning will be. A strategy consists of a small number of strategic objectives (three to five) that frame big areas upon which the system will focus. Under each objective, there is a series of strategic initiatives—specific work the system will undertake toward achieving the objectives. As the rubric from chapter 1 reminds us, the key is for the strategy to be focused on the instructional core, focused on a few things that are coherent and synergistic, and balanced in its solving of problems and pursuit of the system's vision.

We describe this step as "placing bets" to reflect the reality that all of the preceding work positions us to make well-informed guesses about what will be most effective in accelerating student learning. We can't know for sure. There is no silver bullet.

The Moorwood schools team identified some common practices of effective systems and will probably use those to inform its strategy. But again, the work of systemic improvement is deeply contextual. Considering issues of a system's capacity, its political environment, its partnerships, and its culture when designing strategy is critical to choosing the strategy that is likely to be effective. Strategic objectives and their initiatives should be identified with an eye to how easy or hard each is to implement and how great its impact on student learning will be. Considering whether the system has the capacity to implement the initiatives under consideration or will need to develop new capacity helps a system decide what it can realistically do. Needing to build some capacity is fine; needing to fundamentally redesign the system before implementing any part of the strategy sets a system up for failure.

[handwritten margin note: what is sense of pace + sequence]

The system's capacity informs the pace and sequencing of implementing the strategy. What needs to happen first? What builds off of what? What initiatives need to happen simultaneously? What are the politics, and how do they influence this work? What is the nature and strength of key partnerships with other groups, such as unions, institutions of higher education, and community-based organizations, and how can they be mobilized in support of the strategy? These are some of the questions a team needs to talk through to ensure that the strategy it designs is viable and likely to lead to improved student learning.

If this sounds like a lot to weigh simultaneously—if it sounds hard—that's because it is. Holding complexity and managing the emotional challenge of committing and probably disagreeing about the best places to place your bets is difficult. The process leading up to this point will have built individuals' and the team's capacity for this complex work, but it will still be hard, both intellectually and emotionally. In the following pages, we demonstrate how to segment the work and hence help to manage the complexity. The segments are: identify major strategic objectives; map strategic objectives with theory of action; and identify strategic initiatives, weighing ease and impact, synergy, and pacing and sequencing. Again, we look to the Moorwood leadership team's experience as it proceeded through this process.

Identify Major Strategic Objectives

The Moorwood team set aside a full day for this segment of designing its strategy. The team began the meeting by reviewing the rubric it first used to assess the system's work under way, recalling that the four foundational criteria of effective strategy are as follows:

1. *Instructional core:* The focus of the strategy is to improve the quality of the learning and teaching of content.
2. *Focused, coherent, and synergistic:* The design of the strategy focuses on trying to do just a few things deeply; these things are interrelated and add up to a whole that is greater than the sum of the individual parts.
3. *Visionary and problem solving:* The strategy balances addressing identified problems and moves beyond them to pursue the system's vision.
4. *Discussed and understood:* People in the system talk about the strategy, understand it, and have organized their work in support of it.

The team's process was iterative as the conversation moved from the current initiatives and categories to the root causes to the key lessons from outside the system. The idea of the first strategic objective surfaced fairly quickly. All of the data gathered as part of the process spoke to the system's need to create something comprehensive and coherent to guide instruction in the classroom. From their reading and visits, the team members learned that this is called a "comprehensive aligned instructional system."[2] Such a system addresses the curriculum; the instructional materials that are the primary support to teachers as they teach the curriculum; the quality of instruction; and the use of formative assessments aligned to all the other pieces to provide quick, easy-to-use data about student performance and to inform instruction. The last and, perhaps, most important component is the teacher and principal professional development needed to ensure successful execution.

The team's root cause analysis spoke to the lack of clarity about what the system values and supports instructionally. The mishmash of curricular, instructional, assessment, and professional development initiatives reflects this confusion and dissipates the system's resources. Visits to, and literature about, high-performing school systems demonstrated the power of an aligned instructional system to create a foundational level of consistent, quality instruction. Reviewing this data, the group agreed this was a top priority. The debate ensued as the team tried to decide what content areas to focus on first and how fast to scale the system to include all content areas. Some wanted to move forward on all fronts. Others argued this would repeat the system's tendency to spread itself too wide and thin. The team agreed that math and science were good places to start, given the math test scores, the impending state requirements in science, and the work currently under way.

The team was surprised by what emerged as its second strategic objective: the idea of human capital. This was beyond the team's original framing of an early hiring issue and is a term the team hadn't heard much about or given much thought to before the investigatory groups reported back on their visits and reading about schools and school systems with impressive student learning results. The idea that the school system could identify ways to systematically raise the quality of teaching and school leadership (and central office staff) excited the team. It was also clear that this was new territory and the team needed to define what the initiatives would be for this objective and how to think about building the system's capacity to take on this new work. The team brainstormed a list of possible initiatives for this objective:

- Work with higher education to improve teacher and principal preparation.
- Revamp teacher hiring.

- Introduce new teacher and principal induction.
- Rethink tenure review.
- Create teacher career pathways.
- Consider pay-for-performance.

The last bullet generated the most discussion. The team felt is was a radical idea for this system and would require that the system use value-added assessments and build a system for tracking student performance by teacher. Team members were intrigued and also hesitant about the system's ability to pull this off and the political implications. The union's resistance to any effort to treat teachers differently was also a concern.

The newness and stretch required by the second objective raised concerns about overextending the system. Remembering the strategy rubric's emphasis on the instructional core and focus, the team decided the system could probably only handle one more strategic objective. Reviewing the rubric also brought up the issue of synergy. The second objective's focus on recruiting and supporting top talent felt like a nice complement to the first objective's emphasis on supporting effective teaching through comprehensive classroom support. One objective ensures that talent comes into the schools; the other continues to build the talent through support provided once the person is hired. The team speculated, "Is there another part of this equation that will enhance the effectiveness of the first two objectives?"

The issue of data—about student learning, teachers, and principals and the use of data to facilitate student learning—was raised repeatedly in the early stages of this process, and it was front and center in this day's discussion. The importance of this issue to the success of the other two objectives convinced the team that this should be the third objective. Its additional appeal was that it had the potential to push the system to more productively support the work in classrooms and schools and begin to change central office culture.

Moving on, Betty, the chief of staff, raised the issue of support systems—Wouldn't progress be limited by not addressing student support? After deliberation, the team members concluded that the district wasn't prepared to take on student support as a major strategic objective; it was better prepared to address some of the other critical issues first and focus on doing those few things well. They considered building learning about student support into the strategic plan so that down the road, they will be prepared to address student support systemically.

Map Strategic Objectives with a Theory of Action

Stepping back from the conversation, the team tried to articulate its strategy. It had three strategic objectives:

1. Build instructional excellence by building and implementing an aligned instructional management system in math and science.
2. Hire and retain effective educators.
3. Build the information management systems and technology infrastructure required to support instructional excellence and operations that support schools' focus on instructional excellence.

At this point in the process, the team needed to look at what it was choosing to focus on and define the theory of action underlying its choices. The key questions to answer were "By choosing these three strategic objectives, what are we saying we believe about how our system will improve student learning?" and "Do we believe that what we are saying is true?" As the team thought about this, several assumptions surfaced: the belief that student learning is accelerated when instruction is improved and the belief that a comprehensive approach addressing everything that affects instruction (curriculum, instructional materials, pedagogy, assessment, and professional development) will have the greatest effect on instructional improvement. Another underlying belief was that hiring the most effective teachers possible and focusing on supporting all teachers to improve through training will improve instruction. Finally, there was an assumption that technology can be an important tool for improving instruction and accelerating student learning.

At the end of the session, after much discussion and a couple of drafts, the team came up with its theory of action, shown below alongside the team's chosen (and well-aligned) strategic objectives (figure 5.4).

The Moorwood team was excited to have reached this point, but it also realized that the devil is in the details. Whether the system is able to move forward in a coherent, synergistic way depends a great deal upon the details of initiatives yet to be determined. If we think of the theory of action and strategy like a medical treatment plan, then the strategic initiatives are akin to the daily, actual care the system will receive.

Identify Strategic Initiatives

For each strategic objective, school systems choose multiple strategic initiatives. Different systems might choose different initiatives. For example, one system

FIGURE 5.4

THE MOORWOOD TEAM THEORY OF ACTION AND STRATEGIC OBJECTIVES

Theory of action
If we ensure the quality of instruction by hiring high-quality educators, providing them curriculum, instructional and assessment materials aligned to high standards, clarity about effective pedagogy, and training and support to implement the system and if we leverage technology to support instructional excellence and operational support of schools, then every student we serve will be supported to meet high standards and graduate ready for college and career.

Strategic objectives		
Support instructional excellence by building and implementing an aligned instructional management system in math and science.	Hire and retain effective educators.	Build the information management systems and technology infrastructure required to support instructional excellence.

looking to hire and retain effective educators might work with local universities to match the content of their curriculum to the system's needs. Another system might start its own teacher preparation program. A third might work with nonuniversity programs and partners to provide prospective teacher candidates. Still another system might choose some combination of these strategies or might focus on a marketing, recruiting, and incentives strategy instead of the content and quality of teachers' preparation. Weighing all the possibilities involves a similar analytic and decision-making process that we've seen throughout the book—generate a list of ideas and narrow the list, thinking strategically about multiple factors, including these:

Ease and impact: How easy or hard will this initiative be to do? How much of an impact is this initiative likely to have on the instructional core and on student outcomes?

Synergy: Is there a particular combination of initiatives that together is more likely to have an impact on student outcomes?

Pacing and sequencing: What needs to come before what? Where do we start? How quickly can we roll this out? What do we need to do now to lay the foundation for more substantial action down the road?

Ease and Impact

One of our favorite tools for sifting through multiple options is an ease-versus-impact graph. The goal of the ease and impact analysis is to understand the level of impact each initiative has on student learning and the ease or challenge associated with implementing it. The visual and hands-on nature of the analysis allows everyone involved to see the multiple factors the team is weighing and usually generates rich conversations as people debate the placement of each initiative. In the analysis, teams generate a list of potential initiatives in light of their prior discussions and investigations. They write each of these initiatives on a sticky note and then plot the sticky notes on a graph. The Moorwood team's graph for its human capital strategic objective of "hiring and retaining effective educators" is shown in figure 5.5.

When weighing ease, people often consider multiple factors, including capacity, resources, and political will. For *capacity,* systems consider several questions: Do we know how to do this? Are we ready to take this action, or do we need to do some prep work? For *resources,* systems ask, What resources (people, money, and time) are required for this initiative? Can we reallocate existing resources, or do we need to generate new resources? For *political will*, systems ask, What's the current state of overall enthusiasm and energy for this? Are there particular groups of people to whom this is really important? Are there particular groups of people who are likely to need to be persuaded of the merits of this initiative?

When weighing the likely impact, people consider the evidence, including research, from both inside and outside their system. Information and perspectives on these issues emerge as people discuss where they would place an initiative on the graph. As with much of the strategy design process, the conversation is important for making wise decisions that influence likely success and for developing shared understanding and investment in the decisions. The reasoning behind decisions becomes more clear, making it easier to explain to others, including why a system is doing one thing and not another.

It is important to have some parts of the strategy that are easy to implement and have high impact. These are the quick wins that build buy-in and momentum. Initiatives that are hard and have high impact on student learning are important to consider because they generally focus on making substantive change in how the organization functions to serve children better. Hard work that has little impact on student learning is a bad use of people's time. The trick is to make sure all the work has substantial impact.

FIGURE 5.5

EASE VERSUS IMPACT FOR HUMAN CAPITAL STRATEGIC OBJECTIVE

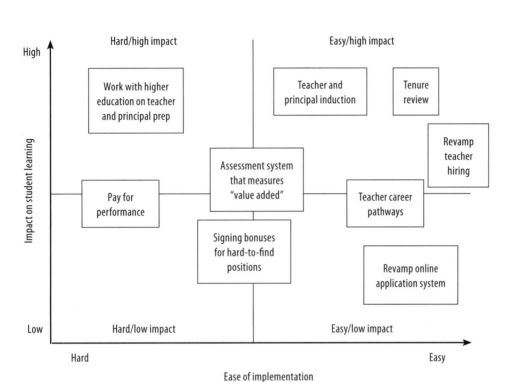

The grid made clear to the Moorwood team that many human capital initiatives are high impact and at least half of them are easy to implement. That's a pretty good ratio. The easy and high-impact initiatives offer relatively quick wins and are a good place to start. There are also some high-impact things that are hard. This doesn't mean they shouldn't be pursued. It simply suggests the importance of people knowing what they are getting into. Mobilizing change in higher education teacher preparation is generally a slow process. The different perspectives, needs, and interests of higher education and K–12 systems need to be explored and negotiated. Yet the potential to transform teacher preparation and the skills of aspiring teachers who want to teach in the system is profound. Claudia, one of the more skeptical

Moorwood team members, pushed the team, asking, "What's our evidence that this would be a good area for us to focus on?" People paused for a moment, and then there was a rapid fire of responses: "Two of the other systems have new-teacher attrition rates at the end of three years of service that are 50 percent lower than ours"; "One of the systems has interview data in which teachers from our system say they want to switch systems because the other system has more career opportunities"; "Two of those systems are notorious for snatching up the best new teachers and principals before we get to them." Some of the data are hard; some anecdotal. But by the end of the conversation, the whole team was convinced that human capital is worth pursuing and that there are some specific ways the system can and should pursue it.

The two initiatives straddling the high- and low-impact line warranted further discussion. Their placement suggests either that their potential impact may not warrant the effort required to implement them or that the team has not been explicit enough about how it envisions the impact of these initiatives. Performance pay is on the line because it is unclear how paying an effective teacher more increases the number of effective teachers, which in turn raises questions about impact on student learning. Plus, the teachers union has grave concerns about differentiating the treatment of teachers. The teacher career pathway initiative is on the line because the team doesn't have a clear view of how a teacher career ladder can be used to drive student learning. The team prioritized engaging the head of human resources, some principals, teacher leaders, union leaders, and key players in teaching and learning to think about this strategic objective and its initiatives before making decisions. Similarly, as the team members discussed signing bonuses, they decided there is mixed evidence about the retention of teachers from signing bonuses, and they worried about union opposition to paying some teachers bonuses. Revamping the online application system seemed relatively easy and needed, but also relatively far removed from student learning, particularly on its own.

Synergy

Synergy, or the idea that some things will be more influential in combination than alone, is helpful for thinking about how to make the work powerful, coherent, and manageable. The Moorwood team, for example, thought the online application system only made sense as part of an overall revamp of teacher hiring and as part of a multiprong effort to assess and value teaching quality. Team members also thought any such system needed to keep track of data in a way that could be combined with a student data warehouse and other human resource data so that the system could ask questions and learn about teachers who were improving student achievement. Currently, their databases don't talk to each other very well.

It is important to think about synergy both within a strategic objective—How might these human capital initiatives work together? Are there any that are essential to do in combination to maximize their value?—and across strategic objectives. Visually, it can help to do an ease-versus-impact graph for the potential initiatives for all strategic objectives (perhaps using different-colored sticky notes for different strategic objectives) and then look for synergy. We've seen some teams draw arrows between sticky notes to show relationships. This serves as both a focusing aide (when prioritizing, focus on high-impact, synergistic initiatives) and a cohering mechanism (there are less likely to be silos down the implementation road if people are clear on how things work in combination).

Pacing and Sequencing

The final consideration when selecting initiatives is pacing and sequencing. Which things can the system do well, and in what sequence and at what pace should they be undertaken to maximize success? You'll do more detailed planning when designing implementation work plans (see chapter 6), but it helps to consider pacing and sequencing when selecting the initiatives. The ease-versus-impact grid helps systems begin to think about the pace and sequencing of strategy implementation. Pursuing some quick wins while simultaneously kicking off harder processes will yield faster results and build energy that will support the harder, longer-term work. Taking on several hard-to-implement initiatives at the same time must be done carefully with consideration of organizational capacity and a clear plan to keep people motivated.

In the Moorwood meeting, as part of this discussion, the facilitator introduced the idea of choosing strategy that both matches and builds the system's capacity to improve student learning. The goal was to find the system's learning edge where it is doing a mix of work that includes things it knows how to do and things it is learning how to do. The facilitator suggested the team think through the initiatives required to implement the aligned instruction strategic objective in terms of the system's capacity and what that means for sequencing and pacing of implementation.

The team talked about the components of the strategic objective. The system knows how to develop a curriculum and choose instructional materials. However, defining what effective teaching looks like is a clear stretch. The system has never done it before, and naming and describing effective teaching is complex. The assessment system work requires additional capacity to ensure that the assessments are aligned to the standards, are benchmarked to the state assessments, and can be used to inform instruction—a trifecta that few assessments have realized. Professional development is something the system has been providing for years, but the quality of it is questionable and there is a need to rethink both its content and its delivery. The critical issue of ensuring that English language learners and students with disabilities are well served through this work also surfaced during the conversation. The team realized this latter concern isn't simply an issue of materials. The system isn't clear about how to most effectively teach those student populations. The team concluded that this is an area where capacity building will be necessary.

Seeing the varied level of capacity for the initiatives, the team realized it would be smart to stagger the pace of roll-out over three years and to differentiate it at the elementary and secondary levels, recognizing that elementary teachers teach all content areas while the secondary level is departmentalized. The system would focus on math in the first year. The current math instructional materials adoption and assessment work would be put on hold while the curriculum was mapped to standards. Then, instructional materials selection and the development of assessments would resume to ensure alignment. The consensus was that the work needed to move to action and observable changes in classroom instruction quickly but not without the infrastructure underneath to support it.

The team reasoned that in the second year, once the math work is up and running and the system has learned from it, the system might start the work in science, using experience from the math initiative to guide the science work. The focus on science in year two would focus on the secondary level. Knowing that many elementary school teachers' discomfort with math would require two years of intensive support to grow roots in that work, the team decided to wait till year three to introduce science at the elementary level. This prompted a longer conversation about phasing the work in—what to roll out to the whole system and what would first be piloted with a smaller group of teachers or schools. It was exciting to see the team dive so deeply into the issues.

At several points during the earlier discussions, the Moorwood team identified areas where feedback from others in the system was needed. Eager to collect this feedback, the team met two weeks later to finalize its strategy statement and was then ready for the vetting process—the last step before sharing the statement more broadly.

4. Vet

Once the strategy statement is well defined, it is then time to assess the integrity of the strategy using the "signs of strategy" rubric introduced in chapter 1.

1. Instructional core

In the introduction to this book, we talked about the instructional core and the importance of organizing systems to make clear that their business is learning. The core work of schools and school systems is the work that happens in a classroom between students, teachers, and content. Strategy must focus on those players and the dynamic relationship that exists between them.

There are several aspects of the Moorwood strategy that focus on the instructional core. One of the strategic objectives steps into the heart of the classroom and provides teachers with support to improve instruction; it addresses teachers and content, two of the three components in the instructional core. The second objective is entirely focused on hiring, developing, and retaining talented educators, touching on the teacher part of the instructional core. The final strategic objective focuses outside the instructional core on technology and support services that directly affect the instructional core. The extent to which all these strategic objectives will actually support the core rather than creating noise and distracting from it will depend upon how that work is designed and implemented. Finally, it's not clear that every initiative is tied to the instructional core, and it's also worth noting that the student element of the core is not explicitly addressed in the strategy, a source of dismay for some team members. The team members returned to the question of student support, something that surfaced in the root-cause analysis and in their generation of potential strategies. They decided that the system needs to signal and support a focus on what is happening in classrooms, and that it can't do *that* well *and* build a comprehensive system of student support, given current capacity. Yet, they didn't want to ignore the issue of student support, knowing that once other elements of their strategy start to work, the issue of student support will become all the more urgent. Rather than repeat the tendency to do too many things, the team decided not to include student support as a strategic objective, but to build toward it. The team scored the strategy 3 on its focus on the instructional core.

2. Focused, coherent, and synergistic

The challenge and opportunity in strategy design is to choose only a few things, ensuring that when they are combined, they create a whole that is greater than the sum of the parts. This means that there is interplay both between the strategic objectives and between the initiatives associated with each strategic objective. This reflects the reality of a dynamic interplay between various problems, solutions and possibilities. As strategy is designed, these pieces must be looked at holistically to ensure that the strategy is robust.

Moorwood's proposed technology work will support the assessments associated with the math and science initiatives, all of which are focused on the classroom. The human capital element is organized to address teacher leadership roles that will be needed to implement both the math and the science work and the assessments. Within these strategic objectives, there is a strong level of focus, coherence, and synergy. The math and science initiatives in the instructional objective build on one another—curriculum, aligned instructional materials, instructional standards, professional development, and assessments—culminating in the implementation of an aligned instructional system, which unites all the pieces and provides comprehensive support and direction for instruction. The human capital objective has a similar focus. Its coherence is reflected in how it progresses from teacher preparation to hiring to induction and then tenure. The synergy is realized when the new teachers meet tenure requirements because of the support provided by the preceding initiatives. Again, the devil will be in the details of implementation, specifically, the level of cross-functional collaboration. During the design of the strategy, team members suggested that this level of collaboration will be new for them. Therefore, the team scored the strategy somewhere between a 3 and a 4 on the focused, coherent, and synergistic criterion, acknowledging that much of the power of this area would be realized or lost in implementation.

3. *Both* visionary *and* problem solving

It is tempting to think that a system's strategy should focus on fixing the root causes of the most pressing issues facing the system. This assumes that the work is neat and linear and that by addressing problems of the past, we can realize our vision for the future. Not so. The work of successful, dynamic organizations is seldom neat, linear, or backward looking. Problem solving needs to be complemented by forward-looking innovation. Addressing the most pressing root causes should be a part of the strategy formulation, but it is not enough.

Strategy must also look forward and encourage innovation, driven by a compelling vision of what is possible. Vision is what inspires; it gets people to stretch in hopes of reaching a new level of performance and learning outcomes for children.

It was immediately clear that the Moorwood team tried to organize a bunch of disparate initiatives, leveraging those that suggest a vision (like the STEM [science, technology, engineering, and math] initiative and "green" [sustainability and protecting the environment] curriculum), while also addressing problems (systemwide provision of math and science instructional materials). The question was, did the team try too hard to make many of its existing initiatives fit, jamming square pegs into circular holes? If it did, this would become apparent during implementation, when conflicts between initiatives might arise. The human capital objective provides a great example of balancing problem solving and the pursuit of a vision. Fixing the teacher hiring process is a clear effort to address a problem, while exploring different approaches to teacher compensation may speak to a more transformational vision. The team scored the strategy a 3 on the balancing vision and problem solving criterion.

4. Ownership and enactment throughout the system

Talking about and building understanding of the strategy must begin during its earliest development and continue throughout its lifetime. It must happen at every level of the organization, focusing on three things: what, why, and how. By building an understanding of what the strategy is, why it has been chosen, and how it will be implemented, everyone in the system knows what they are supposed to do, the rationale behind doing those things, and how the work should play out. At this stage of strategy design, the rubric should be used to assess the extent to which the strategy design process has engaged people from all levels of the organization and reflects their voices. If no one except the senior leadership team knows the system is designing a strategy, there is reason to be concerned that the strategy may not be well enough based in the reality of the system to be useful and that the lack of early work building buy-in may compromise its implementation.

For Moorwood, this criterion was a work in progress. Team members reached out to staff to get ideas and reactions before the strategy design meeting, but there hadn't been a good way to share those ideas and ensure that they inform the strategy design process. Some staff members had been involved in learning about potential ideas for the strategy, but more had not been included. There was clarity that the strategy couldn't be finalized till key department leaders and stakeholders were consulted. This would be important not only for broad understanding of the strategy but also for enhancing its power and the likelihood of its being owned and well-implemented. The team rated the strategy a 2.5 on this criterion, but put plans in place that it hoped would raise the score to a 3.

The team gave a collective sigh of relief that it was in the range of a strategy with integrity and the potential to realize real improvements in student learning. The participants adjourned, planning to meet again once members had shared the strategy statement with their direct reports and solicited feedback, focusing particularly on things to consider in planning execution. Two weeks later, the team met to pool and review the feedback. Principals offered particularly helpful insights on challenges and opportunities that may arise with implementation at the school level.

The team's refined strategy document captured *what* the system was going to do and shows the relationships between the vision, the theory of action, strategic objectives, and strategic initiatives. The theory of action and strategic initiatives became much more streamlined and actionable. The document was much more concise, coherent, and focused than the original plan that had weighed Sonya down. It was exciting to see the strategy clearly articulated on a single page, and this made the group think about how it might use that one-pager to facilitate the work. Most importantly, now the system needed to figure out *how* it was going to really do its strategic work.

FIGURE 5.6

MOORWOOD PUBLIC SCHOOLS STRATEGY FOR IMPROVEMENT OF STUDENT OUTCOMES

Vision
Ensure that our students meet the state academic performance expectations and graduate from high school able to choose college or career and be successful. Our graduates are curious learners who know how to think critically, analyze information, and apply their knowledge in different settings to create things and make new knowledge. They are also good people, capable of empathy, and prepared to be citizens in a diverse democracy.
Theory of action
If the system ensures high-quality teaching through the implementation of an aligned instructional system, the hiring and retention of effective teachers, and an information management system that provides diagnostic and summative data on student learning, teacher practice, and school performance, then students will progress through the system on grade level, graduating from high school ready for college, career, and life as contributing citizens.

Strategic objectives		
Support instructional excellence by building and implementing an aligned instructional management system in math and science.	Hire and retain effective educators.	Build the information management systems and technology infra-structure required to support instructional excellence.
Strategic initiatives		
Develop math and science curriculum maps to align curriculum to standards.	Target partnerships with higher education focused on tailored teacher and principal preparation programs.	Build data warehouse to house all necessary student and teacher data in ways that can be used to support instructional improvement and teacher quality.
Adopt math and science instructional materials aligned to standards.	Revamp teacher hiring process and calendar to hire earlier, focus on customer service, and be competitive with the most talented applicants.	Build technology platform to report formative assessment data in a user-friendly format that teachers can use to guide instruction.
Articulate effective teaching practices, using math and science as a starting point.	Offer comprehensive induction programs for new teachers and principals.	Focus school technology upgrades on supporting math and science work.
Design and implement professional development system to support teachers in integrating curriculum, instruction, and assessments into instruction.	Make granting tenure to new teachers a more rigorous process, and hold principals accountable for the performance of the teachers they recommend.	Upgrade software used to track payroll, benefits, and earned time.
Design and implement information management system that provides teachers with easy-to-use results of student assessments.	Build and implement a student performance measurement system that assesses teachers' "value added."	Develop data literacy professional development and a teacher data leader role.
Develop formative assessments in math and science.	Pilot performance pay initiative for teachers and principals.	
Develop teacher leader roles in math and science to support teacher implementation of aligned instruc-tional system.	Build a teacher leader career track and related pay incentives.	

CHAPTER 6

Execution

Putting Strategy into Action

> If you hold a cat by the tail you learn things you cannot learn any other way.
>
> —*Mark Twain*

Moorwood Public Schools chief academic officer, Patrick, sat with his direct reports at their monthly meeting listening as the department heads gave updates on their departments' work. The head of curriculum and instruction began: "With the new literacy program that we're piloting in K–3, implementation has been challenging. The program has several different components, and we didn't anticipate how time-consuming it would be to train teachers on them. Teachers are hesitant to use the materials. There are reports that the materials are sitting in the corner of classrooms in the boxes they were shipped in." The director of assessment, Jane, spoke next: "We're not sure if the math assessments we've been developing are going to map to the state assessments and be predictive of student achievement on the state test the way we hoped. We're going to keep moving forward, finish the development, and then see how the alignment looks." Next, the director of English language learning services raised the subject of a new assessment designed to assess English language learners' level of English language acquisition. "There's all this confusion at the schools about the test. They think it's to be used to test students out of ELL services, but it's really to measure the pace of English language acquisition. Some schools are refusing to administer the test. Others are administering it, but they aren't inputting the data into the system we created." Patrick sat listening, growing more and more concerned. All three projects were off track. Some of the issues related to planning. It sounded as if the viability of one project to accomplish what was intended was in question. Another seemed like the victim of bad communication. Patrick wondered how all this had happened and what to do about it.

Strategy is not enough. Clear and established methods of executing the strategy, problem solving, learning from the work, and refining the work as you go along are essential to helping the strategy become something that actually helps children move toward the system's vision. As the vignette illustrates, the work of school systems is often quite idiosyncratic and not reflective of a high level of organizational functioning. Often, the way work gets done is defined by who is doing it rather than by principles of effective management. Individuals and departments work independently, deciding on their own how they will function. Their approaches to the work are variably effective and create inefficiencies in the system. The larger the system, the more widespread the inefficiencies since there are a greater number of individuals and departments potentially operating in their own orbits. The issues raised in the chief academic officer's meeting are very common. What is unusual is how frankly they are discussed by this group. Usually, department heads muddle through, heads down, disinclined to talk about or examine the challenges they face. They don't know how to ask for help, what help to ask for, or to whom they should direct their request.

In any organization, moving from idea to reality, from agreeing in a meeting to engaging in action, is challenging. It is usually easier to continue whatever we were doing than to do something different. School systems are particularly prone to inertia, even with a strong strategy in hand. When we ask educators where they get stuck in their improvement processes, they point to execution as the place where the plan goes off the rails. They recognize the problem, but don't know how to get back on track. This chapter is designed to help you execute your strategy. The first step is to recognize and understand the disconnects between intent and action. The chapter then provides key questions and concrete tools to aid in addressing your root causes, reaching toward your vision, and helping children, adults, and the school system get smarter about how they do their work.

WHY STRATEGY EXECUTION IS HARD

You may have noticed by now, one of our favorite questions for informing purposeful and effective action is *why*. *Why* is strategy execution hard? We encourage you to ask that question in your own system. We consistently see systems struggle in four areas: aligning resources to the strategy, implementing systems and structures that facilitate the work, supporting employees through work that demands they change their behaviors, and embracing the dynamic nature of the work.[1]

Strategy without resource alignment is simply words on a page with no hopes of implementation. Strategy comes to life when its execution drives the budgeting process and the allocation of resources, be they time, staff, or money. When systems do not allocate sufficient resources for effective implementation, the initiative is often deemed a failure and there is pressure to shift focus. The system is then thrust back into a reactive cycle searching for the ever-elusive silver bullet. Yet the reality is that the initiative wasn't given a chance to succeed. Allocating resources to a new strategy inevitably requires shifting resources from other less promising or less critical work—work to which some stakeholders within and outside the organization are probably deeply committed; navigating the shift in resources means making difficult, and sometimes unpopular, choices.

Building systems and structures to support strategy execution is another challenge. The technical, managerial disciplines of project planning, managing workflow, and tracking metrics are not well established in most school systems. The concept of cross-functional teams, the lifeblood of high-performing organizations, is unfamiliar and directly challenges the prevailing culture of autonomy and "turf." The importance of group process and how to set teams up to be high functioning and effective is not prioritized, and the related skills are seldom taught.

Strategy execution usually requires significant changes in the way people and the organization do business. Employees have to learn new skills. They have to work in ways that are unfamiliar and perhaps uncomfortable. They need to engage in the productive conflict that generates the best ideas and work. These things can be experienced by employees as an infringement on their autonomy, hurting their sense of professional value, or they can be experienced as the professional practice required to execute strategy and ensure student learning. While we talk a lot about school systems as driven by compliance, it's worth noting that the people working within them are not actually all that compliant. They have well-established ways of doing business, and changing these ways is a challenge.

Finally, there is the reality that strategy execution is dynamic. The strategy written on the page must evolve as it grows into life, responding to the environment, changing conditions, and the learning that occurs along the way. This reality bumps up against the tendency of many school systems to function as if their work is static, linear, and predictable. The vignette illustrates how sometimes people continue on, in spite of data that indicate a problem, ultimately compromising success. There is also a tendency within systems to rigidly adhere to a plan even when the conditions upon which it depends shift. Imagine, for example, a system with the goal of providing a literacy coach to every school. That plan is then challenged by a lack of well-qualified applicants to serve as coaches. The system nevertheless proceeds, functioning in a static way, hiring weak coaches and filling the positions. Senior leadership said every school would have a coach (and convinced the union and persuaded the board and promised principals), so every school must have a coach. The purpose of the plan, to draw upon *skilled* coaches' expertise to help teachers and to make improvements within the instructional core, is sacrificed to the mechanical completion of the task. Given the dynamic nature of this work, this system should respond more deliberately to the changing conditions by revisiting its goal of providing a coach for every school, thinking creatively about alternate ways schools might receive that expertise, or slowing down implementation to give the system time to build the skills of a pool of potential coaches. The system that is able to stop "doing" long enough to respond to the environment will be better able to keep purpose at the center.

Because the work is dynamic, people doing it need to embrace the fact that things will come up that push their learning. Sometimes we don't know enough about the content of the work we are undertaking—for example, how to build the best possible student assessment system when the available assessment instruments don't address all the issues we want to address. Other times we don't know how to build the buy-in, collaboration, and two-way learning required for successful implementation—for example, how to engage and leverage the expertise of four very different stakeholder groups(the information systems department, the assessment department, teaching and learning staff, and teachers) in developing and executing an assessment system. It is not unusual to face both problems simultaneously as we bump up against the limits of individual and organizational energy, capacity, culture, and will. Departing from the relative comfort of predictability and "knowing" to embrace "not knowing," and learning from experience, is a tremendous shift in culture for many school systems.

Addressing all of these issues builds organizational capacity to execute strategy. It also helps change the culture of the system: from idiosyncratic to structured and systematic; from autonomous to interdependent; from laissez-faire to accountable; from static to dynamic and learning; from knowing to not knowing; from reactive "doing" to something more reflective and intentional. The idea of changing culture can feel quite daunting. Culture is amorphous, invisible and pervasive. No wonder the prospect of attempting to change it feels futile. Remember, however, that culture is learned—the byproduct of people's expectations, beliefs, and behaviors. Deliberate steps focused on changing behavior have a cumulative effect. As expectations, beliefs and behavior shift over time, so too will the culture.

This chapter focuses on developing the capacity of school systems to effectively execute strategy. It introduces building blocks of effective strategy execution and provides tools to support that work. We will also return to the Moorwood experience, illustrating the use of the tools in the execution of its strategy.

BUILDING BLOCKS

Effective strategy execution requires the alignment of resources, structures, and systems. These are fairly straightforward technical issues for which there are tools. The more complex aspects of strategy execution relate to engaging key internal and external stakeholders in the work. This involves understanding stakeholders' concerns and communicating the strategy in ways that respond to those concerns. It is also about convincing staff to work differently and providing the necessary support and accountability to build capacity and ensure changes in behavior. Finally, it is about ensuring effective communication of the strategy and learning from its implementation so that the system gets smarter and more effective at improving student learning. The four questions listed below address these issues. Embedded within the questions are key building blocks of effective strategy execution.

- How does strategy drive action?
- How do we organize the work with clear structures and systems?
- How do we build stakeholder support of strategy?
- How does the system manage strategy execution?

How Does Strategy Drive Action?

A system signals its values by what it does and doesn't do, and by how it allocates its precious resources of money, time, and people. Once a strategy is developed, everything the system is currently doing and investing in needs to be assessed for its alignment to the strategy. Some work will be central to the strategy. Other work will need to be repurposed to align to the strategy. Inevitably, some current work won't fit or will no longer make sense to continue. What a system does about the work that doesn't fit speaks volumes about that system's commitment to meaningful improvement of student learning. As hard and politically challenging as this is, it is also an opportunity on several levels. First, it's a chance to stop work that is ineffective. Second, it is a chance to reflect on work that has merit but isn't a high enough priority to be continued: What can be learned from this work that might inform the system in its implementation of the strategic initiatives? For example, a literacy lead teacher program that is identified as no longer a priority can still be honored through the learning it provides regarding how it trained and supported teachers who are very effective in their role.

Evaluating current work against the strategy is similar to pruning shrubs. Sometimes it is obvious which branch needs to be pruned. It is showing signs of stress, withering as it loses its leaves. The choice to clip those branches is fairly easy. The harder work lies in identifying other branches and shoots to cut; they may not be withering and may in fact be big, healthy branches, but cutting them is good for the overall health of the shrub. It can be painful to do, but the shrub is stronger for it.

At this point, we will draw again from Moorwood's leadership team experience, this time to illustrate the process of building coherence and pruning initiative shrubs for effective strategy execution. The team began by comparing its grid of current work (see chapter 1) to the strategy and related initiatives (chapter 5), figuring out what it needed to start doing, stop doing, and continue doing. Determining what work could be repurposed in support of the strategy and what work would to be put on hold was key to their process as well. After much debate, particularly around the "stop doing" column, the team arrived at the list in figure 6.1.

Team members were enthusiastic about how they repurposed things meaningfully rather than with brute force to make things fit. The STEM (science, technology, engineering, and math) and "green" curriculum work was identified as having the potential to enhance the curriculum mapping and instructional materials central to their strategy. They were less enthusiastic about the "stop" list. Team members wondered if the idea of K–8s could really be dismissed after a year of study, even though the evidence is clear that what matters most is what's happening in classrooms, not school structure. The team members were also somewhat concerned that not having a special "school safety" initiative would draw strong reactions from parents and the community, even though the data don't support the need for a special focus on safety. The question was also raised whether a redesign of individual education plans (IEPs) was mandated by the state. Patrick, the chief academic officer, raised a

FIGURE 6.1

MOORWOOD'S LIST OF INITIATIVES TO START, STOP, OR CONTINUE

Start
- Adopt science instructional materials
- Articulate effective teaching practices, using math and science as a starting point
- Implement math coaching to support teachers in integrating curriculum, instruction, and assessment
- Design and implement information management system that provides teachers with easy-to-use results of student assessments
- Develop teacher leader roles in math and science to support teacher implementation of aligned instructional system
- Target partnerships with higher education focused on tailored programs for teacher and principal preparation
- Make granting tenure to new teachers a more rigorous process, and hold principals accountable for the performance of the teachers they recommend
- Build and implement a student performance measurement system that assesses teachers' "value added"
- Pilot performance pay initiative for teachers and principals
- Build a teacher leader career track and related pay incentives
- Build technology platform to report formative assessment data in a user-friendly format that teachers can use to guide instruction
- Develop professional development on data literacy and a teacher data leader role

Stop
- Direct instruction initiative
- "Workshop" pilot in literacy
- Collaboration with external partner on formative assessment system aligned to state assessment in English
- Development of a system for formative assessments in English
- Adoption of English tutorial software (to be completed after curriculum mapped)
- Conversion of 20 percent of elementary schools to K–8
- Mapping curriculum to standards in all English language arts, social studies, K–12
- Redesign of school budgeting process and timeline
- School safety initiative
- Redesign of how individual education plans (IEPs) are written and used

(continued on next page)

FIGURE 6.1 , continued

Continue

- Mapping curriculum to standards in math and science, K–12
- Adopting math instruction materials
- Middle school pedagogy initiative focused on math and science
- Two-year new-teacher induction system (add principals)
- Developing scorecards to measure school and department performance and improvement
- Creating data warehouse for all students and staff to include assessment data
- Developing a system for formative assessments in math
- Revamping teacher hiring process
- Upgrading software used to track payroll, benefits, and earned time

Repurpose

- Science, technology, engineering, and math (STEM) initiative at high school level (integrate into curriculum mapping)
- Development of "green curriculum" for use in upper elementary grades (integrate into curriculum mapping)
- Training of all teachers in instructional strategies that support English language learners (focus on math and science instruction)
- Development of professional learning communities (PLCs) among principals (focus on math and science)
- Conversion of two large high schools into small schools (math/science/STEM foci for schools)
- Upgrade to provide new computer labs in 40 percent of schools (support math/science work once clarified)
- Upgrade of schools' technology infrastructure to ensure Internet access in all classrooms (support math/science work once clarified)

On hold

- Adoption of math tutorial software (to be completed after curriculum mapped)
- Collaboration with external partner on formative assessment system aligned to state assessment in math (wait to see if it can guide or be integrated into math assessments)
- Healthy School Lunch Initiative (engage students in this project as part of science curriculum?)
- New principal evaluation instrument (wait till scorecards are developed)

concern about stopping all of the English and literacy initiatives: "Maybe we could call that category 'Stop/Finish.' I think if we've already spent the money, or it doesn't require much additional money and time and contributes to our strategy, we should think about how to finish the initiative and learn from it to inform our strategy." After twenty minutes of heated debate, the superintendent, Sonya, spoke up: "This is hard, and there will be some backlash. The board and I have been talking about the K–8 issue. But we have to be careful not to add things that are really resource intensive and distract us from the core of the strategy. We developed the strategy because we think it will raise student achievement. It isn't some random act. I need to work with the board and the community to mitigate some of the noise we can anticipate. We need to figure out what we're going to do when and how we're going to pay for it. We have to bring current initiatives to closure in a way that makes sense and honors the work that has been done."

The conversation then shifted to the initiatives in the "start" column. Leadership team members who oversee the departments charged with implementing key initiatives brought rough cost estimates, many of which were developed in concert with the budget office, to the meeting. It quickly became clear which were the biggest-ticket items and that there was a need to prioritize them and pace their execution. For example, the members concluded that there wouldn't be enough money to adopt math and science instructional materials and start math coaching in the same year, so they needed to decide what to start first as the foundation upon which other initiatives would be built. With these questions in mind, they tried to lay the strategy out over its five-year timeline. They agreed to try to be very specific about the first few years, with years four and five serving more as placeholders since no one thought they could plan that far in advance with any degree of accuracy.

Even after the discussion, the team struggled with having more first-year initiatives than the system could support financially, despite some creative reallocation: math and science instructional materials, induction support for new teachers and principals, and building the data warehouse. After much debate, the team agreed to shift induction to year two. It reasoned that the other two initiatives had the potential to touch more teachers and were foundational elements upon which other initiatives would build. Team members also argued that it made sense to have the progression of execution follow the career path: hiring, induction, then career pathways. They assembled a timeline (figure 6.2), agreeing that they were most sure about the first and second years, recognizing the timeline would need to be revisited once real costs were finalized and strategy execution began.

FIGURE 6.2

DRAFT TIMELINE FOR STRATEGIC INITIATIVES IMPLEMENTATION

Strategic objectives		
Support instructional excellence by building and implementing an aligned instructional management system in math and science	Hire and retain effective educators	Build the information management systems and technology infrastructure required to support instructional excellence
Strategic initiatives		
Year 1		
Develop math and science curriculum maps to align curriculum to standards (integrate STEM and "green" curriculum)	Revamp teacher hiring process and calendar to hire earlier, focus on customer service, and be competitive with the most talented applicants	Build data warehouse to house all necessary student and teacher data in ways that can be used to support instructional improvement and teacher quality
Adopt math and science instructional materials aligned to standards		Focus school technology upgrades on supporting math and science work
Develop PLCs among principals (focus on math and science)		
Year 2		
Develop formative assessments in math and science	Offer comprehensive induction programs for new teachers and principals	Build technology platform to report formative assessment data in a user-friendly format that teachers can use to guide instruction
Design and implement math coaching to support teachers in integrating curriculum, instruction, and assessments	Target partnerships with higher education focused on tailored programs for teacher and principal preparation	Upgrade to provide new computer labs in 40 percent of schools (support math science work once clarified)
Middle school pedagogy initiative focused on math and science	Make granting tenure to new teachers a more rigorous process, and hold principals accountable for the performance of the teachers they recommend	Upgrade schools' technology infrastructure to ensure Internet access in all classrooms (support math science work once clarified)
Conversion of two large high schools into small schools (math/science/STEM foci for schools)		Upgrade software used to track payroll, benefits, and earned time

Year 3		
Design and implement information management system that provides teachers with easy-to-use results of student assessments	Build and implement a student performance measurement system that assesses teachers' "value added"	Develop scorecards to measure school and department performance and improvement
Train all teachers in instructional strategies that support English language learners (focus on math and science instruction)	Build a teacher leader career track and related pay incentives	Develop data literacy PD and a teacher data leader role
Years 4–5		
Articulate effective teaching practices, using math and science as a starting point	Pilot performance pay initiative for teachers and principals	

Abbreviations: STEM, science, technology, engineering, and math; PLC, professional learning communities; PD, professional development.

The team stepped back to look at the timeline as a whole, looking first horizontally (is each year manageable, and do the initiatives make sense together?) and then vertically (does each strategic objective progress in a sensible order?). The chief financial officer, Victor, said, "I'm no education expert, but that first column is looking too slow to me. Are we really going to wait until year four to name effective teaching practices? And will it take all of year one to do curriculum maps and choose materials?"

"I agree with you," said Patrick. "We want to be thoughtful, but this first column is where we need to accelerate our work." After more conversation, the team agreed that the second and third columns looked good, and altered the first column. Their revisions are shown in figure 6.3

How Do We Organize the Work with Clear Structures and Systems?

The space between strategy and the day-to-day work of school systems can feel vast. Questions abound: How do we design the initiatives so they move from a bullet on a strategy statement to a well-designed plan? Who is in charge of each initiative? What needs to happen in the next week, month, six months, to make the initiative successful? And how will we learn from our work to get smarter and refine the initiative accordingly? While the system is still considering the strategy as a whole, each initiative needs more detail if it is going to be implemented successfully, and if

FIGURE 6.3

ALIGNED INSTRUCTIONAL MANAGEMENT SYSTEM STRATEGIC OBJECTIVE, REVISED TIMELINE

First draft

Strategic objectives
Support instructional excellence by building and implementing an aligned instructional management system in math and science

Strategic initiatives

YEAR 1
- Develop math and science curriculum maps to align curriculum to standards (integrate STEM and "green" curriculum)
- Adopt math and science instructional materials aligned to standards
- Develop PLCs among principals (focus on math and science)

YEAR 2
- Develop formative assessments in math and science
- Design and implement math coaching to support teachers in integrating curriculum, instruction, and assessments into instruction
- Middle school pedagogy initiative focused on math and science
- Conversion of two large high schools into small schools (math/science/STEM foci for some schools)

YEAR 3
- Design and implement information management system that provides teachers with easy-to-use results of student assessments
- Train all teachers in instructional strategies that support English language learners (focus on math and science instruction)

YEARS 4–5
- Articulate effective teaching practices, using math and science as a starting point

---

Moved to pre–year 1

Year 3
too late to help teachers use assessments: will work well with other initiatives in year 2, but can't do at full scale—pilot in year 2, refine, and scale up in year 3

Moved: too much happening in year 2

Moved from year 3 with the idea that by now will be implementing new math and science curriculum and will start to learn for whom the curriculum is working and not working

Moved from years 4–5 with the idea that system needs to articulate effective teaching sooner

Second draft

Strategic objectives
Support instructional excellence by building and implementing an aligned instructional management system in math and science.

Strategic initiatives

PRE–YEAR 1 (next few months)
- Adopt math and science instructional materials aligned to standards
- Develop math and science curriculum maps to align curriculum to standards (integrate STEM and "green" curriculum)
- **Finish ELA curriculum mapping**

YEAR 1
- **Implement** math and science instructional materials **(including PD for teachers, offered by company providing materials)**
- **Start building coaching corps (look for teacher leaders in curriculum implementation as potential coaches)**
- Develop PLCs among principals (focus on math and science)
- **Finish developing formative assessments in English with partner**

YEAR 2
- Develop formative assessments in math and science
- Design and implement math coaching to support teachers in integrating curriculum, instruction, and assessments
- Middle school pedagogy initiative focused on math and science
- Pilot information management system that provides teachers with easy-to-use results of student assessments

YEAR 3
- Scale up information management system that provides teachers with easy-to-use results of student assessments
- Conversion of two large high schools into small schools (math/science/STEM foci for some schools)
- Articulate effective teaching practices, using math and science as a starting point

YEARS 4–5
- Train all teachers in instructional strategies that support English language learners and students with disabilities (focus on math and science instruction); further differentiate instruction as needed
- **Implement student support system**

Added per Patrick's comment

Added text in bold for clarification

Added to show coach development as part of materials implementation

Added

Added per earlier conversations; team recognized need to think more about how to build toward student support system the initiatives together are going to add up to a powerful strategy that improves the lives of children. There are a variety of tools that can help systems organize at the level of detail needed to execute strategy. Three we find quite helpful are (1) a logic model to help design the initiative; (2) an implementation work plan to lay out the steps of implementation with clear responsibilities, timelines, and benchmarks; and (3) an after-action review to build a feedback loop to ensure that learning from the work of the initiative is surfaced and informs refinements.

Logic Model

A logic model is a kind of map that helps to broadly outline a strategic initiative and assess three things: (1) the soundness of the reasoning about what the initiative will achieve and any refinements that need to be made to the initiative, including the possibility of abandoning it entirely; (2) the initiative's likelihood of realizing its intended outcomes, given the internal and external players, the resources available, and the system context; and (3) the capacity of the organization to execute the initiative, the role of external partners, and issues of capacity building or partnering to ensure success.[2] The elements of the logic model in figure 6.4 are defined as follows:

Activities: what needs to be done to execute the strategic initiative

Resources: the money, time, people, and internal and external resources that need to be directed to the work to ensure its success

Outputs: the immediate results of the program activities; answer the question of whether we did what we said we were going to do

Outcomes: the impact that the outputs have on behavior, knowledge, and skills; can be defined as both short term (one to three years) and long term (four to six years) and include measures of how will we know if we've achieved the outcomes

Assumptions: the little theory of action that drives this particular strategic initiative; a way to vet the strategic initiative

Logic models are useful before undertaking an initiative because they help make explicit what the intended outcomes of an initiative are and how the organization expects the initiative to lead to those outcomes—kind of like a theory of action with concrete details. Like a theory of action, logic models should be constantly revised and updated to reflect reality and learning. The process of designing and refining

FIGURE 6.4

ELEMENTS OF A LOGIC MODEL

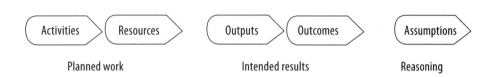

a logic model helps build the capacity of people in the system to plan and think strategically and helps keep execution on track.

Developing a logic model lets you tell the story of what you will do to execute the initiative (activities), what support you will need (resources), what results you expect to achieve (outputs and outcomes), and why you think the activities will lead to the results (assumptions). The "assumptions" column allows you to think through the reasoning that informed each of the other columns and check to make sure it is sound. This column plays the same role of vetting the logic model that the theory of action plays for the strategy. As with theory of action, some people prefer to start with assumptions, but in our experience, for most people, it's easier to talk about assumptions after there is more explicit detail about the *what* and the *how*.

The most valuable parts of the process are the conversations people have as they share their image of how the initiative will look in action, explore points of confusion or potential problems, and ultimately hammer out a shared vision for the initiative—a vision that draws on the best thinking of everyone in the group. While this kind of intentionality may be unfamiliar and may take a couple of tries to get comfortable with, staff often take well to it. The concrete, linear nature (which is a bit deceptive) of the tool can be very grounding, and the resulting one-page visual captures the storyline with some detail. People find the opportunity to think through issues and resolve them up-front satisfying. The process builds confidence and ownership in the work.

Logic models are most valuable when they are developed by a team of people including those who will lead the initiative, representatives from departments that are not the leads but are integral players in the work, people who will be consumers of the initiative, potential external partners in the work, and at least one senior staff person who understands how this initiative relates to the system's overall strategy.

Some external partners may already be familiar with the tool and able to assist in its use.

We recommend using a logic model to vet every strategic initiative a system plans to execute. If that feels overwhelming, there are probably too many initiatives. Anticipate that the logic models will raise difficult questions whose answers are not immediately apparent, and understand that asking and answering these questions will make the strategic initiative far more likely to fulfill its purpose. The few hours spent drafting the logic model and engaging sticky questions now can save much time, money, energy, and frustration later. The process won't bring to light every-thing that may emerge when the initiative is implemented, but it will help those responsible for and involved with implementation be more thoughtful, purposeful, and, probably, more successful.

In our experience, the "outcomes" column is often the most difficult—and the most essential—part of the logic model for educators to complete. In that column, educators ask and answer, "How will we know if we're successful?" Often, educa-tors aren't used to thinking about outcome measures beyond test scores and have to develop that skill and mental muscle. Another challenge is a lack of clear baseline data. One of the advantages of doing the logic model and thinking about mea-sures of success before execution is that a system can collect baseline evidence that answers the question "Where are we now?" and will later help the system measure progress. It's much easier to set improvement targets and to note evidence of success or the need for adjustment if you have a good measure of the current state. Much of the data collected when people are identifying problems and opportunities earlier in the strategic design process will prove helpful as both baseline data and poten-tial data sources for measuring progress on those problems and opportunities (see chapter 3 for a discussion of these data, as well as other types of key indicators that are helpful for measuring results and progress). Making the targets and measures explicit early on helps everyone in the system with accountability—it's clear who is being held accountable for what by whom (and gets increasingly clear as details are hammered out), what the supports for achieving those results are, and how we will know how we're doing along the way so that we can adjust as needed. This approach puts systems in a proactive rather than reactive stance vis-à-vis their data. People ask questions like, "How are we doing with X?" rather than fending off data like a goalkeeper minding a net.

The logic model shown in figure 6.5 was developed by the Moorwood staff for one strategic initiative: Implement math coaching to support teachers in integrating curriculum, instruction, and assessments into instruction. Moorwood developed logic models for each of its strategic initiatives in year one and for the year-two initiatives that they knew would require capacity building in year one, such as coaching.[3]

The group that developed the math coaching logic model included the chief academic officer, the math curriculum director, the head of professional development, the director of staffing from human resources, the director of curriculum and instruction who had experience working with the union on the creation of new positions for teachers, a manager from the budget department, a principal whose school had been making substantial gains in math, and a teacher who was currently serving in a role akin to a math coach.

The process of completing the logic model helped the group build a shared understanding of what the coaching initiative would look like and what it would take to get it up and running. Drilling down into the details helped people see all the pieces and think about who could assist with each detail. It also surfaced capacity issues, for example, who would be on screening teams, who would help with documenting coaches' work, and who would design and implement the coach training. It became clear that costing out the specific pieces of the initiative was a critical next step, as was getting more clarity about what accountability for coaches would look like and identifying outcome measures.

The group unearthed a variety of issues in thinking through the initiative. The issues included:

- Why do we think math coaching is the way to improve instruction and student achievement? What data do we have that backs this up? This is expensive and will place big demands on the system in order to do well, so we better be clear that it's worth doing and that we are doing what's needed to make it effective.
- What do we envision the role of a math coach to be? What does a coach do on a daily basis?
- We shouldn't assume teachers (and principals) are going to be enthusiastic about having math coaches in their school. What can we do to make the staff more agreeable to this change?
- Do we have enough people in the system who are qualified to step into the role of math coach? If not, do we have adequate other sources for coaches, or are we willing to rethink the allocation to schools?

FIGURE 6.5

LOGIC MODEL OF MATH COACHING STRATEGIC INITIATIVE

Activities	Resources	Outputs	Outcomes	Measures	Assumptions
Communicate the idea of math coaches to principals and teachers, and solicit ideas	Communications staff support; union newsletter and staff; mechanisms for gathering input—e.g., focus groups, surveys (require time and staff to design, conduct, and analyze results)	■ Survey of all teachers and principals (target: 60% completion rate) ■ Two focus groups of teachers; two focus groups of principals (8–10 participants in each group) ■ Article in union newsletter	■ Improved coaching plan ■ Principal and teacher buy-in	■ To be determined ■ Survey results	■ Principals and teachers will be open to the idea of a coach working with teachers to improve instruction if they are engaged in the process from the beginning
Define the role, job description, and qualifications of math coaches; recruit highly qualified applicants; develop and execute a rigorous screening process for math coaches	HR support (may need reallocation of half the time of a full-time HR employee to manage recruitment and screening); math expert support (in-house); learn from other systems using a coaching model (no new dollars, but time—draw on existing professional networks and read articles); technology to manage application and screening process (need to update—requires partial technology staff FTE and possibly new monetary resources)	■ Document outlining job description and qualifications ■ Recruiting materials (posted on Web site; also available in print form, distributed internally to all staff and distributed externally to targeted local and national organizations and Web sites as well as partners) ■ Multistep screening process (including interviews) with clear, consistent selection criteria	■ High-quality pool of math coaches ■ Math coach as a teacher leadership opportunity	■ 100 potential candidates who meet qualifications (for 50 positions); 100% of coaches in final pool meet qualifications; 90% of principals satisfied with their options when selecting a coach from pool ■ At least half of pool is drawn from internal candidates	■ HR has the infrastructure and capacity to design and implement a high-quality recruitment and screening process ■ We can identify effective coaches through the screening process
Collaborate with union on any aspects of math coach job that have contractual implications	Senior leadership team time (including superintendent) to meet and communicate with union; possibly more time from senior staff for further conversation; possibly advice of legal counsel (in-house)	■ Meeting between senior leadership team representatives and senior union officials ■ Open meeting between senior leadership team and union membership ■ Modifications to contract as needed	■ Union support of math coaching ■ Longer term: full engagement of teachers in math coaching; appeal of coaching position; fair treatment of coaches	■ Doesn't require union vote; 60% of teachers surveyed support the idea? ■ Participation rates of teachers with coaches ■ Increasing number of internal candidates and increasing percentage of high-quality pool that's internal ■ Coaches report they're respected and treated well in focus groups and surveys	■ Union support is essential to success of math coaching ■ Math coaches are union members

Activity	Resources	Outputs	Outcomes	Indicators	Assumptions
Deploy a math coach to every school	$4.25 million per year: 50 coaches at $80,000 (includes money to pay for time beyond usual teacher hours); $250,000 for math coach manager and support staff	50 math coaches: 100% of schools have math coach by August 1	*Shorter term* ■ Improved math instruction *Longer term* ■ Student achievement results on state tests ■ Integration of math coaching into school improvement strategy ■ Deep math expertise built within the system	■ Evident in observation, coach, and teacher reports; video analysis ■ State test math scores increase within one year; by end of three years, 85% of students proficient, with declining gaps between students ■ Integration evident in school improvement plans	■ Every school needs its own coach ■ Coaching will improve instruction, which will improve results on state math tests
Define the structure, systems, and tools math coaches will use	Math experts within and outside system (will need money for consultants and perhaps some stipends for teacher experts: ~$10,000; central staff and principals need time, not money); tools from other coaching programs	■ Coach handbook (paper and online) with clear coaching model ■ Coach internal Web site with tools and resources	■ Well-designed coaching model ■ Consistent coach work across schools, guided by best practices	■ Consistently high ratings on coach satisfaction by principals and teachers on surveys; consistent practice observed across schools	■ A well-defined coaching model with accountability measures will ensure consistency and quality and will be more effective than letting math coaches design their work individually
Develop and deliver training for math coaches	$100,000 for initial week-long orientation and biweekly day-long training (delivered by external partner); staff to coordinate with partner (content and logistics) (cost captured under "Deploy" row, above)	■ Five-day summer orientation with 97% attendance by coaches ■ Biweekly, full-day training with 95% attendance by coaches	■ Coaches report satisfaction with training ■ Coaches are more effective with teachers	■ Satisfaction rates average of 4 on a 5-point scale in regular evaluation ■ Self-reports from coaches; principal and teacher surveys; observations of coaches working with teachers	■ Coaching requires a set of distinct skills that must be taught
Develop a system to track the work of math coaches, learn from it, and hold coaches accountable	Resources unclear. Suggestions: allocate existing staff in assessment and evaluation; hire outside evaluator; use technology (check if current system suffices)	■ Feedback loop to learn from coaches' work (formal surveys and interviews or focus groups once a year; regular evaluations at biweekly meetings; quarterly: two focus groups of coaches and two of principals/teachers in first year) ■ Monthly meetings of cross-functional team ■ Accountability system for coaches (not sure what this looks like yet)	■ Well-defined coaching model that reflects learning about the most effective coaching tools and processes and the impact on student learning	■ What does accountability look like? How often should we evaluate coaches? Who will evaluate? ■ Adjustments to coaching model	■ We will learn things in the implementation of coaching that will help us make the program better ■ Need time to learn from results

Abbreviations: HR, human resources; FTE, full-time equivalent.

- How will we collaborate with human resources on the screening of coach applicants to ensure that screeners can assess applicants' math skills and that we get the most qualified people?
- How will math coaches be deployed to schools? Will they get to pick the school they go to? Will principals choose the coaches? Will the system choose which coaches go to which school? What are the trade-offs on who decides? How will we ensure that every school gets a coach?
- Do we want a consistent coaching model, or is it better to hire good people and let them shape the work according to their own expertise and experience and their assessment of the needs of the school? Or some combination of those?
- How are we going to learn from the work of math coaches, and who can help us do that?
- How much training do we want for coaches, and who will design and deliver it? How will coaches learn from each other?
- What are the working conditions, for example, the number of hours per day, the length of the school year, professional development commitment, and evaluation process for math coaches? How much will we pay coaches? Will all coaches be paid the same, or will pay vary? If it varies, what criteria do we use—expertise? Effectiveness? How can we use this to help us think about the possibility of paying teachers in different ways down the road?
- How can we define the full cost of the coaching initiative when we haven't decided what the working conditions are?
- What do principals need to know to use and support coaches well? How will they learn it?
- How are we going to know if the coaching is working? How do we get some early indicators? How will we know if instruction is improving? How can we use finer-grained measures of learning than the state tests?

In a three-hour meeting, the members of the group developed the logic model and began to wrestle with the questions. As they filled in details, they realized how much time and money the system needed to invest before coaches showed up at schools. Toward the end of the meeting, the group felt a bit daunted by the capacity development required to successfully execute this initiative and the possibility that amid the sheer logistics and details, they might lose sight of the importance of building relationships for coaching to succeed. An external partner who had been working with the system on math was identified as a possible partner for the coach training. A group member identified a national clearinghouse for math coaching as a possible resource to be explored. As the meeting ended, the team clearly understood the details of the math coaching initiative and possible resources to tap. People left feeling that they had the beginnings of a plan.

Implementation Work Plan

A work plan is the bridge between the logic model and action. For each strategic initiative, it lays out the specific tasks that need to be completed, identifying who is responsible for executing each task, and the timeline for completing tasks, including the completion deadline. Laying out all the elements forces deeper thinking about pacing, sequencing, and capacity. Once a work plan is developed and approved, it then serves as the implementation bible, serving as a constant guide and checklist. People responsible for implementation use the plan to guide their daily work, as it literally lays out what should be happening on a weekly or monthly basis. It is a living document, evolving as the reality of execution replaces planning and best estimates.

Most strategic initiatives have a designated project manager who is responsible for the successful implementation of the initiative. That person isn't responsible for *doing* everything, but is responsible for making sure everything *gets done*. In the math coaching example, there is both a project manager (director of math coaching) and a cross-functional work group (the team that developed the logic model). The project manager usually takes the lead in developing the work plan. While some people definitely have the natural disposition to manage details and follow-through (and personally, we're very grateful that some people love to do that kind of work), project management is a skill set that can also be learned. If you don't have people with this skill set in your system already, training is available, particularly outside the field of education, for people to learn these skills.

Figure 6.6 is an excerpt from the work plan for Moorwood Public Schools' math coaching strategic initiative. The excerpt shows the recruiting and hiring component of the work plan, as well as the project management component.[4] The complete work plan includes all components of the coaching initiative (each activity in the logic model, as well as financial management and communication as part of the overall project management). The work plan extends through the first year of the initiative, including processes for collecting data and learning from them.

FIGURE 6.6

EXCERPT OF WORK PLAN FOR MATH COACHING STRATEGIC INITIATIVE

Math coaching implementation work plan, draft

Project manager:	*Frida fFuentes*
Date of last revision:	
Team members (allocation of FTE):	Project manager (100%), director of math (30%), assistant director of human resources (10%), director of training and development (20%), external partner in math (20%)

	Status	Responsibility	Target start date	Target completion date	Actual completion date
		Project management			
I. Process management					
Develop and manage implementation work plan	On track	Frida (FF)	Feb. 1, 2010	Ongoing	
II. Communication					
Internal					
Manage work group	On track	FF		Ongoing	
Schedule meetings	On track	FF	Feb. 10, 2010	Ongoing	
Set agendas for work group meetings	On track	FF, with work group	Feb. 15, 2010	Ongoing	
Prepare materials for meetings	On track	FF	Feb. 15, 2010	Ongoing	
Manage follow-up between meetings	On track	FF	Feb. 15, 2010	Ongoing	
Prepare initiative updates and reports for CAO, superintendent, and board	On track	FF	March 1, 2010	Ongoing (monthly)	

Math coach recruitment and hiring

	Complete	Work group		
Define role, job responsibilities, job classification, and salary	On track	FF and work group	Feb. 15, 2010	March 15, 2010
Develop job description and applicant qualifications	Off track	HR	March 1, 2010	April 1, 2010
Advertise position and set deadline for applications	Not yet in play	FF and HR	March 15, 2010	April 15, 2010
Develop screening process and criteria	Not yet in play	FF	April 1, 2010	May 10, 2010
Recruit screeners	Not yet in play	FF and HR	April 1, 2010	May 1, 2010
Train screeners	Not yet in play	FF and HR	May 15, 2010	June 1, 2010
Manage paper review of applications	Not yet in play	FF and HR	May 15, 2010	June 15, 2010
Manage stage two screening	Not yet in play	FF and HR	June 15, 2010	June 30, 2010
Tally results of screening	Not yet in play	FF and HR	June 30, 2010	July 1, 2010
Approve final pool	Not yet in play	FF, with work group	July 1, 2010	July 3, 2010
Notify applicants of status	Not yet in play	FF and HR	July 5, 2010	July 10, 2010

Key milestones

Budget finalized	April 15
Survey data analyzed and reported	May 1
Coaching position posted	May 15
Screening teams in place	June 1
Coaches hired and deployed	July 30

Abbreviations: FTE, full-time equivalent; FF, Frida Fuentes; HR, human resources; CAO, chief academic officer.

Notice the level of detail in the work plan, as well as the clarity around *who* is responsible for *what* by *when*. Key milestones and deliverables are also clear. You can read this document and understand the storyline of how the coaching strategic initiative will develop, at least in the district's best guess at the outset, and see how the system will know if the initiative is on track at various points. This level of detail is what's needed to keep the implementation train on track.

Dilemmas raised during creation of the logic model must be addressed, and their solutions reflected in the work plan. Most commonly, the dilemmas boil down to issues of scale, capacity, pace of implementation, and measures. How many schools or departments will be involved, and how fast? When will the whole system be engaged in the work of the initiative? There is often pressure from somewhere in the system (school board, schools, optimistic project manager) to quickly scale up initiatives that show early promise. Yet the more a new initiative takes on quickly, the shallower the work will be. Nascent initiatives need time to develop and be refined. Their credibility and success depend on it.

Scale and pace of implementation relate to organizational capacity. When capacity is high, the pace of implementation can be faster. When capacity is low, a smaller-scale effort makes sense as the organization builds capacity. Big, systemic initiatives often need a multiyear phase-in and, from the outset, clear definition of how they will grow to full implementation over what period of time. When an initiative is phased in, it's important to be sensitive to issues of equity regarding which schools or individuals are involved and the criteria used to choose them. Starting new initiatives in higher-performing schools often maximizes the likelihood of success because the schools function well and have the capacity to take on new work. However, this can also result in a "rich get richer" reinforcing cycle where the schools with higher capacity get more opportunity, and the children who are being well served get even better served, while the children who most need support don't get it. This cycle is particularly troubling in school systems where the higher-performing schools disproportionately serve white students and students of a higher socioeconomic status. The challenge is to get a representative sample of schools involved in the first round of an initiative and differentiate support as needed to ensure broad success.

A related consideration when building a work plan is how to organize it to build and sustain momentum. Quick wins are successes that can be realized in the first weeks or months of an initiative's execution. They help build credibility and ownership of the initiative. Often, quick wins are technical fixes that scrape the surface of the deep work of the initiative, building good will for the harder work of deep execution that lies ahead. Hiring and deploying coaches to all schools in the agreed-upon timeline is an example of a quick win in the math coaching initiative.

Learning from the Work: After-Action Reviews

Work plans lay out the best thinking about how an initiative should be executed. Once implementation begins, the dynamic nature of the work becomes apparent. Work plans must evolve to reflect this reality. This requires building into the implementation process the mechanisms to learn from the work. One of the great ironies of school systems is that they are responsible for children's learning, yet these institutions themselves often struggle to learn as organizations. The tyranny of time prioritizes "doing"; pausing to reflect on action to get smarter gets short shrift. Creating the conditions for learning during the execution of initiatives requires intentionality and the creation of a safe space where people openly discuss their questions, mistakes, and disagreements with the shared goal of improving the quality of the work. In such a setting, the focus is on the work, and people are able to separate themselves from the work.[5]

The U.S. Army developed a very simple process, called after-action review (AAR), which can be used to learn from individual tasks, events, or milestones of execution. The lessons can then be woven back into the overall work of the initiative to inform ongoing execution. This creates a learning loop. The purpose of AAR is to compare what happened with what was planned, to understand why it happened and what could be done to improve it next time. The goal of AAR is not to critique or assign credit or blame for outcomes but, instead, to provide feedback on work done and learn from it to inform future work.[6] The simplicity of the AAR and the rapidity with which it can be completed (as little as thirty minutes) makes it very user-friendly and appealing. It entails bringing together everyone who was involved in the activity and answering these four questions:

1. What was planned?
2. What happened?
3. Why did it happen?
4. What could be done to improve it next time?

To show the AAR in action, let's look at an AAR for one of Moorwood's milestones of the math coaching work plan:

Milestone: Report results from coaching surveys of principals and teachers

1. What was planned?
   - Identify focus areas for survey questions.
   - Design survey and plan for its administration.
   - Administer the survey.
   - Tabulate the results.
2. What happened?
   - Each of the steps planned was accomplished in the timeline outlined.
   - The survey was online for two weeks for people to complete.
   - When the survey results came in, it became clear that the survey questions didn't explore in enough depth several critical areas of feedback that the team wanted from the surveyed principals and teachers.
   - Survey response rates were 45 percent for principals and 22 percent for teachers.
   - Survey respondents faced technology challenges as they tried to complete the survey. Technology issues came to the team's attention two days after the survey went live and were addressed within thirty-six hours. It is not clear how many people tried to complete the survey during this time but were unsuccessful.
3. Why did it happen?
   - Project management was tight, and the timeline was tracked carefully.
   - There was not clear communication between the people developing the survey and those who were researching coaching best practices to calibrate and identify key survey questions.
   - The principal supervisors were effective in communicating about the survey to principals, but the communication and coordination between the principals and teachers, between the work group and the union, and subsequently between the union and its teacher members was limited and not well coordinated.
   - The user interface for the online survey was not thoroughly tested and assumed a higher level of technology comfort on the part of the user than exists.
4. What could be done to improve it next time?
   - More ongoing communication and tighter collaboration between the work group members and the other departments and external partners who are critical players in the work plan execution.

- Research best practices before developing the survey so the research results inform the survey questions.
- Create incentives for participating in the survey.
- Use a more user-friendly technology platform for the survey.

As the team reflected, members talked about how learning from the survey process could help them with upcoming activities related to the initiative. They concluded that the importance of communication and collaboration was a good reminder for the identification and training of screeners for coach hiring and the coordination of coaching work with principals. The issue of incentives encouraged the group to think about how to market coaching and make the coach role appealing to the most effective teachers who work well with their colleagues. AARs often provoke important learning that can be generalized to the overall initiative and to other strategic initiatives (if the learning is shared in team meetings). By surfacing these issues quickly and thinking about how they might show up elsewhere and how they could be addressed, the team might avoid a variety of potential problems.

An AAR supports immediate improvements in work processes and also builds a culture where questions are valued as much as, or more than, answers, and failure is seen as the threshold to learning. We engage in the work knowing we will make mistakes because we simply don't know enough to avoid them. So the goal becomes learning from our mistakes, accelerating progress, and making mistakes that are more sophisticated, while learning along the way. A principal recently captured the sentiment of this concept beautifully when he was talking to his teachers about how to move from the analysis of assessment data to instructional strategies. The teachers were nervous about whether their ideas for improving instruction would be right, and the principal was trying to create a safe space for experimentation and learning. He described trying something and failing as "failing forward," meaning that from this experience, they would learn something that would help them get smarter about the work and be better at it.[7]

How Do We Build Stakeholder Support of Strategy?

While a few people are busily planning strategic initiatives at a level of detail necessary for success, the majority of people who will soon be involved in execution or who have some interest in execution may know nothing about the initiative. Building stakeholder support is critical to implementation and largely about communication. Too often, critical stakeholders are left out of the loop when strategy and related initiatives are developed, engendering misunderstanding and mistrust. Throughout the strategy development process, we have indicated ways to engage different stakeholders along the way to build understanding, support, and ownership. This is something to continue (not begin!) in strategy execution. To do so effectively requires (1) understanding the interests of various stakeholders and aligning communication to them; (2) balancing a message of urgency and agency; and (3) ensuring the flow of communication up and down, in and out, and throughout the organization.

Ensuring communication in all directions is essential. Too often, communication in a school system, particularly a large one, is akin to a game of telephone. Carefully conceived, well-aligned strategy often lives a rich life in the heads of six to ten of the most senior people in the school system. Employees two levels (and sometimes only one level) down in the organization don't understand the strategy and related initiatives, much less why these things have been chosen, how they affect the staff's daily work, and how they lead to results. Strategy execution requires people in the system to understand what they are being asked to do and why. The people charged with executing the strategy need to have a voice in shaping how it will be executed, bringing together the big picture plan for the system with the on-the-ground reality of daily work. Some of the suggestions earlier in the book to engage staff from middle management, schools, and classrooms in strategy development are designed to build the multilateral communication needed for successful strategy execution.

Every group of stakeholders has interests. Sometimes they are defined by the group's responsibility (e.g., the board and staff whose work is affected by an initiative). Other times they are defined by commitments and investments that stakeholders have made to the work (e.g., funders and programmatic partners). The key to communication is figuring out what different people care about and focusing your communication to them on those things. Developing a stakeholder map that identifies all the different stakeholders, their interests, and the communication approach for each is a great way for a leadership team to think about a communication plan for the overall strategy. It can also be used when thinking about individual strategic initiatives.

Stakeholder mapping consists of three steps: (1) brainstorm all the stakeholders, internal and external, who have a vested interest in the strategy and their relationships to one another; (2) identify the interests of each stakeholder; and (3) define the communication approach for each stakeholder. The stakeholder mapping in figure 6.7 reflects the Moorwood leadership team's assessment of the stakeholders for their overall strategy.

FIGURE 6.7

STRATEGY STAKEHOLDER MAP

Stakeholders	Interests	Communication approach
School board	■ Responsiveness of strategy to needs ■ Financial implications ■ Results; how to measure the effect	■ Superintendent continues briefings started during strategy development ■ Introduce strategy with clear tie to system needs, budget, and metrics to measure effect
Principals	■ To ensure positive impact on students ■ Implications of strategy for their daily work	■ Superintendent meets with principals to discuss strategy and talk about their role in its execution; include time for Q&A ■ Develop a one-pager to accompany strategy document that outlines implications of strategy execution for principals' work
Teachers	■ To ensure positive impact on students ■ To know what's expected of them ■ To ensure that it supports their practice ■ Respect for their competence and professionalism	■ Joint system/union communication (newsletter, school union leaders meeting) ■ Principals asked to discuss strategy with staff in light of their meeting with the superintendent and given talking points and sample protocol for that meeting; principals share teachers' response with deputy superintendents ■ Every teacher gets the strategy statement and summary that highlights how initiatives in years 1–3 will support teachers' practice
Teachers union	■ To ensure that union rules are followed ■ To ensure that strategy supports and respects teachers	■ Superintendent continues discussion of strategy begun in regular meetings with union president ■ Impact bargaining as necessary (nothing foreseeable in year 1; possible bargaining implications for "value added" and career ladder in year 3, to be addressed soon)
Central office staff	■ Vision for system, strategy, and implications of both for their work	■ Leadership team members convene all staff in departments they oversee, present and discuss strategy ■ Leadership team members meet with direct reports to discuss implications of strategy for their department's work ■ Department heads discuss implications with their staffs and share their response with leadership team supervisor
Parents	■ To ensure positive impact on students	■ Superintendent presents strategy and implications for families with leaders of parent organizations ■ System highlights it in newsletter or other communication with parents ■ Superintendent and head of parent outreach engage in monthly parent forums

(continued on next page)

Stakeholders	Interests	Communication approach
Funders	■ To ensure alignment of their investments with strategy ■ To identify areas for possible additional investments	■ Superintendent or senior staff talk one-on-one with any funder who has invested in work that is being stopped ■ Superintendent meets with current and potential funders to outline strategy, highlighting areas for investments
State department of education	■ Compliance with state regulations	■ Superintendent or senior staff talks to state department staff about any aspect of strategy that requires a state waiver (look into IEP question) ■ Develop and share document that explains how strategy addresses state mandates and priorities
Other community (business, citizens, mayor and elected officials)	■ Workforce development; educated citizenry ■ Overall community health	■ Superintendent presents strategy to local business organizations, e.g., chamber of commerce with clear tie to system needs, budget, and metrics to measure effect ■ Superintendent meets with mayor to share strategy ■ Develop visually appealing materials for Web site and paper distribution summarizing strategy

The beauty of having completed this grid is that the Moorwood team now has the beginnings of its strategy communication plan (third column), and the team is clear about communication priorities and the responsibilities of individual team members relative to them. Stakeholder mapping is something that can be done pretty quickly and can help the system avoid land mines.

Having defined stakeholders, their interests, and the communication approach, the team faces the next task of developing the tone and message. The trick in communicating strategy is to simultaneously communicate a sense of urgency combined with a sense of agency to improve, answering the questions "Why change?" and "How to change?" John Kotter described the importance of urgency: "Without an organization-wide sense of urgency, [leading change] is like trying to build a pyramid on a foundation of empty shoeboxes."[8] Agency is equally important; it gives people the confidence to believe they can effect the change needed.

Balancing urgency and agency is tricky. In high-performing systems, there is often a strong sense of agency as aggregate student achievement results make people feel successful and confident. In these same systems, the good news about achievement often evaporates once the issue of the achievement gap is raised. The system's success in certain areas makes it hard for the adults to feel a sense of urgency about the children who are not being well served. The result is often a sense of complacency. In low-performing systems, the opposite is true. Urgency is a constant drumbeat. Performance is continually deemed low. Interventions for improvement are commonplace. Yet people are beaten down by the circumstances and often lack a sense of their capacity to influence these circumstances and improve student outcomes. If people don't believe they can do it, they can't.

Engaging a broad range of actors in the work is critical. Smart, thoughtful people who carry out the daily work of the system know a lot about execution and the shoals on which other initiatives have crashed. Inviting their feedback and creating ways for it to move throughout the system to inform design and execution ensures that both the big-picture vision of the system and the on-the-ground reality are represented. It also builds a mechanism for sharing learning among the different levels of the organization. Simple ways to build communication include these:

- Survey of teachers and principals to assess implementation
- Study or work groups that have representation from all levels of the system to develop implementation plans for initiatives
- Focus groups to present ideas and plans to people who will be affected by them for reaction and refinement before execution
- Piloting initiatives with clear mechanisms to learn and refine in light of learning
- School visits by central staff to observe initiatives in action and to get feedback from teachers and principals
- Monthly principal/teacher breakfasts at different school sites hosted by senior leadership team members (and monthly superintendent meetings for the community, when relevant)
- An open online communication system where people in the system can express suggestions, concerns, and questions and see a posted response
- An incentive system that periodically rewards employees whose suggestions, large and small, for improvement have been implemented

Developing and executing strategy in a way that builds trust, empowers people, and makes them hopeful about the possibilities leads to a high-functioning organization that does great work. This is accomplished through lots of simple actions. Invite people from the schools into the conversation in a meaningful way. Take their lead some of the time. Ask someone how they're doing, and take the feedback seriously. Frame strategy to be as much about pursuing greatness in the future as it is about addressing problems of the past. Describe problems as opportunities for learning and improvement rather than blaming people. Pay less attention to assigning blame and more attention to moving forward productively. Remember, when you get hot under the collar, that none of this is about you. It is about children and what they need and deserve.

How Does the System Manage Strategy Execution?

Successful strategy execution requires a balance of support and accountability. Support is provided through resource allocation (money, staff, and time), technical assistance, and collaborative problem-solving. Accountability is ensured through regular tracking of work, timelines and benchmarks, and assessing organizational learning. Successful execution also requires vigilant management and communication at every level and between levels of implementation. It is only through this thoughtful and regular analysis of work progress and pitfalls that the system can learn and adjust its strategy accordingly.

Efficient management of individual initiatives, many of which are happening simultaneously, is the bedrock of effective execution. Coordination across the initiatives to ensure coherence and alignment, to track work, and to solve common dilemmas is the next critical level of management. Finally, the leadership team's management focus during execution is to aggregate the work, challenges, and results of all initiatives, holding the vision and overall strategy in mind. The team tracks implementation and results and refines the strategy as needed. There is much to be learned at each level: the implementation of each individual initiative, the experiences that are similar and distinct across initiatives, the successes and challenges encountered, the way the overall strategy is being executed, and the results it is achieving (figure 6.8). And, there needs to be an intentional approach to capturing that knowledge and funneling it back into strategy improvements.

Individual Strategic Initiatives

At the level of implementing individual initiatives, project managers for each initiative are a big help. As described earlier, project managers develop the work plans and oversee all aspects of implementation. They lay out in detail all of the steps involved in bringing an initiative to life, the timeline for the work, and key benchmarks and identify the people responsible for each step of implementation. They

FIGURE 6.8

SYSTEM LEARNING SPIRAL

Overall strategy execution and refinement
(leadership team)

Across strategic initiatives
(project managers and strategy
implementation coordinator)

Individual strategic initiatives
(project managers and initiative work groups)

work with everyone involved in the initiative to keep things on track, manage the implementation team, and ensure its functioning. Tracking all the work of the initiative and reporting results through the organization are additional responsibilities. The strength of a project manager often defines the success of an initiative. He or she needs to have strong organizational and interpersonal skills and the ability to hold the big picture and purpose of the initiative in mind while addressing the day-to-day tasks required for execution. In addition to selecting project managers carefully, it can be quite helpful to train them in the use of the tools introduced earlier in the chapter to ensure consistency and quality of strategy implementation.

Project managers are also responsible for creating opportunities to surface learning from implementation efforts, document it, and use it to inform future work. At the level of specific activities, after-action reviews are helpful in this effort. Establishing regular implementation meetings is also useful (depending on the timeline and complexity of the initiative, "regular" can mean monthly or biweekly). Everyone involved in the initiative participates in these meetings. The participants describe their work, the problems encountered, the solutions developed, the next steps, and outstanding questions. The regularity and structure of these meetings leverage the expertise of the group to solve problems and build its sense of owner-ship, commitment, and collaboration.

Across Strategic Initiatives

Coordination across initiatives leads to better results. The people leading the instructional materials adoption process need to be talking with the people lead-ing the formative assessment development to ensure these two efforts are aligned so that they are of maximum value to teachers. Similarly, the people developing the data warehouse need to be working in concert with the people developing the formative assessments. Sometimes, coordination across initiatives happens within a strategic objective. Other times, it must happen across objectives. The best results generally arise when the people responsible for implementation identify the others with whom they need to be working. and this information is mapped to the leader-ship team's sense of necessary collaboration. Senior managers often manage this level of coordination, typically through monthly meetings. The work of these cross-initiative meetings is to talk about the points of intersection to ensure they are well conceived and carried out. Project managers and key staff from work groups participate and often share dilemmas that the other participants in the meeting are well positioned to help them address.

Overall Strategy Execution and Refinement

Finally, the work of all initiatives must be aggregated to the system level. This allows the leadership team to do a broad review of initiatives, objectives, and the strategy as a whole. Systems often identify one person or a small team (depending on the size of the system and the complexity of the strategy) to coordinate overall strat-egy execution. This person or team works with all project managers, coordinates meetings across initiatives, and solicits and collects monthly status reports for each initiative. The person or persons consolidate the reports into a single account of key successes, including quarterly metrics on how the initiatives are doing relative to their benchmarks and results, and challenges and other issues that need immediate attention for discussion among the senior leadership team. The information pro-vided by the overall coordinator, combined with information from senior leaders who manage the departments engaged in strategy execution, helps the leadership team assess overall strategy execution, problem solve, and make refinements to the strategy as needed. Leadership team meeting agendas are set up with adequate time to look at the work across initiatives in a fairly superficial, check-in manner, as well as to dive deeply into specific initiatives, the results achieved, and the roadblocks encountered, all with an eye to solving problems and identifying the organizational learning that can inform other work. Project managers often present their work and results to the leadership team as part of the deep dives. The team's job during these discussions is to both ensure its understanding of the work and identify opportunities and expectations for improvement. Projects that aren't meeting benchmarks and targets are highlighted for additional attention.

While all of this coordination within and across initiatives is helpful, it is not enough. If we want to learn about how things are going in classrooms, we know that students are a key source for that information. In much the same way, asking the people involved in implementation on the ground level how things are going is often the best way to gauge implementation, what to learn from innovations, and what adjustments to make. For example, ensuring that the voice of teachers and principals is heard as the team in charge of curriculum mapping is reviewing its work is essential to making the assessment accurate. The team's sense of how things are going must be triangulated with the experience of people on the ground trying to use the tools. Focus groups, surveys, classroom and school observations, pilots of new work, and other conversations are just a few tools that provide great feedback and broaden the learning loops. The goal of all these learning loops is to ensure that information about the work of strategy execution is moving up, down, across, in and out of the system. This must include information moving all the way from classrooms to the superintendent and vice versa.

Clearly, execution requires a high level of collaboration and interdependence. It also requires a high level of personal, team, and organizational responsibility and accountability. The supports and communication just described are intended to help with those. Additionally, accountability measures for the team's process, outputs, and outcomes are a good way to encourage productive team behavior and action. This can happen at several levels. At the individual level, people's contribution to teams they participate in and the team's overall performance should be part of their annual performance evaluation. This can be accomplished by a mix of metrics that range from 360-degree feedback from other team members on performance to self-evaluations of an individual's contribution to the team. This provides a strong incentive for individuals to contribute and clearly signals the system's commitment to this work. It is also important to measure the team's performance in terms of meeting milestones, reviews of the team's work by the people whom it's supposed to serve, and the team's demonstrated ability to solve problems and adapt plans as needed. The teams themselves should get a group performance rating based on the same metrics above. These metrics are aggregated up the organization to the performance evaluations of the senior managers who champion specific initiatives.

Strong execution is marked by careful planning, ongoing learning, and nimble adjustments along the way. It's not just "implementation"—it's deliberate, energetic action that translates strategy from words on a page to real improvements in classrooms for children.

Look, Leap, and Learn

When we talk with educators about where they get stuck or where things fall apart, they frequently point to choosing a few things to focus on and executing them well. These challenges are about making hard choices, taking a chance, creating conditions for success, and committing to learning. Too often, systems hedge their bets by committing to more things than they can manage and creating a compliance culture where *doing* trumps and sometimes precludes *learning*. In high-performing systems, choosing what to do, doing it well, and learning from the doing are iterative processes that are inextricably linked. It is here that the paradoxes emerge. How do you make choices knowing that what you learn from executing them may make you revisit them? How you do dive in to execute while stepping back to learn and adjust? How do you insist on the concrete details of a plan while also acknowledging that reality is more unpredictable and complex than any plan? Below are some suggestions for managing these paradoxes while placing strategic bets and executing.

DIVING IN VERSUS STEPPING BACK

Partner with the professionals. Driving improvement requires us to dive in and develop ideas about what we most need to do to improve student learning and to constantly be looking beyond ourselves for better ideas. It is surprising how seldom we think to ask the professionals closest to the work how they think things can be improved. And yet we know that they have a unique perspective because of how close they are to the action. It is appropriate for a leadership team to drive where the system is going and, in broad terms, what steps it will take to get there. It is also important that the people charged with execution define the specifics of how the steps should be taken. It is not enough to "run ideas by them." The individuals who will do the work should be involved in the design of that work. For example, you could engage them in these ways:

- Ask principals and teachers how a math coach could be best used to help teachers improve their math instruction (and if they have other ideas for supporting teachers to improve their math instruction).
- Charge human resources staff with convening a cross-functional team to lay out how the hiring process will be revamped and induction services will be developed.
- Ask parents what they would find most helpful to support them in extending classroom learning at home.

Inviting other people to dive into designing the specifics of what the strategy will look like on the ground gives you a chance to get some perspective on your own ideas, benefit from the ideas of others, and build investment in, and commitment to, execution.

Be a learner. The success of strategy depends on your making smart bets, learning from the work, and then shaping and refining it accordingly. This is a continual process of diving in (focusing on a few key things), stepping back (learning and refining), and diving in again to apply the learning. Simultaneously executing and learning allows you to learn as you deeply own and drive the work. It requires you to ask a question about how things are going even if you're unsure that you want to hear the answer. Moving from strategy as a concept to strategy as a set of initiatives under way brings the strategy into reality. Plans that make sense on paper may not play out quite as well in reality, or they may not stand up to the reality test at all. This is not a problem as long as you notice it and respond thoughtfully. Taking a stance as a learner also keeps you sane. If you take a strategy at its word, assuming execution will look exactly like what is written in the logic model and implementation work plan, you will be forever frustrated. The inevitable roadblocks are learning opportunities, full of data that can inform your actions. Seeing them through this lens will both help you feel more efficacious and allow you to respond in ways that maximize success. One retired superintendent we know said that the highest compliment she had ever received was that she was the "lead learner." Be a lead learner. Saying "I don't understand," asking authentic questions—questions you really don't know the answer to—and noting aloud when you learned something or were wrong about something gives other people in the system permission to do the same. That is how the system (and the individuals within it) get smarter.

Shift from compliance to accountability. There is a strong culture of compliance in many school systems. This is particularly true in the central office, where people work at a distance from both senior leadership and the schools. Strategy execution can turn into a compliance exercise when people don't see the connection between their work and children or the overall system strategy or don't feel empowered to do meaningful work. They are less inclined to think critically about what they are doing, to ask tough questions, and to refine plans in light of early indicators of a problem. Compliance is a way of deflecting responsibility and protecting ourselves from fragmented, cacophonous systems that don't make sense. When faced with challenging goals and urgency, it can be easy to slip into compliance mode. Compliance is about *doing something.* Accountability is about *achieving results.* While accountability can sometimes reinforce a compliance mind-set, at its best accountability encourages diving into the work, fully committing to it, and also stepping back to assess its impact on children. Three simple questions can make the connection between the work and children clear and push learning and improvement:

- How does what I'm doing support children and their learning?
- Is this working for children?
- How do I know?

Stepping back to answer these questions helps to ensure that the work is responsive and purposeful rather than a mere compliance activity—in other words, it helps you dive in. It empowers you to make changes as needed and reminds you why you're doing it in the first place.

COMPLEXITY VERSUS SIMPLICITY

Look and leap. Designing strategy requires taking the time to be thoughtful and thorough. It also requires the courage and decisiveness to take a leap once you've done your best thinking. Thoughtful action requires holding complexity and simplicity, honing in on a few clear strategic objectives while recognizing the complexity that precedes and follows the decision to commit to those objectives. There are many ways to encourage thoughtful action. For example:

- Collect evidence and study promising practices so that your bets are well informed.
- Debate the options, understand different perspectives, and dig deeply into the pros and cons and trade-offs of each choice.
- Set aside time and create the conditions for this kind of due diligence. And then it is time to decide.
- Be clear about decision points, and push to make them. Avoid setting aside niggling issues with the intention of dealing with them later; take them on.

Understand that to not decide is simply a passive way of deciding. Have faith. Practicing looking and leaping for smaller-scale decisions, like small action items at a meeting, will help you have the skill and confidence to do so when it comes to larger decisions, like committing to a strategy for the system.

Give strategy room to grow. For strategy to be effective, it cannot be immutable. It must evolve in response to needs and changes in the environment. Yet if people in the system interpret refinements to the strategy as reflecting the same old reactive behavior of many school systems, the credibility of the strategy will be compromised. The trick is to simultaneously be clear, consistent, and emphatic about the vision for the work, allow flexibility about how it can best be executed, and learn from and share promising practices as a way of supporting people in the work. For some people, this will feel like too much complexity and ambiguity. They will yearn to be told what to do and will interpret revision as a change of strategy rather than as a way of being strategic. Creating learning loops that focus on helping people (and the organization) get smarter as they do the work and regularly reviewing strategy execution makes it clear that learning is a critical part of doing the work well and helps people begin to see the work as both coherent and dynamic.

Measure process and results. Measuring results is simultaneously simple and complex. It is a matter of answering the question "Are students learning more as a result of our efforts?" Many of our tools for measurement (student test scores) are quite blunt, and our ability to make clear correlations between specific actions and results is often not as precise as would be helpful. Nevertheless, as educators, we are getting smarter about how to measure results effectively. What is equally important and much harder is measuring the processes that are expected to lead to the results. How do you know if instruction is improving, if leadership is improving, if central office capacity is improving? How do you keep the measures simple enough that educators can use them, yet valid and reliable enough that you would want educators to use them? A few examples of how to measure work along the road to improved student learning include these:

- Break big instructional improvement priorities down into manageable pieces, and prioritize specific instructional strategies for focus (e.g., questioning techniques instead of "rigor"; assessment and grouping strategies instead of "differentiated instruction"). Organize teacher professional development and support to help teachers implement those strategies. Have people in the system (teachers, coaches, principals, central office staff) observe in classrooms to see the extent to which the strategies are being integrated into instruction, using a clear rubric to guide them. And then have them talk with one another (and their supervisors) about what they see and how to accelerate the work.
- Create benchmarks for school improvement and to measure the impact of the principal's leadership. Has the principal developed a leadership team to guide improvement efforts? Does the team function well and make meaningful decisions? Is there evidence that decisions are data-driven?
- Start surveying principals about their satisfaction with central office services. They will have lots to say. Create the expectation that central offices will refine their improvement efforts based on survey data by following up to see what central offices did in response.

When we ferociously commit to acting and learn from that action, both become easier because they feed on and reinforce one another. It's easier to commit because we know we'll get smarter as we go. It's easier to *do* because we know the goal isn't perfection. It's easier to learn because we know it will help us improve. And in the end, we are more effective in realizing what we care most about: the success of all children.

Toward Realizing the Potential of Strategic Action

Although social change cannot come overnight, we must always work as though it were a possibility in the morning.

—*Rev. Dr. Martin Luther King, Jr.*

Every chapter of this book, up to this point, has focused on how to design a strategy that accelerates student learning. We have emphasized the technical work of how to assess a system's current practices and its problems and opportunities. We have advocated for developing a vision in a way that lets you think boldly and audaciously about what you want to make possible for children. And we have laid out a process for actually designing and executing the strategy. Throughout the chapters, and quite explicitly in chapter 2, we have talked about why this work is hard and offered some ways to make it easier. The two paradoxes we have woven through the book hint at the complexity of strategic thinking and the reality that it is an endeavor done by people, which adds additional layers of personal and interpersonal complexity.

As we bring this book to a close, we want to do three things. First, we want to bring the conversation about strategy to a close by surfacing tensions that are common to strategy work. Second, we want to revisit the instructional core and talk about how systems can organize themselves on the core after the initial work of designing strategy is done and execution is under way. Finally, we want to revisit the paradoxes, suggesting ways to manage them—ways that will serve school systems well in their strategy work and beyond.

BALANCING TENSIONS IN STRATEGY

In execution, strategy comes to life. And through that process, it evolves. In chapter 6, we talked about how strategy is refined in light of learning during execution. Beyond those refinements, strategy evolves more substantially over time because the system's needs and capacity change and its understanding of the fundamental work of instructional improvement deepens. A system that starts its strategy work needing to build an aligned instructional system will need something more sophisticated to continue to accelerate student learning once that first building block is put in place. A system that uses a strategy that focuses on autonomy and accountability will surely evolve as it learns from the innovations some schools initiate and the struggles other schools face.

Two tensions (dare we say paradoxes) surface in the strategy design and execution work of school systems and warrant discussion. Understanding them can help you balance them in strategy design and evolution. The first relates to how loosely or tightly the system is going to manage schools. The second relates to the strategy's focus on *all* children and, at the same time, on *each* child. Looking closely at the evolution of two systems' strategies provides the chance to see these tensions in living color.

The Redstone Public Schools followed a tightly managed curriculum for close to ten years.[1] Everyone used a prescribed set of curriculum and instructional materials, which came complete with pacing guides and repercussions for teachers who were not on track. Student achievement rose dramatically and made the system a standout among its peer group. Over time, though, the gains started to level out. The system decided that the way to drive the next jump in performance was to pursue a strategy focused on innovation, providing schools freedom and flexibility to make choices about curriculum, instruction, and assessment within some established boundaries for accountability.

The system gave schools that met certain performance guidelines freedom from system policies and expectations. These schools were encouraged to innovate by implementing new ways to accelerate student learning that could then inform the practices of other schools. The system intentionally didn't ask these schools to focus their innovations on a couple of problems of practice common to the district. It wanted to give them leeway to decide on their own the areas of innovation they thought would be most worthwhile.

Within six months of initiating this change in strategy, the system knew something was amiss. Schools were tinkering at the edges—after-school programming, tutorials, small adjustments to staffing—rather than focusing deeply on the instructional core. As the system leaders set about to learn what had gone wrong, they learned several important things. Schools didn't really know what to do with the freedom they had been given. Central office departments were not prepared to shift from a heavy top-down compliance orientation to responding to schools' requests. And policies and state mandates that limit flexibility were not fully considered or addressed.

Under the system's tightly managed curriculum, everyone was expected to do the same thing at the same time, under close monitoring. With the shift to freedom and flexibility, schools were given enormous autonomy with little guidance. The system faltered because the pendulum swung too widely from tight to loose. Schools that excelled in the tight system, those that were expected to lead the way when things were loosened up, were unprepared to take advantage of the flexibility the new system offered. Similarly, central office staff who had overseen compliance for years were in many cases unable to shift to a supportive and responsive role. The system's initial inclination that giving schools more flexibility might lead to innovation that would accelerate student achievement was reasonable. But the arc of the pendulum was too wide, swinging from tight prescription to complete freedom. The system didn't fully consider what the right balance of tight and loose was or what support people would need to make the transition.

The good news is that the system learned from its experience. Several months into the implementation of the freedom and flexibility initiative, the system gathered data, analyzed them, identified a problem, and tried to better understand it and figure out how to address it. The system was also strategic in inviting outside colleagues who had a broader perspective on the work to serve as critical friends. Together they examined the circumstances to better understand the problem and consider solutions. They ended up with an approach that provided a better balance between tight and loose management.

The challenge of balancing the second tension, *all* children and *each* child, is reflected in the experience of the Boston Public Schools, the place where Liz and

Rachel first met. The tension most clearly arose in the part of Boston's strategy that focused on the instructional core. The initial strategy targeted literacy (reading, writing, and speaking) in grades K–12, because of student achievement results and the reality that literacy skills support learning in all content areas. Literacy instruction and achievement improved over several years, most notably at the elementary level. With this foundation, the next iteration of the strategy expanded beyond literacy to address math, K–12. It took several years to seed the math work and begin to see results because many of the teachers had to build their math content knowledge and comfort with the subject to teach the curriculum and instructional materials.

Once the math work gained traction, the system decided to shift its focus from developing aligned instruction systems in specific content areas to addressing effective teaching. The system decided to scale up "workshop," the model of instruction that was a centerpiece of both the literacy and the math initiatives, across all content areas. This decision was made to provide a model of effective teaching and ensure consistency from classroom to classroom. With the workshop initiative in place, the system then moved to define effective teaching and set teaching standards.

The strategy shows a clear evolution: from an initial focus on building an aligned instructional system in one content area to several and then extrapolating from that work to define teaching standards for the system. And the focus of all of it was to build high-quality teaching in all classrooms. The priority was to scale up improvements systemwide; the emphasis was on *all* students, *all* teachers, and *all* schools. And the results overall showed steady growth in student achievement.

However, a look beneath the overall data revealed that progress was uneven and that English language learners and students with disabilities were in trouble. Classroom observations confirmed that many teachers serving those students were struggling to apply workshop instruction effectively in their classrooms. At the school level, some schools had accelerated their overall performance significantly while others were persistently low-performing. The system needed to balance *all* with *each* by differentiating support in response to the specific needs of struggling students, teachers, and schools.

These tensions are ones that every system needs to be mindful of. Anticipating and trying to balance them as strategy is developed can lead to accelerated results. But it is not always possible to plan for them in advance. Sometimes, systems don't have the capacity. Sometimes, they don't yet know enough to avoid the problem.

What both examples make clear is that the journey of strategy design and evolution is not always linear and logical. Sometimes, pendulums swing in wide arcs, unable to find their center. Sometimes, through efforts to build the overall system, the needs of certain children are inadvertently overlooked. Given this reality, it is important to be on the lookout for these tensions and to intentionally think about ways to balance them. This can best be accomplished by ensuring that at the same time that you are *executing* strategy you are also intentionally *learning* from it so that you stay conscious, keep learning, and make good decisions.

FOCUSING ON THE INSTRUCTIONAL CORE

Digging deeper into the instructional core will help to ensure that the focus of strategy and the system's work is on students, teachers, and the content. In this book, we have advocated for leadership teams to dip their collective toes into the instructional-core water by visiting schools and classrooms in their own and other systems. Simple visits can be quite enlightening and begin to build the habit of seeing the work in action to better understand it and guide its improvement. Wading into the instructional-core waters to your knees can best be done by visiting schools and classrooms as a team, looking for particular characteristics of effective instruction: expectations, rigor, student engagement, quality of teacher questioning, and so on. Debriefing these visits builds a common understanding of effective instruction and helps to make concrete the strengths and weaknesses of the system's instructional program. Systems that wade into the instructional-core waters up to their waist focus in a way that is deep, systemic, and purposeful. The goal is to deeply understand a problem, become smarter about what the research and best practices suggest are the best ways to address it, and to focus intensely on improving. Everyone in the system organizes to solve the problem, believing that collective action has the power to transform the quality of instruction.

These forays into the instructional core can be quite discrete, occasionally done by senior leadership or others in the system, or they can permeate the organization. The early forays are more likely driven by individual interests than by a systemic commitment. A few principals visit one another's schools in search of colleagueship and ideas. The leadership team visits for specific purposes—for example, to see the great implementation of the math curriculum, to visit high- and low-performing schools, to get ideas to inform the system's vision. When the idea becomes more pervasive, the system is likely to engage the leadership team and some groups of principals or teachers or both. At the point at which the effort is systemic, everyone in the system is organized to solve a common problem.

A simple example of this is a system that decides to focus intensively on better understanding the learning needs of English language learners (ELL) and the instructional strategies that have been found to be most effective in facilitating their learning. Everyone in the system reads research and explores best practices in this area. Teachers meet to review their ELL students' work and performance on assessments to better understand their needs and develop effective responses. Principals share their schools' performance data for ELL students, visit one another's schools, and develop and implement plans for schoolwide action. And finally, central office staff and the senior leadership team are engaged in visiting classrooms to better understand the problem and figure out the most helpful departmental and systemic response.

When systems reach this point, the instructional core is the context in which everything else in the system happens. Decisions are made according to what best supports the content, teacher practice, and student learning. The system is constantly trying to get smarter about how children learn, the elements of effective instruction, and what it can do to strengthen both. Questions about the instructional core are not answered and set aside. They are explored in increasing depth to help the system respond with increasing precision and speed.

MANAGING THE PARADOXES

Committing to the Work: Dive In/Step Back

Managing the paradoxes woven through the book can ground strategy work and how the organization functions. The diving in/stepping back paradox relates to commitment. It is about bringing our best selves to the endeavor while maintaining a boundary between ourselves and the work. Our best selves are interested and engaged. We feel invited into the work and included. We grow and learn from the work, and it ends up having meaning. And slowly we begin to own it and identify with it. At the same time, we can separate ourselves from it, understanding that our involvement matters only to the extent that it serves children well. They come first. At best, we rate a distant second. Our job is to hold a vision for them and to help make it possible for them. And we must every day be inspired by who they are and the potential *each* of them holds. Bringing our best selves to the work and placing children first requires us and the systems we work in to change. Change requires trust and risk-taking, two things that are often in short supply in school systems. Change also requires that we anticipate and acknowledge the real losses individuals will experience in this process. And finally, change provokes conflicts between what people say and do. These conflicts must be anticipated, understood, and addressed.

Building trust requires getting to know our colleagues and having faith that their actions are driven by good intentions. So often, the pace of school systems makes it quite difficult to know our colleagues in a meaningful way. Changing that requires committing time and energy to it, but doing so can start with simple steps—starting a meeting by asking everyone to share what work they left unfinished to come to the meeting or something fun they did over the weekend. Additionally, we build trust through our actions. Do we listen? Are we respectful in our behaviors? Are we transparent about our interests, and do they relate to children and their learning? Do our actions match our words? Do we deliver results? Do we admit our mistakes? Do we honor our commitments? Do we acknowledge problems and work to solve them?[2]

It is worth saying a bit more about the issue of aligning what we do with what we say. Robert Kegan and Lisa Lahey have studied this inconsistency extensively. They explain the difference between what people say they want to do and what they actually do as not simply an act of subversion but an "immunity to change."[3] People have every intention of changing—and their language reflects their intentions—but they still have trouble doing it because they are committed to other things that compete for their allegiance. Building people's understanding of this immunity can be a powerful way to accelerate change and build trust.

Trust also exists at the level of the organization. We talked earlier in the book about the power of transparent, multidimensional communication as a powerful way to build trust. The way a system responds to risk-taking also influences organizational trust. Doing things differently requires people to try new things. And, inevitably, these attempts result in some failure. The system can take its cue from the principal mentioned earlier in the book and think of failure as progress, "failing forward," or it can ignore mistakes or punish them. The former response builds a culture of risk-taking while the latter signals that it is not safe to take risks.

Loss is a real part of change. Regardless of how compelling the reason (children!) for the change or how the change is expected to result in more effective and rewarding work for people, change will result in some type of loss. Some losses are substantial. In systems where people are identified by the position they hold and the authority that they wield, asking them to work collaboratively implies a loss of identity. They may have to give up making the final decision, and they lose control and a sense of competence. People's ability to name and understand these losses is often compromised, particularly in time of stress (which is how most would describe change). Simply acknowledging these losses and making them discussable can help people grieve them and then move forward productively.

Learning: Embrace Complexity and Simplify

The complexity-versus-simplicity paradox is about living and acting well in the context of uncertainty and imperfection while looking for every opportunity to simplify things. It requires examining things thoroughly to build understanding, look beyond the obvious, and avoid generalizations. That can be kept simple by answering the questions "What?" "How?" and "Why?" When synthesizing what is learned to figure out the most important issues and actions to address them, the simple question that provides clarity is, "What is best for children?" Answering that question and having it drive the system's actions is not an end point. It is a new starting point to begin learning from. To balance this paradox, school systems and the people who work in them must be learners, visionaries, and problem solvers.

Learning is the work of school systems. They exist to facilitate students' learning. Yet systems are far less intentional about facilitating adult learning or taking a learning stance as an organization. This reality is important because there is a striking correlation between adult and student learning. This connection becomes clear if you are sitting in a faculty meeting in a school. If teachers are actively engaged in the meeting, learning new things, and assuming leadership, it is quite likely you will see students behaving in the same way in classrooms. If teachers are sitting passively, being lectured to by administrators, then the teachers probably lecture to their students, leaving students disengaged. If staff meetings are combative affairs where unproductive disagreement and confrontation are the norm, the school is likely to have a student behavior problem.

This reality doesn't just exist within a school. It happens in the central office and the senior leadership team as well. We once watched as the full implications of this truth hit a school system leader like a ton of bricks as she realized that the lack of rigor of the system's senior leadership team meetings was probably a good reflection of the level of rigor happening in classrooms and schools across the system. The senior team seldom used data to inform conversations, often accepting opinion as fact. Research and best practices were infrequently tapped to guide decisions about the best way to proceed. It was uncommon to discuss and debate important issues. Little wonder this system struggled to build students' critical thinking skills.

This book is about strategy: what it is, why it's important, and how to go about designing and executing it. But it is also about being strategic: acting in purposeful ways to focus first and foremost on children; looking within and beyond the system to imagine what is possible and be inspired; organizing work in ways that value people, engage them, and hold them accountable; and reflecting in action and learning to guide improvement. These are all habits of high-performing organizations that will serve school systems well.

The potential of weaving purpose, commitment, and beliefs together with strategy, systems, structures, and continuous learning is tremendous. That power can be realized in adults who are driven by a common vision of and belief in what is possible, a commitment to realize that vision, and the knowledge and skills required to do just that. Ultimately, it can be realized in students who can pass high-stakes assessments, have promising postsecondary careers and educational opportunities, and believe in, participate in, and contribute to a democratic society. The second outcome cannot be realized without the first. And so we must dive into the work.

Summary of Protocols and Tools by Chapter

Chapter 1

Making Sense of the Work Under Way Protocol (appendix B; and chapter 1 text)
"Signs of Strategy" Rubric (figure 1.4)

Chapter 2

Team Membership Characteristics for Consideration (figure 2.1)
Quick Check on Team Functioning (figure 2.7)

Chapter 3

Affinity Protocol (appendix B; and chapter 3 text)
5 Whys (appendix B; and chapter 3 text)

Chapter 4

Vision Assessment Tool (figure 4.1)
Back-to-the-Future Protocol (appendix B; and chapter 4 text)
Sample Visitation Protocol (figure 4.4)

Chapter 5

Ease Versus Impact for Human Capital Strategic Objective (figure 5.5)
"Signs of Strategy" Rubric (reprise) (chapter 5 text)

Chapter 6

Start/Stop/Continue (figure 6.1)
Logic Model (appendix B; and figure 6.5)
Implementation Work Plan (figure 6.6)
After-Action Review (chapter 6 text)
Strategy Stakeholder Map (figure 6.7)

APPENDIX B

Selected Protocols
with Tips on Implementation

MAKING SENSE OF THE WORK UNDER WAY PROTOCOL

Objective:	To articulate the work the system is currently doing and assess the level of strategy it reflects
Materials:	Flip chart paper, sticky notes, and markers
Time needed:	3–4 hours
Roles:	Facilitator or timekeeper; if group has more than ten people, break into groups of around five

1. Brainstorm
   - Share the definition of *initiative*, and share some examples from the system.
   - An initiative is something the system is doing on its own or in collaboration with partners and is focused on improving some aspect of how the system functions. It may directly involve a set of schools or all schools. It might be a pilot program or full-scale implementation. It may focus on reengineering how a central office does all or some part of its work.
   - Ask participants to brainstorm all the initiatives they can think of, writing one on each sticky note. When they are done, have them post the sticky notes on several pieces of chart paper posted on a wall.
   - Once everyone's stickies are up, ask the group to review all of them and to eliminate duplicates.

2. Sort
   - Run through the initiatives to see if there are any with which people are unfamiliar. If so, ask someone in the know to explain the initiative in two sentences. This should be a very quick step focused on making sure everyone has a basic understanding of the initiatives.

- Ask participants to group like initiatives together and label the categories they choose. The grain size of the categories will vary according to the number and focus of the initiatives. Examples of broad categories might include teaching and learning, human resources, and operations. Categories more fine-grained might include curriculum, instructional materials, professional development, assessment, technology, data, teacher hiring, teacher evaluation, school budgeting, new schools, and closing schools.

3. Assess
    - Once the categories are firmly established and the stickies are posted in the appropriate categories, ask team members what they notice as they look at the categories and initiatives.
    - Introduce the rubric for signs of strategy (figure 1.4). Explain that it shows four characteristics of a robust strategy that has integrity.
    - Ask everyone to individually review each of the characteristics in the rubric and then use the rubric to rate the extent to which the categories and initiatives reflect a strategy.

4. Synthesize
    - Engage the team in a conversation about how it assessed the system's work using the rubric. You may want to have people share their scores or to simply use the scoring activity as a starting point for the conversation. Surface common themes from people's individual analysis as well as differences of opinion. Encourage conversation about the differences in opinion to build greater understanding. The purpose of this conversation is both to assess the extent to which the system has a robust strategy and to identify some ways to develop or strengthen the system's strategy.

Tips

- *Group size:* This protocol can be used with the senior leadership team or with a broader team of system leaders and middle managers. If the group has more than ten people, the conversation will be richer if you use a combination of small groups and the whole group. For a large group, complete steps 1 and 2 in smaller groups of about five people. Then have the teams compare, contrast, and consolidate their categories so there is one final list of categories and initiatives from which to work. Once the categories are finalized, have people return to their small groups to do step 3. Reconvene as a full group to share rubric scores and the highlights of small-group conversations focused on how to strengthen the strategy.
- Even having defined *initiatives*, people will suggest initiatives of different sizes and importance. This is okay, as what matters most is that the big initiatives are listed. The group will naturally give less attention to smaller initiatives.

- When teams try to group initiatives, they sometimes try to fit everything into one or two categories, which leads to a less fine-grained analysis. The facilitator can encourage teams to consider subcategories if there's time.
- Conversation using the rubric can get abstract, particularly when discussing the third and fourth indicators. If that starts to happen, have teams examine a specific initiative to make the discussion more concrete.
- When using the rubric, remind teams to cite evidence to back up their ratings, always asking and answering the question "What are our data and evidence to justify this score?"

THE AFFINITY PROTOCOL

Objective: To generate hypotheses about the causes of problems
Materials: Flip chart paper, sticky notes, and markers
Time needed: 30–45 minutes
Roles: Facilitator or timekeeper; groups of four to seven participants

1. Brainstorm
   Ask teams to write at the top of a piece of chart paper the symptom to be explored. Ask individuals to work independently to brainstorm hunches and hypotheses about what might be the causes of the symptom. Individuals write each of their ideas on separate sticky notes. Once everyone has finished brainstorming hypotheses individually, have them place their sticky notes randomly on their chart paper.

2. Sort
   Ask individuals to sort the sticky notes into categories, with minimal discussion. Sticky notes that list items over which the team has no control should be put in their own category. It is okay for some notes to stand alone. If there is an idea that goes under more than one grouping, participants can duplicate the idea on a separate sticky note and include it in two categories.

3. Categorize
   Ask teams to create a header for each category and to write it on the chart paper. Large categories can be divided into subcategories with subheadings.

4. Prioritize
   Ask teams to choose their top three hypotheses of causes for the problem, remembering that the best causes to choose are
   - things they have control over; and
   - things they believe that, if fixed, would have the biggest impact on fixing the problem.

5. Share

   If there is more than one team, have all teams share their top causes. Ask for a few comments about what people notice. Ask about whether there is any pattern in where these choices came from.

Source: From Kathryn Parker Boudett, Elizabeth A. City, and Richard J. Murnane, eds., *Data Wise: A Step-by-Step Guide to Using Assessment Results to Improve Teaching and Learning* (Cambridge, MA: Harvard Education Press, 2005).

Note: This protocol is useful for many kinds of brainstorming and narrowing purposes in addition to root-cause analysis. For example, a group might use the protocol to brainstorm potential strategic initiatives or to collect evidence from classroom observations and analyze for common themes. The protocol is useful for generating many ideas quickly and then narrowing those ideas. Much of the richness of the protocol lies in the conversations people have as they sort the ideas.

5 WHYS PROTOCOL

Objective:	To identify actionable causes of problems
Materials:	Flip chart paper, sticky notes, and markers
Time needed:	90–120 minutes, depending on the number of hypotheses investigated for a problem and how they are divided up between team members
Roles:	Facilitator or timekeeper; groups of four or five participants

1. Create groups of four or five people. If you have done some of the earlier protocols, you may want to mix the groups up at this point to bring varied perspectives to the work.
2. Give each group chart paper, sticky notes, and markers. Draw the 5 Whys grid on chart paper, and ask each group to copy it (see below), or provide a graphic organizer of the 5 Whys grid.

	Hypothesis 1	*Hypothesis 2*	*Hypothesis 3*	*Hypothesis 4*
Why 1				
Why 2				
Why 3				
Why 4				
Why 5				

3. For each hypothesis that the teams are working on, ask the team to ask why the hypothesis exists. The team's answer is recorded in the Why 1 column. That answer becomes the statement that Why 2 focuses on. This process is repeated four more times, with each subsequent answer recorded in the next row and serving as the focus of the next *why*. With each *why*, the team digs deeper to reach the root cause of the hypotheses.

4. By Why 5, (and sometimes before it), teams will probably identify a root cause that resonates as the core issue and something that can be addressed.

Tips

- Why 3 and Why 4 can be difficult for people, especially when they're new to the protocol and not used to digging this deeply. Press on!
- Keep people focused on things the system has influence over. You're trying to get to actionable causes, and that means action within the system.
- Knowing when to stop can be challenging. You're looking to get to something actionable, which usually pops up between Whys 4, 5, and 6.
- People are often both annoyed and amused with this protocol. It pushes the discourse and analysis beyond the usual surface-level conversation. Often, people have fun with this protocol after they've used it once or twice, with the refrain "why-why-why" popping up in regular conversation.
- The 5 Whys is a widely used protocol. If you want to see examples or learn more, Google "5 Whys."

BACK-TO-THE-FUTURE PROTOCOL

Objective:	To envision an audacious future and provide some ideas about how to get from the present to that future
Materials:	Flip chart paper, markers
Time needed:	45–60 minutes
Roles:	Facilitator or timekeeper

1. In small groups of about five people, project into the future X years, and thoroughly describe what "it" (see "Tips" for guidelines on what "it" should be) looks like, sounds like, and feels like. *Use the present tense when describing!* (about10–15 minutes)

2. Look "back" from your "projected present," and describe how it looked when it started. *Use the past tense! You're describing what's happening now as if it were past.* (5–10 minutes)

3. Continue looking back from the projected present, and discuss how the system addressed the starting place and how the system moved from that to the projected present. Be as specific and concrete as possible. *Again, use the past tense!* (about 10 minutes)

4. Chart your responses, and prepare to share your ideas with the whole group. (usually done while doing the other steps)

5. Have small groups share with the whole group, either verbally or in a gallery walk. (10 minutes)

6. Have the whole group discuss what it noticed from the small groups' ideas. (10 minutes)

Tips

- Define the "it" for the exercise according to what is most relevant for this conversation—what are you trying to create a vision of. For example describe what "all children learning at high levels" or "a system where everyone is engaged in learning" or "a system that supports curiosity, questioning, risk taking, and knowledge creation" or "a human capital system that hires and retains effective educators" looks like, sounds like, and feels like.

- We often use five, seven, or ten years as the timeline for the future. Choose something that feels relevant for your context.

- Before doing this protocol, warn people that it will feel a little funny, but that the language is intentional and will help us create a vision. Encourage them to "try on" the language, and have a facilitator or two circulate while small groups are working to nudge people on language. The protocol is a bit challenging for people at first because it asks them to use verb tenses in unusual ways—talking about the future as the present and the present as the past—but this unusual language creates some distance from reality that frees people.

- Another challenge people have is being absolutely audacious when they're doing the first step of talking about the future as if it were the present. People may need a nudge—what does our system really look like when all children are learning at high levels? What do classrooms look like? What do the schools look like? What do faculty meetings look like? What does HR look like? There are no limits on this step except our own imaginations. When people start laughing and thinking they're talking crazy, they're getting warm.

Source: This protocol is adapted from the National School Reform Faculty's Future Protocol. See www.nsrfharmony.org/protocol/doc/future.pdf for the protocol.

LOGIC MODEL

Objective:	To lay out the plan for what will be done and what will be accomplished and to check the logic of the plan
Materials:	Logic model template
Time needed:	60–90 minutes to complete logic model; additional 60–90 minute to address related questions
Roles:	Facilitator or timekeeper; group of six to eight participants

Sample Logic Model Template

Activities	Resources	Outputs	Outcomes	Measures	Assumptions

Tips

- *Choose the right people.* Make sure the right people are at the table to create the logic model. They should include any senior leadership team member(s) who oversee the departments implicated in the initiative, key staff who will drive execution, budget staff responsible for estimating initiative costs, consumers of the initiative (in the math coaching example, it would be principals and teachers), and any likely external partners.

- *Consider outcomes first.* Start drafting the model with outcomes first, which is hard for many educators, but is often helpful for framing the work. Then move to activities, resources, and outputs, with assumptions surfacing along the way. When people are learning to use the logic model, they can get hung up in one column. If that happens, move on to another column, and move back and forth between columns as the conversation progresses.

- *Distinguish between outputs and outcomes.* People often get confused between outputs and outcomes. Outputs are connected to activities and will answer the question "Did we do what we said we were going to do?" Did we have three meetings, make the coaching handbook, conduct the survey, and the like? Outcomes are about results and will answer the question "Did we get the result we wanted?" Seeing an example (as in chapter 6) can be helpful for differentiating. The point is not to get hung up on the distinction, but to be clear about what you're hoping the activities will accomplish.

- *Push for details.* "Communication with principals and teachers" is different from "four focus groups, an internal Web site, FAQs, and a one-pager distributed at monthly meetings." "Improved student achievement" is different from "In years 3–5, 85 percent of students will be proficient or advanced in math on the state test." When someone says, "high-quality pool of math coaches," ask, "How will we know the pool is 'high-quality'?" Push for measurable details when appropriate. Measures can be hard for people to articulate, especially once you move beyond test scores. Baseline data from the root-cause analysis can be a helpful place to start. One group we worked with was filling out a logic model for its coaching initiative about six months into the initiative (not ideal to be doing it so late in the process, but better late than never!). After a lengthy conversation about outcomes—a conversation that finally achieved some level of detail—a coach said to the larger group of coaches and system leaders assembled, "Oh. If *that's* what you're hoping the outcome will be, I should be spending my time differently." While you want some detail, part of the logic model's power is in being relatively short—one or two pages, tops. You'll put more detail in the work plan.

- *Test the logic.* When the logic model is filled in, read horizontally: Will these activities and resources lead to these outputs? Are there gaps? Read vertically: Does the system have the capacity to do the combination of the things in this column? What already exists that the system can draw on? What will be new for the system? Tune the model as needed.

- *Follow up on loose ends.* Questions will inevitably pop up when people are completing the logic model. If there isn't time to answer the questions, or certain questions have to be referred to other people, decide how the questions will be addressed and assign people responsibility for addressing them and reporting back to the team. If there are other loose ends at the end of the meeting, schedule another meeting to happen within a week or two to continue the work and maintain momentum.

- *Value the process.* Finally, remember that part of what makes the logic model so valuable is the conversation that people have while they're completing it and revising it over time. The process is as important as the product because it is in the dialogue that people articulate outcomes, test their logic, identify gaps, and come to a shared understanding of how the strategic initiative will lead to particular results.

Further Resources

This list shares some of the resources that we find helpful. It is intended to provide a starting point for your additional learning and is not intended to be comprehensive.

Strategy

These are some of our favorite books and articles on strategy and how to develop it:

Christensen, Clayton. "Managing Strategy: Learning by Doing." *Harvard Business Review,* November–December 1997.

Kotter, John. "Leading Change: Why Transformation Efforts Fail." *Harvard Business Review,* January 2007.

Kotter, John, and Leonard Schlesinger. "Choosing Strategies for Change." *Harvard Business Review,* July–August 2008.

Magee, David. *How Toyota Became #1.* New York: Penguin, 2007.

O'Reilly, Charles III, and Michael Tushman. "The Ambidextrous Organization." *Harvard Business Review,* April 2004.

Porter, Michael. "Operational Effectiveness Is Not Strategy." *Harvard Business Review,* November–December 1996.

The following three pieces focus specifically on strategy in public education:

Childress, Stacey, and Geoff Marietta. *A Problem-Solving Approach to Designing and Implementing a Strategy to Improve Performance.* Cambridge, MA: Public Education Leadership Project at Harvard University, 2008.

Childress, Stacey, Richard Elmore, Allen Grossman, and Caroline King. *Note on the PELP Coherence Framework.* Cambridge, MA: Public Education Leadership Project at Harvard University, 2006.

Knapp, Michael S. et al. *Leading for Learning Sourcebook: Concepts and Examples.* Seattle, WA: Center for the Study of Teaching and Policy, 2003. http://depts.washington.edu/ctpmail/PDFs/LforLSourcebook-02-03.pdf.

Teams

These are a few of our favorite books, articles, and online resources to support team development and functioning:

Covey, Stephen M. R., with Rebecca R. Merrill. *The Speed of Trust.* New York: Free Press 2006.

Edmonson, Amy. "The Competitive Imperative of Learning." *Harvard Business Review,* July–August 2008.

Garvin, David, Amy Edmondson, and Francesca Gino. "Is Yours a Learning Organization?" *Harvard Business Review*, March 2008.

Hill, Linda A., and Maria T. Farkas. *A Note on Team Process.* Cambridge, MA: Harvard Business Publishing, 2001.

"Is Yours a Learning Organization?" Web site includes a sample survey to assess your organization and related video: http://harvardbusinessonline.hbsp.harvard.edu/flatmm/hbrextras/200803/garvin/index.html.

Katzenbach, Jon, and Douglas Smith. *The Wisdom of Teams: Creating the High-Performance Organization.* New York: HarperBusiness Essentials, 2003.

Lencioni, Patrick. *Overcoming the Five Dysfunctions of a Team.* San Francisco: Jossey-Bass, 2005.

Wageman, Ruth, Debra Nunes, James Burruss, and J. Richard Hackman. *Senior Leadership Teams.* Cambridge, MA: Harvard Business School Press, 2008.

The following personality/behavioral styles inventories can be used to develop team members' understanding of the styles and preferences of themselves and others:

Compass Points Protocol: www.turningpts.org/tools.htm (a more informal inventory).

Disc Assessment: www.professionalchange.com.

Keirsey Temperament Sorter: adaptation of Myers-Briggs, www.keirsey.com.

Data

Of the many books available about data use, these are a few of our favorites:

Bernhardt, Victoria L. *Data Analysis for Continuous School Improvement*, 2nd ed. Larchmont, New York: Eye on Education, 2004.

Boudett, Kathryn Parker, and Jennifer L. Steele, eds. *Data Wise in Action: Stories of Schools Using Data to Improve Teaching and Learning.* Cambridge, MA: Harvard Education Press, 2007.

Boudett, Kathryn Parker, Elizabeth A. City, and Richard J. Murnane, eds. *Data Wise: A Step-by-Step Guide to Using Assessment Results to Improve Teaching and Learning.* Cambridge, MA: Harvard Education Press, 2005.

Johnson, Ruth S. *Using Data to Close the Achievement Gap: How to Measure Equity in Our Schools.* Thousand Oaks, CA: Corwin Press, 2002.

There is an increasing volume of research available on district-level use of data. A few resources on this topic include:

Data Quality Campaign. "Data Use Drives School and District Improvement." 2006. www.dataqualitycampaign.org/files/Meetings-DQC_Quarterly_Issue_Brief_092506.pdf.

The New Schools Venture Fund Web site includes research about systemic use of data, including "Achieving with Data: How High-Performing School Systems Use Data to Improve Instruction for Elementary Students" (February 2007). See www.newschools.org/about/publications.

The University of Texas at Austin Data Use Web site: http://edadmin.edb.utexas.edu/datause/.

Vision

For a good overview of the history of twentieth-century schooling in America, see:

Patricia A. Graham, *Schooling America: How the Public Schools Meet the Nation's Changing Needs* (New York: Oxford University Press, 2007).

For information about what skills and knowledge students need to be successful in the twenty-first century, see:

Conley, David T. *College Knowledge: What It Really Takes for Students to Succeed and What We Can Do to Get Them Ready*. San Francisco: Jossey-Bass, 2005.

Levy, Frank, and Richard J. Murnane. "Education and the Job Market." *Educational Leadership*, October 2004.

Murnane, Richard J., and Frank Levy. *Teaching The New Basic Skills* New York: Free Press, 1996.

Partnership for 21st Century Skills. www.21stcenturyskills.org.

For data about student achievement in the United States, see the National Assessment of Education Progress (NAEP) (http://nces.ed.gov/NATIONSREPORTCARD/).

For data about how the United States compares internationally on student achievement, see TIMSS (http://nces.ed.gov/timss/) and PISA (http://www.pisa.oecd.org).

For a description of some of the most salient features of high-performing educational systems globally, see "How the World's Best-Performing School Systems Come Out on Top" (McKinsey & Company, 2007), www.mckinsey.com/clientservice/socialsector/resources/pdf/Worlds_School_systems_final.pdf).

For a description of innovation and what it might look like in education, see Clayton Christensen, Curtis W. Johnson, and Michael B. Horn, *Disrupting Class: How Disruptive Innovation Will Change the Way the World Learns*. (New York: McGraw-Hill, 2008).

Instructional Core

We often use frameworks as a starting point for conversations about the instructional core. We find these texts helpful:

Anderson, Lorin W. et al. *A Taxonomy for Learning, Teaching, and Assessing: A Revision of Bloom's Taxonomy of Educational Objectives.* Columbus, OH: Allyn & Bacon, 2000.

Marzano, Robert J., and John S. Kendall. *Designing and Assessing Educational Objectives: Applying the New Taxonomy.* Thousand Oaks, CA: Corwin Press, 2008.

Wiggins, Grant and Jay McTighe. *Understanding by Design,* 2nd ed. New York: Prentice Hall, 2005.

Additionally, the following books provide both context and practice for how to improve the instructional core:

City, Elizabeth A., Richard F. Elmore, Sarah E. Fiarman, and Lee Teitel. *Instructional Rounds in Education: A Network Approach to Improving Teaching and Learning.* Cambridge, MA: Harvard Education Press, 2009.

Darling-Hammond, Linda, and John Bransford, eds. *Preparing Teachers for a Changing World.* San Francisco: Jossey-Bass, 2005.

Execution

Our current favorite books on managing the human aspects of change include:

Bridge, William. *Managing Transitions: Making the Most of Change.* New York: Da Capo Press, 2003.

Dweck, Carol. *Mindset: The New Psychology of Success.* New York: Ballantine, 2008.

Heifetz, Ronald A., and Donald L. Laurie. "The Work of Leadership." *Harvard Business Review* (January–February 1997): 124–134.

Kegan, Robert, and Lisa Laskow Lahey. *Immunity to Change.* Cambridge, MA: Harvard Business School Press, 2009.

The following Web sites provide further information about tools introduced in the book or additional complementary tools that support strategy execution:

Logic models are prevalent in the foundation and nonprofit worlds. The W.K. Kellogg Foundation Logic Model Development Guide (www.wkkf.org/Pubs/Tools/Evaluation/Pub3669.pdf) is very helpful. The University of Wisconsin has a treasure trove of information about logic models (www.uwex.edu/ces/pdande/evaluation/evallogicmodel.html), including examples and a self-study online module.

Dashboards and balanced scorecards are becoming quite popular in education. Some examples include www.dashboardzone.com/school-summary-dashboard-charlotte-mecklenburg-school-metrics (Charlotte-Mecklenburg Schools), www.seminolecountyeducation.com/dashboards.html (Florida Education Dashboards), www.richmond.k12.va.us/indexnew/

sub/bsc_mou.cfm (Richmond Public Schools), and www.strategy2act.com/solutions/
education_excel.htm. Demetrius Karathanos and Patricia Karathanos, "Applying the Balanced Scorecard in Education," *Journal of Education for Business* (March/April 2005):
222–230, provides a helpful overview of the balanced-scorecard approach as well as examples of scorecards.

The After-Action Review process designed by the U.S. Army is used by many organizations. A
Google search will generate several examples to peruse. Among the many Web resources
are www.nwlink.com/~Donclark/leader/leadaar.html, and http://pdf.dec.org/pdf_docs/
PNADF360.pdf (link to U.S. AID *After-Action Review Technical Guidance* report, February 2006, PN-ADF-360).

We also use success analysis as a way of helping educators learn from their work, using success as
a starting point. See the National School Reform Faculty Web site (www.nsrfharmony.org/
protocol/doc/success_ana_individuals.pdf) for a success analysis protocol.

On the topic of strategic resource use, a few of our favorite resources include:

City, Elizabeth A. *Resourceful Leadership: Tradeoffs and Tough Decisions on the Road to School
Improvement.* Cambridge, MA: Harvard Education Press, 2008.

Education Resource Strategies, www.educationresourcestrategies.org, includes research, readings, and a nifty Web-based tool called DREAM (District Resource Allocation Mod-
eler), which lets you run different scenarios to think through how to focus resources
strategically.

Miles, Karen Hawley, and Stephen Frank. *The Strategic School: Making the Most of People, Time,
and Money.* Thousand Oaks, CA: Corwin Press, 2008.

Additional Resources to Stay Current in the Field

*A few of our favorite regular publications and Web sites provide access to current education news,
research, and policy debates:*

Association of Supervision and Curriculum Development's (ASCD) SmartBrief: daily briefing on
top stories in K–12 education; www.smartbrief.com/ascd.

Center for Comprehensive School Reform and Improvement: various resources, including briefs
(policy, issue, and research) and database of 5,000 research articles; www.centerforcsri.
org/.

Education Next: The Hoover Institute's quarterly magazine, which addresses current education
research, ideas about school and system improvement, and debates and policy in the education sector; www.hoover.org/publications/ednext.

Education Week: weekly newspaper that reports national K–12 education news; www.edweek.
org/ew/index.html.

Marshall Memo: weekly synthesis of articles about improving teaching, leadership, and learning
in K–12 education drawn from 44 publications; www.marshallmemo.com/.

Public Education Network Weekly Newsblast: weekly briefing on top stories about education policy, practice, and research; www.publiceducation.org/subscribe.asp.

Voices in Urban Education: quarterly publication of the Annenberg Institute for School Reform, which serves as a "roundtable in print" to air diverse viewpoints and share new knowledge on vital issues in urban education; www.annenberginstitute.org/VUE/index.php.

Introduction

1. For more on instructional rounds, see Elizabeth A. City, Richard F. Elmore, Sarah E. Fiarman, and Lee Teitel, *Instructional Rounds in Education: A Network Approach to Improving Teaching and Learning* (Cambridge, MA: Harvard Education Press, 2009).

2. We gratefully acknowledge our colleagues Kathy Augustine, Tom Payzant, and Larry Stanton, who helped boil down our messy thinking into the three *what, why,* and *how* questions.

3. Stacey Childress, "Note on Strategy in Public Education," Case PEL-011 (Boston: Harvard Graduate School of Education and Harvard Business School, 2004).

4. D. Cohen and D. Ball, *Instruction, Capacity, and Improvement*, Research Report Series RR-43 (Philadelphia: Consortium for Policy Research in Education, University of Pennsylvania, 1999).

5. One of the superintendents participating in the Executive Leadership Program for Educators (ExEL) at Harvard University in association with the Wallace Foundation used the phrase "simplify, simplify, focus, focus" to describe to colleagues what he had learned in the first year of his work at ExEL.

6. For a more extensive discussion of the instructional core and its role in the systemic improvement of learning and teaching, see City et al., *Instructional Rounds in Education,* chapter 1.

7. We gratefully acknowledge our colleague Deanna Burney for several conversations about the instructional core, including one in which she emphasized the importance of acknowledging the prevalence of within-school variation.

8. See P. Peterson and F. Hess, "Few States Set World-Class Standards," *Education Next* 8, no. 3 (summer 2008), available at www.hoover.org/publications/ednext/18845034.html.

9. See also Julia B. Smith, BetsAnn Smith, and Anthony S. Bryk, *Setting the Pace: Opportunities to Learn in Chicago Elementary Schools* (Chicago: Consortium on Chicago School Research, 1998).

10. W. L. Sanders and J. C. Rivers, *Cumulative and Residual Effects of Teachers on Future Student Academic Achievement* (Knoxville: University of Tennessee Value-Added Research and Assessment Center, 1996).

11. This is the second of seven principles of the instructional core described by City et al., *Instructional Rounds in Education.* The seven principles are these: (1) Increases in student learning occur only as a consequence of improvements in the level of content, teachers' knowledge and skill, and student engagement; (2) if you change any single element of the instructional core, you have to change the other two; (3) if you can't see it in the core, it's not there; (4) task predicts performance; (5) the real accountability system is in the tasks that students are asked to do; (6) we learn to do the work by doing the work, *not* by telling other people to do the work, *not* by having done the work sometime in the past, and *not* by hiring experts who can act as proxies for our knowl-

edge about how to do the work; (7) description before analysis, analysis before prediction, and prediction before evaluation.

12. Richard DuFour, "Leading Edge: Are You Looking Out the Window or in a Mirror?" *Journal of Staff Development* (Summer 2004).

Chapter 1: Strategy, Part 1

1. Stacey Childress, "Note on Strategy in Public Education," Case PEL-011 (Boston: Harvard Graduate School of Education and Harvard Business School, 2004).

Chapter 2: Teams

1. Ruth Wageman, D. Nunes, J. Burruss, and J. R. Hackman, *Senior Leadership Teams* (Boston: Harvard Business School Publishing, 2008).
2. Ibid.
3. Ibid.
4. Ibid.
5. Patrick Lencioni, *Overcoming the Five Dysfunctions of a Team: A Field Guide* (San Francisco: Jossey Bass, 2005).

Chapter 3: Data

1. Teachers have long used student work, classroom test scores, and other classroom-level assessments, but these kinds of data have usually been used by individual teachers in isolation, not to inform schoolwide or systemwide decisions. The use of data to inform systemic decisions is a relatively recent trend in education, as is the urge for more consistent and collaborative use of classroom-level data.
2. As we write this book, Massachusetts, like many states, is revising its assessment system to include improvement measures.
3. See, for example, Council of the Great City Schools, "Managing for Results in America's Great City Schools: A Report of the Performance Measurement and Benchmarking Project," 2008, www.cgcs.org/Pubs/ManagingResults_1008.pdf.
4. See, for example, surveys of Chicago Public Schools by the Consortium on Chicago School Research (http://ccsr.uchicago.edu/content/page.php?cat=4); and surveys of students by the Tripod Project (www.tripodproject.org).
5. This question is taken from Elizabeth A. City, Richard F. Elmore, Sarah E. Fiarman, and Lee Teitel, *Instructional Rounds in Education: A Network Approach to Improving Teaching and Learning* (Cambridge, MA: Harvard Education Press, 2009). It is the key question in prediction, the third step in the four-part process of "instructional rounds," a collaborative process of observing and analyzing classrooms.
6. See Stacey Childress and Geoff Marietta, "A Problem-Solving Approach to Designing and Implementing a Strategy to Improve Performance," Case PEL056 (Boston: Harvard Business School, 2008), for a discussion of how to use the 5 Whys as part of a school district's strategic work.

Chapter 4: Vision

1. John Kotter, *Leading Change* (Boston: Harvard Business School Press, 1996).
2. Mortimer J. Adler, *The Paideia Program* (New York: Macmillan, 1984).
3. Richard J. Murnane and F. Levy, *Teaching the New Basic Skills: Principles for Educating Children to Thrive in a Changing Economy* (New York: Free Press, 1996).
4. The system's measurable goals: 95 percent of students will enter grade one ready to read; 90 percent of students will be proficient in reading by the end of grade three; 75 percent of students will be proficient in state math test at grades five and six; 80 percent of students will be proficient in state writing test at grade seven; 70 percent of students will take Algebra 1 in grade eight; 50 percent of students in Advanced Placement courses will attain a score of 3, 4, or 5; 75 percent of high school students will take the PSAT; high school graduation rate will be at 90 percent; districtwide daily student attendance rate will be 95 percent.
5. This protocol is from the National School Reform Faculty. See www.nsrfharmony.org for a complete description of the protocol, and appendix B of this book for our modified version of it. We gratefully acknowledge Jonathan Travers of Education Resource Strategies, with whom Liz collaborated in "Cityside." The Oprah line is Jonathan's.
6. Patricia A. Graham, *Schooling America: How the Public Schools Meet the Nation's Changing Needs* (New York: Oxford University Press, 2007).
7. No Child Left Behind is the name of the current version of the Elementary and Secondary Education Act (ESEA). Any reauthorization would be of ESEA.
8. We thank and acknowledge our colleague Adrienne Looft for this insight.

Chapter 5: Strategy, Part 2

1. For a more detailed discussion of theory of action and its role in systemic improvement, see Elizabeth City, Richard Elmore, Sarah Fiarman, and Lee Teitel, "Theories of Action," in *Instructional Rounds in Education: A Network Approach to Improving Teaching and Learning* (Cambridge, MA: Harvard Education Press, 2009), chapter 2.
2. Louise Bay Waters, *The Bellevue Story* (Stupski Foundation, January 2008).

Chapter 6: Execution

1. For a helpful visual for thinking about the connections between strategy and systems, structures, resources, stakeholders, and culture, see the PELP Coherence Framework (www.hbs.edu/pelp/framework.html). Stacey Childress, Richard Elmore, Allen Grossman, Modupe Akinola, and Caroline King, "Note on the PELP Coherence Framework," Case PEL010-PDF-ENG (Boston: Harvard Business Publishing, 2004), includes many helpful questions for thinking about coherence, alignment, and strategy.
2. For more information on logic models, see W.K. Kellogg Foundation, *Logic Model Development Guide* (Battle Creek, MI: W.K. Kellogg Foundation, January 2004), available at www.wkkf.org/Pubs/Tools/Evaluation/Pub3669.pdf. See appendix C of this book for other logic model resources.

3. Our thanks to Sarah Alvord for teaching us about logic models and providing helpful feedback on this sample logic model.
4. Our thanks to Adrienne Looft, from whom we have learned many things about project management and from whom we adapted this work plan template.
5. David A. Garvin, A. C. Edmondson, and F. Gino, "Is Yours a Learning Organization?" *Harvard Business Review* (March 2008): 109–116.
6. For more information on after-action reviews, see D. Clark, "After Action Reviews," May 1, 1997; revised November 29, 2008, www.nwlink.com/~Donclark/leader/leadaar.html.
7. John Price, interview with author, Audubon School, Chicago, October 8, 2008.
8. Michael McLaughlin, "Meet the MasterMinds: John Kotter on How Change Is Changing," interview of John Kotter by Michael McLaughlin, Management Consulting News, no date, www.managementconsultingnews.com/interviews/kotter_interview.php.

Conclusion

1. "Redstone" is a pseudonym.
2. Stephen M. R. Covey and Rebecca R. Merrill, *The Speed of Trust* (New York: Simon and Schuster, 2006).
3. Robert Kegan and Lisa Laskow Lahey, *Immunity to Change* (Boston: Harvard Business School, 2009).

ACKNOWLEDGMENTS

We joke that it took a village to write this book. It is not far from the truth. It was truly amazing how often we found ourselves thanking our lucky stars that a colleague or friend shared an insight, pushed our thinking, or offered encouragement, always with the intention of helping us make this book better. We are beyond grateful.

The idea for this book first came from our friends and colleagues at the Executive Leadership Program for Educators (ExEL) at Harvard University. With support from the Wallace Foundation, they have spent the last three years helping school systems and state departments of education across the country to develop strategy and to be more strategic. Sarah Alvord, Janice Jackson, Sarah Joblin, Susan Kenyon, Harry Spence, and Lee Teitel have supported us all along our journey both as thought partners and as patient readers of multiple drafts.

Then there are the ExEL coaches—Sally Anderson, Adrienne Bailey, Irwin Blumer, Tom Buffett, Deanna Burney, Dean Damon, Deidre Farmbry, Tobey Fitch, Gail Gerry, Jackie Jackson, Angela Kenyatta, Susan Long, Patricia Magruder, Chris Mazzeo, Harriette Thurber Rasmussen, Larry Rowedder, and Cheryl Wilhoyte—a fun, thoughtful, and truly committed group of colleagues who got excited about the idea of this book before there was much tangible evidence of its existence. As it began to take shape, they helped us refine our thinking and provided feedback on draft chapters.

Kathy Augustine, Deanna Burney, Dan Katzir, Angela Kenyatta, Patti Magruder, Tom Payzant, Ted Preston, Larry Stanton, Elliot Stern, and Judy Wurtzel served as readers, providing feedback on drafts. They showed us the greatest respect by telling us when we were on to something worthwhile and calling us out ever so nicely when we were wandering aimlessly.

Others colleagues whose ideas helped us as we charted our course include Richard Elmore, Sarah Fiarman, Adrienne Looft, Stefanie Reinhorn, Angela Smith, Bob Schwartz, and Stacey Childress.

We thank the many educators we have had the privilege to work with over the years. We have learned so much from them, and they inspired this book.

And then there are the people behind the scenes without whom this book would probably never have been published: Susan Kenyon, editor extraordinaire, waded tirelessly and ever so graciously through our wordiness and helped us hone our story. Robert Rothman stepped in at the eleventh hour and took a scalpel to our words in a way that was decisive and masterful. Tai Sunnanon served both as a research assistant and the generator of the graphics, bringing ideas to life through clear images. Matt Fiteny also provided research assistance and made sure we knew what we were talking about. And we must thank Caroline Chauncey and her colleagues at the Harvard Education Press. Caroline's faith in this book propelled us in moments when we lacked clarity, and her cheerleading in the final days helped us get the darn thing done.

Behind the people are the resources to create the time and space to support the writing and editing of this book. We gratefully acknowledge the support of the Merck Dean's Dissemination Fund at the Harvard Graduate School of Education, which made the book possible.

Finally, there are our family and friends. They have heard more about strategy in education than they ever imagined possible. They cooked for us, gave us quiet places to write, and pretended not to notice life piling up around us. Most importantly, they made us laugh, cheered us on, took us for walks when we needed fresh air and perspective, and generally loved us well.

ABOUT THE AUTHORS

Rachel E. Curtis works with school systems, foundations, higher education, and education policy organizations on district improvement strategy, leadership development, and efforts to make teaching a compelling and rewarding career. Her clients include The Aspen Institute, the Broad Center for the Management of School Systems, the Executive Leadership Program for Educators at Harvard University, and a variety of traditional and charter school systems. Rachel worked for the Boston Public Schools for eleven years, during which time she devised the district's instructional coaching model for literacy and math; developed a data-driven school planning process; founded the School Leadership Institute, which included the nationally recognized Boston Principal Fellowship; developed teaching standards and a new-teacher induction program; and oversaw professional development for teachers and school administrators. She holds a masters degree in Leadership and Organizational Development in the Context of School Reform from the Harvard Graduate School of Education. Her publications include *The Skillful Leader II: Confronting Conditions That Undermine Learning* (Ready About Press, 2008), *Ensuring the Support and Development of New Teachers in the Boston Public Schools* (Boston Public Schools, 2006), *Preparing Non-Principal Administrators to Foster Whole-School Improvement in Boston* (Boston Public Schools, 2005), *Professional Development Spending in the Boston Public Schools* (Boston Public Schools, 2005), and a forthcoming edited volume on human capital management in education (Harvard Education Press, 2010).

Elizabeth A. City helps educators improve learning and teaching through leadership development, the strategic use of data and resources, and instructional rounds networks. She is Director of Instructional Strategy at the Executive Leadership Program for Educators at Harvard University and lecturer at the Harvard Graduate School of Education. Liz has served as a teacher, an instructional coach, and a principal. She holds a doctorate in Administration, Planning, and Social Policy from the Harvard Graduate School of Education. Her publications include *Instructional Rounds in Education: A Network Approach to Improving Teaching and Learning*, coauthored with Richard F. Elmore, Sarah E. Fiarman, and Lee Teitel (Harvard Education Press, 2009); *Resourceful Leadership: Tradeoffs and Tough Decisions on the Road to School Improvement* (Harvard Education Press, 2008); *The Teacher's Guide* *to Leading Student-Centered Discussions: Talking About Texts in the Classroom*, coauthored with Michael S. Hale (Corwin Press, 2006); and *Data Wise: A Step-by-Step Guide to Using Assessment Results to Improve Teaching and Learning,* coedited with Kathryn Parker Boudett and Richard J. Murnane (Harvard Education Press, 2005).

The authors can be reached at rachelecurtis@gmail.com and cityel@gse.harvard.edu.

INDEX

access period, 104

accountability, 12, 59–61, 181

achievement, student

    data, 78

    as focus of education in America, 104, 105

    and focus on learning, 6–7

adjustment period, 104

Adler, Mortimer, 99

affinity protocol, 84

after-action review, 167–169

agendas, meeting, 53–56, 54f, 55f

assessment, benchmark, 74, 183

assignment-level/grade-level gap, 10f

assimilation, 104

attainment, student, 78

authority, 43

behavior norms, meeting, 50–52, 50f, 51f

beliefs, 94–95, 130

benchmark assessments, 74, 183

big-picture thinking, 47

brainstorming, 52

Brown v. Board of Education, 104

buy-in. *See* ownership

capacity, system, 132

change, 191–192

charter schools, 4

citizenship, 99

City, Elizabeth, 1–2

clarity, 128

communication, 170, 171f–172f

complex communication, 99

complexity and simplicity, 6, 13, 111–112,
    181–183, 192–193

compliance, 181

conflict, 58–59

content, instructional, 7f, 8–9

crises, 20

culture, school, 146–147

current initiatives assessment

    assessment, 30–35, 31f

    brainstorming, 27f, 28

    protocol, 26–36

    sorting ideas, 28–30, 29f

    synthesis, 35–36

Curtis, Rachel, 1–2

data

    external data, 78–79

    forms of, 71

    habit of using evidence, 70–72

    hypothesis actionability and vetting, 88–91,
        89f, 90f

    hypothesis generation from, 82–84, 85f

    hypothesis support from, 86–88, 87f

    initiative data, 78

    key indicators to scan, 76–80

    problem-identification, 80–81, 81f

    synthesis of, 81–82

    types of, 72–76

    and vision, 109

ease and impact analysis, 132–134, 133f

ego, 46

English language learners, 190

excellence, 105
experimentation, 25
expert thinking, 99

facilitators, 28
5 Whys tool, 86, 88, 89f, 90f
focus groups, 74–75

grade-level standards, 10f
Graham, Patricia Albjerg, 104

human capital, 128–129

imagination, 94–95
implementation work plan, 163–167, 164f–165f
independent schools, 4
initiatives. *See* strategic initiatives
instructional core, 5, 7f
    components of, 7–10, 7f
    in current initiatives, 32
    focus on, 10–14, 189–190
    strategic initiative development and, 137
    theories of action and, 116–118
interaction dynamic, 11

leadership, 5–6, 125–126, 174–178
leadership inventories, 57–58
learning. *See* student learning
logic models, 156–163, 157f, 160f–161f
loss, 192

Massachusetts, 73
meetings
    agendas, 53–56, 54f, 55f
    engagement, 63–64
    norms of behavior, 50–52, 50f, 51f
    typical, 37–38
mission, 41

National Assessment of Educational Progress, 105
Nation at Risk report, 104–105

No Child Left Behind, 93, 94

observation, classroom, 75–76
outcomes, team, 59–61
ownership, 34–35, 139–140

pay-for-performance, 129
planning fatigue, 22
political will, 132
politics, school, 20, 44
problem, 71
problem-identification
    data synthesis, 81–82
    hypothesis generation, 82–84, 85f
    narrowing focus on, 86–88, 87f
    vetting hypothetical solutions, 88–91, 89f, 90f
problem solving, 33–34
project management, 163, 174–178

race, and achievement, 94, 112
regulations, 12
resources, system, 132, 145

schooling, history of, 104–105
school systems. *See also* current initiatives assessment
    capacity, resources, and political will, 132
    focus on all children/each child, 187–189
    hectic and distracting, 20
    instructional core focus, 12–14
    organizational functioning, 144–147
    ownership throughout, 34–35
    school autonomy, 186–187
    structural and system support for strategy, 153–169
    system change, 2–5, 69–70
    system of collaboration, 39
    visits to other, 101–102, 103f, 110–111
senior leadership teams
    accountability, 59–61
    agendas, 53–56, 54f, 55f

children-focused, 65
engagement in, 63–64
generalizations, 66
imperfections in process, 65–66
individual contributions, 64
membership, 43, 44–49, 48f
purpose clarity and importance, 40–43
quality functioning of, 38–39
structural norms, 50–52, 50f, 51f
trust, 56–59
visiting other schools, 101–102, 103f,
        110–111
simplicity and complexity, 6, 13, 111–112,
        181–183, 192–193
sphere of control, 85
stakeholder support, for strategy, 169–174,
        171f–172f
standardized testing, 73
standards movement, 8–9, 10f, 105
strategic initiatives. *See also* strategy execution
    about, 130–131, 131f
    after-action review, 167–169
    ease and impact of, 132–134, 133f
    implementation work plan, 163–167,
        164f–165f
    lack of focus in, 22
    logic models, 156–163, 157f, 160f–161f
    management, 174–176
    pacing and sequencing, 135–136
    synergy, 134–135
    timeline of implementation, 153–156,
        154f–155f
strategy
    balancing tensions in, 186–189
    defined, 3, 20–21
    difficulties of, 24–25
    example of complete, 140f–141f
    importance, 4–5
    and instructional core, 189–190
    lack of, 3
    measuring results, 182–183
    school autonomy, 186–187

and theory of action, 116–118, 117f
strategy development
    assessing strategy, 137–140, 140f–141f
    diving in, 179–181, 190–191
    formulate, with theories of action, 126–136,
        131f, 133f
    idea generation and research, 123–126, 124f
    identify objectives, 127–129
    initiative identification and evaluation,
        130–136, 131f
    map objectives with theories of action, 130
    synthesis of information and analysis,
        119–123, 120f–122f
    vs. strategic planning, 21–24, 23f, 25
strategy execution
    after-action review, 167–169
    difficulties of, 144–147
    implementation work plan, 163–167,
        164f–165f
    logic models, 156–163, 157f, 160f–161f
    stakeholder support, 169–174, 171f–172f
    strategy drives action, 147–153, 149f–150f,
        152f–153f
    structural and system support, 153–169
    system management of, 174–178, 175f
    timeline of implementation, 151–153,
        152f–153f
student learning
    curious learners, 102
    data, 78
    history of, 104–105
    primacy of, 5
    standards and assignment gap, 9, 10f
    students as learners, 9–11, 10f
style inventories, 57–58
superintendent, 46–47, 56
surveys, 74
synergy, 32–33, 134–135

teaching, quality
    and classroom observation, 75–76
    hiring and retention, 124, 133–134

teaching, quality *(continued)*
  primacy of, 5, 125, 128–129
  variability in, 7–8
teams
  accountability, 59–61
  checklist, 60f
  children-focused, 65
  engagement in, 63–64
  generalizations, 66
  imperfections in process, 65–66
  importance, 38–39
  individual contributions, 64
  meeting agendas, 53–56, 54f, 55f
  membership, 43, 44–49, 48f
  purpose clarity and importance, 40–43
  structural norms, 50–52, 50f, 51f
  trust, 51, 56–59
test scores, 73
theories of action
  about, 114–116
  assessing strategy and, 137–140, 140f–141f
  designing, 118–119
  examples, 115
  formulate strategy with, 126–136, 131f, 133f
  idea generation and research, 123–126, 125f
  and strategy, 116–118, 117f

synthesis of information and analysis, 119–123, 120f–122f
timeline of implementation, 151–153, 152f–153f
transparency, 41
trust, 51, 56–59, 191
twenty-first century skills, 99–101

vision
  about, 94–96
  assessing present, 96–99, 97f, 98f
  considerations, 105–108
  in current initiatives, 33–34
  and data, 109
  imagining future, 99–104, 101f
  importance of, 24–25
  initiative development, 138–139
  personalizing, 109–110
  process, 100–101, 106
  and teams, 41
visits, school, 101–102, 103f, 110–111
vulnerability, personal, 58

whole-school improvement plans (WSIPs), 1–2
work plan, implementation, 163–167, 164f–165f
work style inventories, 57–58